Creative Cooking

CONTENTS

Creative Cooking

America's Best Homemade Recipes!

CONTENTS

OVER 600 FAMILY–PROVEN RECIPES!

EXCLUSIVELY DISTRIBUTED BY:

P.S.I. & ASSOCIATES, INC.

13322 S.W. 128TH ST.
MIAMI, FL 33186
(305) 255-7959

Address all correspondance to the address above.

© 1992

ISBN# 1-55993-202-3

28282

Appetizers

APPEALING

HOT HAMBURGER DIP

1 pound ground beef
½ cup chopped onion
1 (8-ounce) can tomato sauce
¼ cup ketchup
1 (8-ounce) package cream cheese
1 cup grated Parmesan cheese
1 clove garlic, mashed
1 teaspoon oregano
1 tablespoon parsley
1 tablespoon sugar
1 (4-ounce) can mushrooms, chopped
Salt to taste
Pepper to taste

Sauté beef until brown. Add onion and garlic; cook until tender. Add all other ingredients and stir over low heat until cream cheese melts. Pour into Crockpot and keep warm. Serve with corn chips or taco chips.

JEZEBEL

1 (18-ounce) jar peach jam
2½ ounces horseradish
1 ounce dry mustard
1 tablespoon ground white pepper
1 (8-ounce) package cream cheese

Mix all ingredients well, except for cream cheese. When ready to serve, pour over a block of cream cheese and serve with crackers.

CHILI POPCORN

1 tablespoon margarine, melted
⅓ teaspoon chili powder
⅛ teaspoon salt
⅛ teaspoon garlic powder
⅛ teaspoon paprika
6 cups popped corn

Combine margarine, chili powder, salt, garlic powder and paprika; drizzle over warm popcorn. (41 calories per 1-cup serving)

DOUBLE SHRIMP MOLD

1 can cream of shrimp soup
1 envelope unflavored gelatin
2 (8-ounce) packages cream cheese, softened
1 cup mayonnaise
1½ tablespoons green onion, chopped
¾ cup celery, finely chopped
2 (6-ounce) cans small deveined shrimp
Dash salt and pepper, to taste

Heat undiluted soup to boiling point. Add gelatin to ½ cup cold water. Add to soup; mix well. Add cream cheese; blend well. Cool slightly. Add remaining ingredients; mix well. Spoon into mold or molds. Refrigerate for several hours. Unmold and serve with assorted crackers. May be frozen.

BARBECUED MEATBALLS
Makes 80

3 pounds ground beef
1 (12-ounce) can evaporated milk
1 cup oatmeal
1 cup cracker crumbs
2 eggs
½ cup chopped onion
½ teaspoon garlic powder
2 teaspoons salt
½ teaspoon pepper
2 teaspoons chili powder
2 cups ketchup
1 cup brown sugar
½ teaspoon liquid smoke
½ teaspoon garlic powder
¼ cup chopped onion

Combine beef, milk, oatmeal, crumbs, eggs, ½ cup onion, ½ teaspoon garlic powder, salt, pepper and chili powder (mixture will be soft). Shape into walnut-size balls. Place meatballs in a 13 x 9 x 2-inch baking pan.

To make sauce, combine ketchup, brown sugar, liquid smoke, garlic powder and ¼ cup onion. Pour this over the pan of meatballs. Bake in a 350-degree oven for 40–45 minutes.

To freeze for later use: Line cookie sheets with waxed paper; place meatballs in single layer; freeze until solid. Store frozen meatballs in freezer bags until ready to cook. Place frozen meatballs in baking pan; pour on sauce. Bake at 350 degrees for 1 hour.

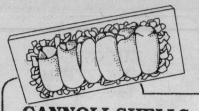

CANNOLI SHELLS AND FILLINGS

4 cups flour (sifted)
1 tablespoon sugar
1/4 teaspoon cinnamon
3/4 cup wine (Italian red)
Egg white for sealing

Sift flour, sugar, and cinnamon together onto a bread board or table top. Make a well in center, and fill with wine. With a fork, gradually blend flour into wine. Knead dough until smooth and stiff, about 15 minutes. If dough is too dry, add a little more wine. Cover dough and let stand for 2 hours in the refrigerator. Then roll 1/3 of dough to paper thinness, making a 16-inch round. Cut into eight, 5-inch circles. Wrap circles loosely around a 6-inch long cannoli form or dowels, 1 inch in diameter. Seal with egg white, and fry 2 cannoli at a time in deep fat for 1 minute or until brown on both sides. Lift out gently with a slotted spoon or tongs, drain on paper towels to cool. Remove forms *gently*. Continue until all dough is used. Then fill with Ricotta Filling or Cream Filling.

Ricotta Filling:

3 pounds Italian Ricotta
1-3/4 cups confectioners' sugar
1/2 teaspoon cinnamon
2 tablespoons citron (chopped)
1/4 cup chocolate bits (semi-sweet)

Beat Ricotta cheese in a large bowl for 1 minute. Add sugar and beat until very light and creamy, about 5 minutes. Add cinnamon, citron and chocolate bits and mix until thoroughly blended.

Cream Filling:

1 gallon milk
1 box cornstarch
4 cups sugar
1/4 cup chocolate chips (semisweet)
1 stick cinnamon (remove later)

Cook milk on a low heat and mix all ingredients except chocolate bits. Cook slowly until mixture thickens. Cool, then add chocolate bits and put filling into cannoli shells.

PEANUT DEVILED-HAM BALL

1 (8-ounce) package cream cheese, softened
1 (4½-ounce) can deviled ham
2 tablespoons grated onion
1 teaspoon horseradish
¼ teaspoon liquid hot pepper seasoning
¼ teaspoon dry mustard
¼ cup chopped, salted peanuts
1 tablespoon dried parsley

Combine first 6 ingredients; beat until smooth and well-blended. Chill. Shape into a ball. Roll in peanuts and parsley to coat outside of cheese ball. Chill for 30 minutes before serving. Serve with party rye bread or assorted crackers.

MACARONI PIZZA

Serves 6

2 cups uncooked macaroni
15-1/2-ounce jar spaghetti sauce
1 egg
1/2 teaspoon salt
1/2 cup milk
3 tablespoons Parmesan cheese
1/2 pound ground beef
1/2 cup chopped green pepper
1/2 cup onion, chopped
4-ounce can mushrooms
8-ounce package Mozzarella cheese, grated

Cook macaroni according to package directions; drain. Beat together egg, milk, 1 teaspoon Parmesan cheese and salt. Blend into macaroni and spread in greased 9 x 13-inch baking pan. Pour spaghetti sauce over macaroni. Add small bits of raw ground meat. Sprinkle on green pepper, onion, mushrooms and remaining Parmesan cheese. Top with Mozzarella cheese. Bake at 350 degrees for 20 minutes. Let stand 5-10 minutes before cutting.

SHRIMP BALL

1 (8-ounce) package cream cheese, softened
1 small can shrimp (rinsed, drained, shredded)
2 tablespoons grated Romano/Parmesan cheese
1 teaspoon parsley flakes
1/2 teaspoon onion salt
1/2 teaspoon garlic salt
2 tablespoons catsup
Chopped walnuts

Mix all ingredients thoroughly (a food processor is helpful). Form into a ball. Roll ball in chopped walnuts. Chill 24 hours before serving. This appetizer freezes well.

SPICY STUFFED EGGS

Makes 8

6 large eggs, hard-cooked
1 green onion, including top, finely chopped
1 tablespoon reduced-calorie mayonnaise
1 tablespoon minced parsley
2 sweet gherkin pickles, finely chopped
½ teaspoon prepared mustard
⅛ teaspoon salt
⅛ teaspoon black pepper
8 sprigs parsley (optional)

Cook eggs; peel and halve lengthwise. Place 1 yolk in small bowl; discard remaining yolks. Mash the yolk with a fork, then add 4 of the white halves and mash. Mix in onion, mayonnaise, parsley, pickles, mustard, salt and pepper. Mound the mixture into remaining white halves, dividing it equally. Garnish each half, if desired, with a sprig of parsley. Cover loosely and refrigerate until ready to serve.

CHINESE ROLL-UPS WITH HOT MUSTARD SAUCE
Makes 10

1 pound ground beef
1 can water chestnuts, chopped
2 tablespoons chopped onion
1 package onion and mushroom soup mix
1 tablespoon beef bouillon
1 can bean sprouts, drained
3 packages crescent rolls
1/4 cup prepared mustard
1/4 cup mayonnaise
1 clove garlic, chopped
1/4 teaspoon hot sauce
2 teaspoons horseradish

Brown ground beef. Add next 5 ingredients. Simmer for 5 minutes. Remove from heat. Place 1 tablespoon meat mixture in center of each crescent triangle. Pull corners over meat mixture; pinch together to seal. Place on baking sheet. Bake at 350 degrees for 15 minutes, or until browned. Combine remaining ingredients; mix well. Refrigerate until serving time. Serve hot mustard sauce over roll-ups while still warm. May be frozen for use later.

MUSHROOM MUNCHIES

1/4 cup vegetable oil
1/4 cup vinegar with lemon
1 tablespoon sugar
1/2 teaspoon onion powder
1/4 teaspoon garlic powder
Pinch of oregano
1 (10-ounce) can whole mushrooms, drained

Mix ingredients together in small bowl. Add mushrooms and marinate for 1 hour. Toothpicks will assist with serving or snacking of the whole mushrooms.

FANCY DOGS
Serves 12

1 (6-ounce) jar mustard
1 (6-ounce) jar currant jelly
1 pound hot dogs, cut diagonally

Combine mustard and jelly in fondue pot; mix well. Heat to boiling point. Add cut hot dogs. Heat until warm. Place over fondue flame, stirring occasionally.

ZUCCHINI APPETIZERS
Makes 4 dozen

3 cups thinly sliced zucchini
1 cup Bisquick
1/2 cup chopped onion
1/2 cup grated Parmesan cheese
2 teaspoons snipped parsley
1/2 teaspoon salt
1/2 teaspoon seasoned salt
1/2 teaspoon oregano
Dash of pepper
1 clove garlic, chopped
1/2 cup oil
4 eggs, slightly beaten

Heat oven to 350 degrees. Grease an oblong 9x13x2-inch pan. Mix all ingredients and spread in pan. Bake until golden brown for about 25 minutes. Cut into pieces, about 2x1-inch.

SAUSAGE BALLS
Makes 4 dozen

1 pound hot sausage, at room temperature
10 ounces extra-sharp Cracker Barrel cheese, grated
3 cups Bisquick mix

Mix Bisquick and grated cheese; add sausage. Blend well. Shape into small balls. Freeze on cookie sheet. Store in a plastic bag in the freezer. Place frozen balls on greased cookie sheet. Bake at 300 degrees for 35-45 minutes. Serve hot.

NUTTY BLEU CHEESE DIP
Makes 2 cups

1 cup mayonnaise
1 (8-ounce) container sour cream
1/4 cup (1 ounce) bleu cheese, crumbled
1 tablespoon finely chopped onion
2 teaspoons instant beef bouillon
1/2 to 3/4 cup walnuts, coarsely chopped
Assorted fresh vegetables

In medium bowl, combine mayonnaise, sour cream, bleu cheese, onion, and bouillon; mix well. Stir in nuts; cover and chill. Stir before serving. Garnish as desired. Serve with vegetables. Refrigerate leftovers.

QUICK PEANUTTY POPCORN BALLS
Makes 8 (2-1/2-inch) balls

1/2 cup light corn syrup
1/4 cup sugar
3/4 cup peanut butter
2 quarts plain popped corn

In a saucepan mix corn syrup and sugar. Cook over medium heat; stir constantly until mixture comes to a boil and sugar is completely dissolved. Remove from heat. Stir in peanut butter until smooth. Immediately pour mixture over popcorn in large bowl. Stir until well-coated. Grease hands and shape into 8 (2-1/2-inch) balls.

BACON-WRAPPED CHESTNUTS

2 cans water chestnuts
½ cup soy sauce
18 slices bacon, cut in half

Marinate water chestnuts in soy sauce for 1 hour. Wrap each chestnut with bacon. Secure with toothpick. Place in pan and bake at 400 degrees for 30 minutes. Drain on paper toweling. Serve.

FAVORITE SPOON BREAD
Serves 8

1 1/3 teaspoons sugar
1 1/2 teaspoons salt
1 cup cornmeal, sifted
1 1/3 cups water, boiling (cool 5 minutes)
1/4 cup butter *or* margarine
3 eggs, lightly beaten
1 1/4 cups milk
1 teaspoon baking powder

Preheat oven to 350 degrees. Mix together sugar, salt and cornmeal. Pour water over meal mixture, stirring constantly. Mix in butter; let stand until cooled; add eggs, milk and baking powder, blending well.

Pour into buttered pan (2-quart). Place in shallow pan of hot water. Bake in a 350-degree oven for 35 minutes, or until crusty. Spoon out; serve.

This spoon bread has a light texture, soft center, and crusty top. Most delicious!

NO–KNEAD ROLLS
Makes 2 dozen

1/2 cup scalded milk
3 tablespoons shortening
3 tablespoons sugar
2 teaspoons salt
1/2 cup water
1 cake yeast *or* 1 package active dry yeast
1 egg
3 cups all-purpose flour
Melted shortening

Blend together milk, 3 tablespoons shortening, sugar, and salt. Cool to lukewarm by adding water. Add yeast, and mix well. Add egg. Add flour, gradually, mixing until dough is well-blended. Place in greased bowl. Brush top with melted shortening and allow to rise until light. Knead dough a few times to make smooth ball. Form into desired shapes and bake in 400-degree oven for 15-25 minutes or until golden brown. Easy and very tasty.

POPPY SEED BREAD

1 package Duncan Hines Yellow Cake Mix
1 package toasted coconut instant pudding (Royal brand)
1/4 cup (scant) poppy seeds
4 eggs
1 cup hot water
1/2 cup Crisco oil

Mix well; pour into 2 well-greased loaf pans 9x5-1/2x2 1/2-inches. Bake at 350 degrees for 40-50 minutes. This is a very moist bread!

This is very delicious spread with Philadelphia Cream Cheese, plus makes a nice bread to serve along with fruit salad!

CHOCOLATE FUDGE MUFFINS

1 cup butter or margarine
4 squares semisweet chocolate
1-1/2 cups white sugar
1 cup flour
1/4 teaspoon salt
4 eggs, beaten
1 teaspoon vanilla

In a saucepan over low heat, combine margarine and chocolate. Melt, stirring frequently, so the chocolate does not burn or stick.

In a bowl, combine sugar, flour and salt. Stir in chocolate mixture. Beat eggs, then add them to batter with the vanilla. Stir until eggs are well-blended, but do not beat the mixture. Line muffin tins with paper liners. Fill each one about two-thirds full. Bake at 300 degrees for 30–40 minutes. Check to see if muffins are done by inserting a toothpick in one near the center of the muffin. If the toothpick does not come out clean, bake for another 5 minutes. Let muffins cool 5 minutes before removing them from the pan. These taste much like brownies. Keep any leftovers in a covered container, then rewarm them.

CRANBERRY BANANA NUT BREA[D]

2 cups flour
3 teaspoons baking powder
1/2 teaspoon salt
1/2 teaspoon cinnamon
1 cup fresh cranberries, ground
1 teaspoon grated orange rind
1 cup mashed very ripe bananas (large)
1/2 cup milk
4 tablespoons butter
1 cup sugar
1 egg
1 cup chopped pecans

Sift together flour, baking powde[r], salt and cinnamon. Blend orange ri[nd] with ground cranberries. In 2-qua[rt] bowl, blend bananas and milk. Crea[m] butter and sugar together; blend [in] egg. Sift dry ingredients alternate[ly] with banana mixture, stirring un[til] just blended. Stir in cranberry mi[x]ture and pecans. Bake in 9x5x3-inc[h] pan at 350 degrees for 1 hour and 1[5] minutes. Store at least 24 hours be[fore slicing.

BUTTERMILK CORN BREAD

3/4 cup Lysine cornmeal
1 cup white flour
3 tablespoons sugar
1 teaspoon soda
3/4 teaspoon salt
1 cup buttermilk
1 egg, beaten
2 tablespoons melted margarine

Preheat oven to 400 degrees. Si[ft] together cornmeal, flour, sugar an[d] salt. Set aside.

Dissolve soda in buttermilk. Ad[d] beaten egg and melted margarine; sti[r] until mixed, then add to dry ingredi[ents and mix well. Turn into grease[d] 9x9-inch pan, or into greased muffi[n] pan. Bake 20 minutes, or until golde[n] and done.

These are delicious and healthfu[l] eating.

RYE CRACKERS

2 cups rye flour
2 cups wheat flour
Salt to taste
1/4 teaspoon baking soda
1/2 cup vegetable oil
1 cup (or more) water
1 tablespoon caraway seeds

Mix together. Roll out thinly on floured surface. Cut into desired shapes. Bake on cookie sheets at 275 degrees for about 30 minutes.

DILL CRACKERS

2/3 cup Wesson oil
1 envelope ranch-style dry salad dressing
1 teaspoon dill
1/2 teaspoon lemon pepper
1/4 teaspoon garlic salt
10 ounce package oyster crackers

Mix all together, except crackers. Coat crackers with mixture, tossing until well coated, about 5 or 6 minutes.

NUT BALLS

1 stick butter
1 cup pecans
1 teaspoon vanilla
2 tablespoons sugar
1 cup flour

Mix all ingredients and roll into tiny balls and bake at 250 degrees for one hour. Cool slightly and roll in confectioners' sugar. Roll in sugar again about half-hour later.

TUNA SPREAD

1 can tuna (water packed), drained

---

1 (8-ounce) package cream cheese, softened
1 small onion, finely chopped
Salt and pepper to taste

Blend all ingredients until smooth. Serve with crackers. This can be rolled into a log and used for all types of festive entertaining.

NUTS, BOLTS AND SCREWS

1 pound pecans
1 large box Cherrios
1 medium box stick pretzels
1 tablespoon Worcestershire sauce
1 box Wheat Chex
2 tablespoons salt
1 tablespoon garlic salt
1 pound oleo or butter

Melt butter in large roaster. Pour in all cereals, nuts and pretzels and seasonings. set oven at 200 degrees. Stir every 15 minutes for 1 hour.

WHEAT GERM CRUNCHIES
Makes 3-1/2 dozen

1/2 cup all-purpose flour
1/2 teaspoon soda
2 teaspoons baking powder
1/4 teaspoon salt
1 cup brown sugar, firmly packed
1/2 cup shortening
1 egg, beaten
1/2 teaspoon vanilla
1/2 cup coconut
1/2 cup uncooked oatmeal
1 cup wheat germ
1-1/2 cups corn or wheat flakes

Sift flour, soda, baking powder and salt. Cream shortening and sugar. Add egg and vanilla. Add dry ingredients and wheat germ. Mix well. Stir in coconut, oatmeal and cornflakes just enough to mix. Drop by teaspoons on greased cookie sheet or roll into walnut-sized balls with fingers and place on greased cookie

---

sheet. Bake 15 minutes at 350 degrees.

TAFFY APPLES

1 large can crushed pineapple (save drained juice)
2-1/2 cups miniature marshmallows
1 egg
1 tablespoon flour
12 ounces Cool Whip
3/4 cup cocktail or Spanish peanuts
1-1/2 tablespoons vinegar
1/2 cup sugar
4-6 apples, unpeeled and chopped

Combine drained pineapple and marshmallows; refrigerate overnight. Beat pineapple juice, egg, flour, vinegar and sugar; heat until thick, stirring constantly. Cool and refrigerate overnight, separate from pineapple.

Next day: Mix sauce and Cool Whip; add peanuts, marshmallow mixture and apples; stir. Refrigerate at least 2 hours before serving.

CELERY PINWHEELS

1 medium stalk celery
1 (3-ounce) package cream cheese
2 tablespoons crumbled Roquefort cheese
Mayonnaise
Worcestershire sauce

Clean celery and separate branches. Blend together the softened cream cheese with the Roquefort cheese. Add mayonnaise to make the mixture of spreading consistency and season with a dash of Worcestershire sauce. Fill the branches of celery with cheese mixture. Press branches back into the original form of the stalk. Roll in waxed paper and chill overnight in refrigerator. Just before serving, slice celery crosswise forming pinwheels. Arrange pinwheels on crisp lettuce for serving.

HAM BALLS

Makes approximately 48 appetizers

4 cups ground lean ham
1/2 cup finely chopped onion
1/4 teaspoon pepper
2 eggs
1 cup plain bread crumbs

Combine and mix all ingredients. Shape into 1-inch balls. Place in a shallow pan and bake at 400 degrees for 25 minutes.

Sour Cream Gravy:
2 tablespoons shortening
2 tablespoons flour
1/4 teaspoon dill seed
1/4 teaspoon marjoram
1/2 cup water
1 1/2 cups sour cream

Melt shortening; add flour and seasonings. Cook until it bubbles. Add water and sour cream, stirring constantly. Cook until thick. Makes 2 cups sauce.

Serve *Ham Balls* with *Sour Cream Gravy;* provide toothpicks for dipping.

DEVILED TURKEY BONBONS

1 cup cooked, finely chopped turkey
1 cup finely chopped nuts
1 tablespoon chopped onion
2 tablespoons chopped pimiento
1/4 teaspoon salt
Hot pepper sauce to taste
1/4 cup cream of mushroom soup.

Combine turkey and 1/2 cup nuts. Add remaining ingredients except remaining nuts; mix well. Shape into small balls and roll in remaining chopped nuts. Chill until serving time.

SIMPLE HORS D'OEUVRES

It's true that these tempting tidbits have a French name, may be very elaborate, and are usually met in hotels, but that's no reason for not serving them simply, in the home, for a little variety.

Try a bit of pink, moist salmon on a piece of rye toast . . . some ripe olives . . . celery, stuffed with cream cheese flavored with mayonnaise, salt and paprika, or filled with a mixture of equal parts cream cheese and Roquefort cheese which has been seasoned with Worcestershire sauce . . . slices of salami. . . . All these are as truly and delightfully "hors d'oeuvres" as the most elaborate arrangement of caviar and egg.

CHEESE SURPRISE APPETIZERS

2 cups grated sharp cheddar cheese
1/2 cup softened butter
1 cup flour
1 small jar green, pimiento-stuffed olives

Mix cheese, butter and flour to form dough. Shape into small balls about 1 inch in diameter. Flatten ball with hands; place one olive in center, wrap dough around it, sealing edges completely. Freeze until just before ready to serve. (These *must* be frozen.)

When ready to serve, place frozen appetizers on baking sheet and immediately place in 375-degree oven. Bake about 10 minutes, or until golden. Cheese will puff up and melt.

ASPARAGUS ROLLS

Makes 20 appetizers

20 slices bread
1 package frozen asparagus
1 5-ounce jar processed pimiento cheese spread

Trim crusts from bread slices; spread each with cheese. Cook asparagus until just tender. Chill. Lay one piece asparagus diagonally across slice of bread. Turn opposite corners over asparagus, overlapping. Press firmly to seal. Wrap several sandwiches together in waxed paper. Place in covered container and chill for several hours.

MEATBALL APPETIZERS

Makes about 8 dozen tiny meatballs and 2 cups sauce

1 1/2 pounds ground beef
2 eggs
1/4 cup milk
1 cup plain bread crumbs
1/4 cup chopped onion
1 1/2 teaspoons chopped parsley
1 1/2 teaspoons salt
1/8 teaspoon pepper
3 tablespoons oil
10-ounce bottle chili sauce
1/2 cup grape jelly
1 tablespoon instant coffee

Combine meat, eggs, milk, crumbs, onion, parsley, salt and pepper and mix well. Shape into tiny meatballs and brown well on all sides in skillet in hot oil. Remove meatballs from pan. Drain excess drippings, leaving just 2-3 tablespoons. Add chili sauce, jelly and instant coffee to pan drippings and simmer, stirring occasionally, until jelly melts (about 4 minutes). Add meatballs and simmer 10 more minutes. Serve on toothpicks.

Meatballs can be browned, refrigerated, then cooked with sauce just before serving.

ANTIPASTO

2 cans tuna fish, undrained
1 can anchovies, undrained
1 small jar stuffed olives, drained
1 small bottle cocktail onions, drained
1 medium can mushrooms, cut up and drained
1 jar sweet pickled cauliflower, drained and cut in small pieces
1 small jar tiny sweet pickles, drained and cut in small pieces
1 No. 2 can green beans, drained
1 cup carrots, cooked crisp, cut in small rings
1 bottle chili sauce
1 bottle catsup

Mix all ingredients. Add a little salad oil if not moist enough. Marinate in refrigerator for at least one day. Eat with crackers. Makes a delicious hors d'oeuvre.

BRAUNSCHWEIGER BALL

(8-ounce) package cream cheese, softened
pound braunschweiger, at room temperature
¼ cup mayonnaise
¼ teaspoon garlic salt
tablespoons dill pickle juice
¾-¾ cup chopped dill pickle
¼ cup (or more) chopped onion
drops Tabasco sauce
tablespoon Worcestershire sauce
½ cup salted peanuts, chopped

Combine half the cream cheese with the remaining ingredients, except peanuts; mix well. Spread in a mold. Chill for several hours. Unmold. Frost with remaining cream cheese. Garnish with chopped peanuts. Snack with assorted crackers or slices of party loaf bread.

SAVORY CHEESE BITES
Makes 7 dozen

1 cup water
1/8 teaspoon salt
4 eggs
1/2 cup butter
1 cup flour
1 cup shredded Swiss cheese

Combine water, butter, and salt in a pan; bring to a boil. Stir until butter melts. Add flour; stir vigorously until mixture leaves sides of pan to form a smooth ball. Remove from heat. Add eggs, one at a time; stir until well-blended. Return to heat and beat mixture until smooth. Remove from heat; stir in cheese. Drop batter by heaping teaspoonfuls onto a greased baking sheet. Bake 400 degrees for 20 minutes, or until puffed and golden brown.

SALMON LOG

1 (1-pound) can salmon
1 (8-ounce) package cream cheese, softened
1 tablespoon lemon juice
2 tablespoons grated onion
1 teaspoon prepared horseradish
1/4 teaspoon salt
1 teaspoon liquid smoke seasoning
1/2 cup chopped walnuts
3 tablespoons snipped parsley

Drain and flake salmon, removing skin and bones. Combine salmon with the next 6 ingredients; mix well. Chill several hours. Combine walnuts and parsley. Shape salmon mixture into 8x2-inch log, or use a fish mold. Roll in nut mixture. Chill well. Serve with crisp crackers.

DILL WEED DIP

2/3 cup real mayonnaise
2/3 cup sour cream
1 tablespoon dried onion
1 tablespoon dried parsley
2 teaspoons dill weed
1 teaspoon Lawry's seasoning salt
Dash pepper
2 drops Tabasco sauce
1/2 teaspoon Worcestershire sauce
1/2 teaspoon Accent

Mix together and let set at least 2 hours before serving. Fresh vegetables and bread cubes are great to serve with the dip.

SAUSAGE TEMPERS IN APPLESAUCE
Makes 4 dozen

1   pound pork sausage
2   cups applesauce

1   ounce cinnamon red candies
2   drops red food coloring

Form sausage in ¾-inch balls. Brown and cook meatballs in a skillet. Turn them so they brown evenly. Place a toothpick in each ball. Heat applesauce, candies and food coloring until candies dissolve. Place sausage balls in sauce, toothpick side up. Serve hot.

Note: A chafing dish would be ideal in which to keep sausages hot while serving.

CRAB PUFFS

1   cup water
1   stick margarine
1   cup flour
4   eggs

Bring water to boil and add margarine, return to boil. Add flour all at once. Remove from heat and beat in 1 egg at a time. Then add all the following ingredients:
3   scallions, chopped
1   teaspoon dry mustard
1   (6½-ounce) can crabmeat
1   teaspoon Worcestershire sauce
½   cup sharp cheddar cheese, grated

Drop on cookie sheet by spoonfuls. Bake at 400 degrees for 15 minutes. Turn oven down to 350 degrees and bake 10 additional minutes.

These can also be frozen.

CANAPE PUFFS
Makes about 25 puffs

1/2 cup water
1/4 cup (1/2 stick) butter
1/2 cup flour
2 eggs

Heat water and butter to boiling; reduce heat and stir in flour all at once. Stir about 1 minute until mixture forms ball around spoon. Remove from heat and beat in eggs, one at a time, until mixture is smooth.

Place by rounded teaspoonsful onto ungreased cookie sheets. Bake in a preheated 400-degree oven for about 25 minutes or until golden. Remove and cool on racks.

Slice off tops; remove any doughy insides. Fill with any sandwich filling; chill until serving time.

EGG & HAM HORS D'OEUVRES
Makes 20 appetizers

5 hard-cooked eggs
1 teaspoon minced chives
Salt and paprika
1-2 drops hot pepper sauce
Mayonnaise
1/2 pound boiled ham

Separate yolks and whites of eggs. Force yolks through a sieve; add chives, seasonings and mayonnaise to moisten. Beat to a smooth paste. Chop egg whites and ham together and mix with yolks. Form into 1-inch balls and garnish with additional mayonnaise.

BLUE CHEESE MUSHROOMS

1 pound mushrooms (1-1 1/2 inches in diameter)
1/4 cup green onion slices
2 tablespoons butter or margarine
1 cup (4 ounces) crumbled blue cheese
1 small package (3 ounces) cream cheese, softened

Remove stems from mushrooms; chop stems. Saute stems and green onion in margarine until soft. Combine with cheeses, mixing well. Stuff mixture into mushroom caps. Place on a broiler pan rack and broil for 2-3 minutes or until golden brown. Serve hot.

SWEET AND SOUR MEATBALLS

1 pound lean ground beef
1 envelope dry onion-soup mix
1 egg
Combine beef, soup mix and egg and form into tiny meatballs. Brown in skillet; discard all but 1 tablespoon fat.

Sauce:
8-ounce can tomato sauce
16-ounce can whole-berry cranberry sauce

Combine ingredients for sauce with reserved tablespoon of fat from meat in saucepan. Heat; add meatballs. Cover and simmer for about an hour. Serve with toothpicks.

PEPPERONI BALLS

1 package hot roll mix
1/4 pound mozzarella cheese, cut in cubes
1/4-1/2 lb. pepperoni, thinly sliced

Prepare roll mix according to package directions, but *omitting egg* and using *1 cup water*. Dough does *not* need to rise. Place one cheese cube on one pepperoni slice. Pinch off a piece of dough and shape carefully around cheese and pepperoni, forming a ball. Repeat until all ingredients are used.

Fry in deep hot oil for about 5 minutes, or until golden brown, turning once. Drain on paper towels and serve warm.

BLUE CHEESE BITES
Makes 40 appetizers

1 package (10-count) refrigerated biscuits

1/4 cup margarine
3 tablespoons crumbled blue cheese or grated Parmesan cheese

Cut each biscuit into four pie[ces] Arrange pieces on two greased 8×[×]2-inch round baking pans. Melt m[ar]garine; add cheese and stir to ble[nd] Drizzle cheese mixture over bisc[uits] Bake in 400-degree oven for 12 minutes.

CHICKEN WINGS

1 pound chicken wings
1/4 pound (1 stick) butter
1/4 teaspoon garlic powder
2 tablespoons parsley
1 cup fine, dry bread crumbs
1/2 cup Parmesan cheese
1 teaspoon salt
1/4 teaspoon pepper

Cut off tips from chicken win[gs] and discard; split remaining porti[on] of wing at joint to form two piec[es] Melt butter, mixing in garlic powd[er] Combine bread crumbs, Parmes[an] cheese and seasonings. Dip chick[en] wing portions in seasoned butter, th[en] roll in crumbs. Bake on a greas[ed] baking sheet (use one with edges) i[n] preheated 325-degree oven for abo[ut] 50 minutes.

These can be frozen and bak[ed] later.

DEVILED EGGS

4 hard-cooked eggs
1/3 cup grated Parmesan cheese
1 teaspoon prepared mustard
Pepper
Skim milk
Paprika

Halve the eggs lengthwise; remo[ve] yolks and mash. Add the chees[e,] mustard, few grains pepper, an[d] enough milk to moisten well. Bea[t] until fluffy and refill the egg whites May want to garnish with paprika fo[r] added color. (65 calories per egg hal[f]

DIPPETY DOO DIP

1 squeeze tube of hickory smoked cheese
1 cup sour cream
1 can bean with bacon soup (undiluted)
2 or 3 minced green onions (use all)

Combine all ingredients and warm over double boiler or in Microwave. Mix well. Serve with tortilla chips. You can't eat just one!

SNACKIN DIPS FOR CHIPS
Serves 4

1 can (6 1/2 ounce) chunk tuna
1 envelope instant onion soup mix
1 cup dairy sour cream
1 tablespoon prepared horseradish
Parsley for garnish
Potato chips - celery sticks - cherry tomatoes

Drain tuna. Combine tuna with soup mix, sour cream, and horseradish. Garnish with parsley. Arrange potato chips, celery sticks, and tomatoes on platter.

LOW CAL CLAM DIP
Makes 2 cups

1-8 ounce can minced clams
1-1/2 cups cottage cheese
1/2 teaspoon seasoned salt
2 teaspoons lemon juice
1 teaspoon Worcestershire sauce
1 tablespoon minced green onions
Assorted crisp vegetable dippers

In blender container, combine clams with liquid, cottage cheese seasoned salt, lemon juice, and Worcestershire sauce. Cover and whirl around until smooth. Stir in green onions. Cover and chill at least two hours to blend flavors. Serve with cauliflower, broccoli, and strips of carrots, zucchini, and cucumbers.

BLUE CHEESE DIP

3 ounces blue cheese, crumbled
1/2 cup sour cream
1/2 cup mayonnaise
Dash of paprika
Dash of garlic powder
Assorted vegetables, cut in strips

Mix together all ingredients except vegetables and chill 2 hours to blend flavors. Serve with vegetables.

RAW VEGETABLE DIP
Yield - 2-1/2 cups

2 cups applesauce
1/2 pint dairy sour cream
2 tablespoons minced onion
1 teaspoon Worcestershire sauce
1/2 teaspoon salt

Slowly cook applesauce abut 5 minutes to evaporate some of the liquid; chill. Combine the applesauce, sour cream, onion, Worcestershire sauce and salt. Mix well. Use as a dip for fresh, raw vegetables of your choice.

CHEESE BALL

8 ounce cream cheese
6 ounce blue cheese, crumbled
6 ounce jar Old English cheese
2 tablespoons mayonnaise
Dash of garlic salt
2 tablespoons finely chopped onion
6 ounce chopped walnuts

Mix all three (3) cheeses together with an electric mixer. Add mayonnaise, garlic salt, onion, and walnuts to cheese mixture. Shape into a ball and wrap with plastic wrap. Refrigerate twenty-four (24) hours before serving. When ready to serve, sprinkle paprika.

CHEESE DIP
Makes 3-1/2 cups

2 cups sour cream
1-1/2 cups shredded Cheddar cheese
1/4 cup sliced pimiento-stuffed olives
1/2 teaspoon salt
1/4 teaspoon sage

Blend sour cream with remaining ingredients. Serve chilled. Especially good with saltine crackers!

FRUIT DIP
Make 3 cups

2 cups sour cream
1/4 cup drained crushed pineapple
2/3 cup chopped red apples
1/2 teaspoon curry powder
1/2 teaspoon garlic salt
Apple slices for garnish

Blend sour cream with apple, pineapple, curry powder, and garlic salt. Place in bowl and chill. Garnish with sliced apples around outer edge of bowl.

Good with corn chips or shredded wheat wafers.

FRESH MUSHROOM DIP

1-8 ounce package cream cheese, softened
2 tablespoons snipped ripe olives
2 tablespoons snipped parsley
3/4 teaspoon seasoned salt
4 drops bottled hot pepper sauce
1/2 cup sour cream
1/2 pound fresh mushrooms, finely chopped

Combine cream cheese and seasonings; fold in sour cream and chill. Stir in mushrooms just before serving.

CHEESE-COCONUT BALLS

Makes about 30

2 packages (3 ounces each) Roquefort cheese
1 package (4 ounces) shredded cheddar cheese
1 package (8 ounces) cream cheese, softened
1 package (3 1/2 ounces) flaked coconut

Mash cheeses and combine them thoroughly with electric mixer. Chill for at least one hour. Shape into 1-inch balls and roll in coconut. Serve with fresh apple slices.

PINEAPPLE CHICKEN WINGS

Serves 4

12 chicken wings
3 tablespoons butter
1 small onion, sliced
8 1/2-ounce can pineapple chunks, drained, juice reserved
Orange juice
1/4 cup soy sauce
2 tablespoons brown sugar
1 tablespoon vinegar
1 teaspoon ground ginger
1/2 teaspoon salt
1/2 teaspoon ground mace
1/2 teaspoon hot pepper sauce
1/4 teaspoon dry mustard
1 1/2 tablespoons cornstarch

Fold chicken wing tips under to form triangles. Melt butter in large skillet; add wings and onion. Cook until wings are brown on both sides, about 10 minutes. Measure reserved pineapple syrup and add enough orange juice to make 1 1/4 cups liquid. Blend in soy sauce, sugar, vinegar, ginger, salt, mace, hot pepper sauce and mustard. Pour over chicken.

Cover and simmer 30 minutes, or until chicken is tender, basting top pieces once or twice. Remove chicken to hot plate. Add a small amount of water to cornstarch, blending to dissolve. Add slowly to the hot liquid in pan, stirring, and bring to boil to thicken. Return chicken to skillet, along with pineapple chunks.

Serve chicken wings and sauce with steamed rice.

BROILED CHICKEN LIVER ROLL-UPS

2 cans water chestnuts
1 pound chicken livers
1/2 pound bacon (cut each slice into thirds)
1 bottle soy sauce
1/2 cup brown sugar

Drain water chestnuts and slice each into 3 pieces. Wrap each water chestnut with a small piece of chicken liver and bacon piece. Secure with a toothpick and marinate in soy sauce for at least 4 hours.

Just before serving, remove roll-ups from soy sauce and roll each in brown sugar. Place on broiler rack and broil for about 10 minutes, or until crisp. Serve at once.

MUSHROOM TARTS

Makes 60

⅔ cup butter
2½ cups flour
½ teaspoon salt
⅓ cup sour cream
1 egg, slightly beaten

Cut butter into flour and salt. Add sour cream and egg. Cut with pastry blender until well-blended. Using 1 teaspoon dough, press into bottom and side of tart muffin pans. Bake at 400 degrees for 12–15 minutes, or until golden. Remove from tart pan and cool.

Filling:
2 tablespoons chopped green onions
½ pound chopped mushrooms
¼ cup butter
¼ cup flour
½ teaspoon salt
1 cup heavy cream

Sauté mushrooms and onions in butter. Stir in flour and salt. Add cream; stir until thick and smooth. Fill shells; garnish with parsley and serve. Can be frozen. To serve, heat 10 minutes at 400 degrees.

ROLLED SANDWICHES

Makes 25-30 sandwiches

1 loaf of bread, sliced into lengthwise slices
Filling:
1/4 pound (1 stick) butter, softened
4 ounces cream cheese
1/4 teaspoon paprika
1/4 teaspoon salt
1 tablespoon mayonnaise
3/4 cup minced nuts, raisins, dates and/or figs

Slice crusts from long pieces bread. Combine *Filling* ingredien well. Spread on bread slices. Roll u from narrow ends. (Before rollin strips of sweet pickles or olives ma be placed over filling for colorf variations.) Press end of roll firml and wrap each roll tightly in plasti wrap. Store in refrigerator overnigh

Before serving, slice each roll int 1/4-inch slices. Arrange on servin plate.

Note: Instead of the nuts-and-dried fruit filling, you can use one of th following: 1 1/2 cups tuna salad, crab shrimp, salmon, finely chopped raw vegetables, grated cheddar cheese chicken, turkey or ham filling.

SHRIMP PUFFERS

Makes 60 appetizers

8 tablespoons softened butter or margarine
2 eggs, separated
3 cups shredded sharp cheddar cheese
15 slices white bread (thin-sliced)
60 cooked shrimp, shelled and deveined

Blend butter, cheese and egg yolk until smooth. Beat egg whites until stiff; fold into cheese mixture.

Trim crusts from thinly sliced bread; cut each piece in quarters diagonally. Top each slice with a shrimp and 1 teaspoon of the cheese mixture. Bake in a preheated 350-degree oven on lightly greased cookie sheets for about 15 minutes, or until puffy and golden.

Beverages

REFRESHING

FIRECRACKER PUNCH
Serves 30

- 4 cups cranberry juice
- 1½ cups sugar
- 4 cups pineapple juice
- 1 tablespoon almond extract
- 2 quarts ginger ale

Combine first 4 ingredients; stir until sugar is dissolved. Chill. Add ginger ale just before serving.

JELL-O FROSTY

- 1 (8-ounce) glass cold milk
- 1 heaping teaspoon flavored gelatin (not lemon or lime)
- 1 teaspoon sugar

Mix well. Place in refrigerator until thickened. Add a scoop of ice cream.

COCOA MIX

- 2 cups powdered milk
- 1 cup white sugar
- ⅓ cup cocoa
- ½ teaspoon salt (optional)

Sift the ingredients together 3 times. Use 3 tablespoons to a cup of hot water—not boiling. Serve cold for chocolate milk. Put cocoa mix in a container and place on kitchen shelf.

STRAWBERRY COOLER
Serves 6

- 2 large (6-ounce) packages strawberry gelatin
- 2 cups hot water
- 1 cup cold water
- 1 large bottle ginger ale, chilled
- 1 quart vanilla ice cream

Dissolve gelatin in hot water; add cold water. Chill for about 1 hour until syrupy. Pour ½ cup gelatin syrup into each of 6 chilled (16-ounce) glasses. Divide half the ginger ale equally among the glasses; stir well. Divide ice cream equally into glasses; fill with remaining ginger ale. Garnish with whole strawberries, if desired.

HOT MULLED CIDER

- 1 quart apple juice
- 1 quart pineapple juice
- 2 cinnamon sticks
- 12 whole cloves

Combine all ingredients and simmer gently for about 5 minutes. Save time by mixing the day before and then heating when ready to serve on the day of the breakfast.

HOT SPICED CIDER

- 1 gallon apple cider
- ½ cup brown sugar
- 2 lemons, sliced
- 2 oranges, sliced
- 8 whole cloves, studded into orange/lemon slices (1 clove to a slice)
- 4 cinnamon sticks

Combine all ingredients in a saucepan. Bring to a boil over medium heat; reduce and simmer for about 10 minutes.

ORANGE APPLE CIDER

Mix the following ingredients together:

- 1 gallon apple cider
- 1 cup sugar
- 1 small can frozen orange juice, diluted
- 1 small can frozen lemonade, undiluted

Take out 2 or 3 cups and add:

- 2 teaspoons whole cloves
- 2 sticks cinnamon

Bring to a boil for a few seconds; then turn off heat and let sit for a little while. Strain and return to other liquid.

Keep in refrigerator until needed and heat up as desired.

CHOCO-NUTTY STEAMER
Serves 2–4

3 tablespoons creamy peanut butter
2 tablespoons chocolate syrup
2 cups milk

Mix peanut butter and chocolate syrup in saucepan. Gradually stir in milk. Heat over medium heat until hot. Do not boil.

FRUIT JUICE SURPRISE
Serves 4

A nutritious drink.

3 cups unsweetened fruit juice (grape, pineapple, apple, etc.)
1 cup fruit pieces, such as apple, banana and orange

Cut up fruit and place some in each glass; add juice.

WEDDING PUNCH
Makes 1 gallon

3 cups sugar
6 cups boiling water
¼ cup green tea leaves
3 cups fresh *or* prepared orange juice
1 cup fresh *or* frozen lemon juice
3 cups pineapple juice
Food coloring (optional)
1½ quarts ginger ale

Combine sugar and 3 cups of boiling water; stir until sugar is dissolved. Boil about 7 minutes; do not stir. Pour remaining boiling water over tea leaves; cover and let steep about 5 minutes. Strain and cool. Combine fruit juices, sugar mixture, tea and food coloring. Add ginger ale and enough ice cubes to keep chilled.

BANANA MILK SHAKE
Serves 1

Frosty and refreshing!

1 cup milk, made from non-fat dry milk
1 banana

Mash banana well; add milk and blend with beater or shake in jar. Serve immediately or refrigerate and serve later.
Variations: One-half teaspoon vanilla extract may be added.

Mary Linger, Jacksonville, Fla.

HOT TEA PUNCH

½ cup sugar
½ cup water
1 (2-inch) stick cinnamon
1 teaspoon grated lemon rind
1½ teaspoons grated orange rind
¼ cup orange juice
2 tablespoons lemon juice
¼ cup canned pineapple juice
3 cups boiling water
3 tablespoons tea leaves *or* 9 tea bags

In saucepan combine sugar, water, cinnamon, lemon and orange rinds; boil 5 minutes. Remove cinnamon stick. Add orange, lemon and pineapple juice; keep hot. Pour boiling water over tea; steep 5 minutes; strain. Combine with juice. Serve hot, float orange slices with cloves on top.

HONEY-SPICED TEA
Makes 1 quart

1 quart boiling water
2 large tea bags
½ cup honey
2 tablespoons lemon juice
¼ teaspoon ground allspice
⅛ teaspoon ground nutmeg
Lemon slices, halved

Pour boiling water over tea bags; cover and let stand 4 minutes. Remove tea bags. Add next 4 ingredients, stirring until honey dissolves. Stir over low heat until thoroughly heated. Serve with lemon slices.

PEANUT BUTTER MILK SHAKE
Serves 3 (1-cup servings)

1¼ cups milk
⅓ cup creamy peanut butter
1 pint vanilla ice cream

Put milk and peanut butter into electric blender container. Blend on high speed until smooth. Add ice cream and blend until desired consistency.
Note: 1 cut-up banana and/or ⅓ cup chocolate syrup may be added to milk.

ORANGE-FLAVOR ANGEL
Serves 3

3 cups reconstituted Birds Eye® Awake
3 tablespoons vanilla *instant* pudding
1 tablespoon lemon juice

Combine all ingredients in bowl. Beat until well-blended. Pour mixture over ice in tall glasses. Garnish with orange slice, if desired.
Note: Beverage may be made ahead of time and chilled. Stir before serving.

KOOL-AID FIZZY

1 (0.14-ounce) package unsweetened Kool-Aid, any flavor
1 cup sugar
6 cups cold water
1 (12-ounce) can Mountain Dew
  soda pop
  Ice

Combine all ingredients in 2-quart pitcher and mix well.

PINK PUNCH
Makes 8 cups

2 (6-ounce) cans frozen pink lemonade
1 (46-ounce) can pineapple
  juice
1 (46-ounce) can Hawaiian
  Punch
4 cups ginger ale

Add water to lemonade to make 8 cups. Add other ingredients and mix well. Chill.

PEACH 'N PINEAPPLE SHAKE

1 pint vanilla ice cream, softened
¾ cup drained, chilled, canned,
  sliced peaches
¾ cup chilled unsweetened
  pineapple juice
1 cup cold milk
½ teaspoon vanilla extract
  Fresh mint, if desired

Place ice cream, peaches and pine-apple juice in blender and cover. Blend on high speed until smooth. Add milk and vanilla. Blend well again. Serve at once in chilled, tall glasses garnished with fresh mint.

TOMATO JUICE COCKTAIL
Serves 6

2½ cups tomato juice
  1 teaspoon grated onion
  ½ teaspoon salt
1½ teaspoons sugar
  ½ teaspoon seasoned salt
  ½ teaspoon Worcestershire
    sauce

Combine all ingredients; stir well. Chill for several hours; serve in juice glasses.

ORANGE EGGNOG
Serves 2

1 egg
½ cup orange juice
1 tablespoon lemon juice
  Crushed ice
2 tablespoons sugar
  Dash nutmeg

Dissolve sugar in the fruit juices. Add egg and crushed ice. Shake until egg is thoroughly beaten and foamy. Strain and serve over crushed ice. Put a few grains of nutmeg on top.

COTTONTAIL MILK SHAKE
Serves 1

1 banana
1 egg
1 cup cold milk
1 tablespoon honey
1 tablespoon peanut butter

Put all ingredients in blender and blend on high speed for 30 seconds. Pour into glass and serve.

ORANGE-FLAVORED EGGNOG
Makes 4 cups

⅓ cup frozen orange juice
  concentrate
1 pint vanilla ice cream
1 egg
2 cups milk
  Ground nutmeg

Blend concentrate, ice cream and egg together with electric mixer. Add milk slowly, beating constantly. Serve in chilled mugs with sprinkle of nutmeg.

JUICY FRUIT SHAKE
Serves 4

1½ cups sweetened pineapple
  juice
2½ cups milk

In blender, blend chilled sweetened pineapple, apricot and strawberry or raspberry juice and milk. Serve over ice.

HOT CRANBERRY SIPPER
Serves 6–8

½ cup sugar
1 cinnamon stick
3 cups cranberry juice
1 (6-ounce) can frozen orange
  juice concentrate, undiluted
¾ cup water
1 tablespoon lemon juice

In 8-cup glass measure combine all ingredients. Cook on HIGH for 8 minutes in the microwave oven.

FROZEN FRUIT SLUSH
Serves 12

- 2½ cups water
- 1 cup sugar
- 1 (6-ounce) can frozen lemonade
- 1 (6-ounce) can frozen orange juice
- 1 (10-ounce) carton frozen strawberries
- 1 large can crushed pineapple
- 3 bananas, sliced

Cook water and sugar until dissolved. Add the rest of the ingredients. Mix well. Keep frozen until 30 minutes or more before serving. Serve while slushy. You can use any kind of fruit in place of strawberries, especially fruit in season.

HEALTHFUL FRUIT DRINK

- 5 pounds finely chopped rhubarb
- 1 gallon water to cover rhubarb

Cook rhubarb and water until soft; strain. You can use the remaining fruit as a sauce.

To the rhubarb juice add:

- 1½ pounds sugar
- 1 (46-ounce) can orange juice
- *or*
- 1 large can frozen orange juice plus the water as directed
- 1 cup Real Lemon juice

Stir and heat to dissolve sugar; bring to just the boiling point. Pour into hot sterilized jars; seal. Keeps well and is a good drink anytime.

FROSTED AMBROSIA

Roll scoops of vanilla ice cream in flaked coconut. Put in sherbet glasses. Pour a little defrosted, but not diluted, orange juice concentrate around the ice-cream ball.

FRUIT-FLAVORED MILK
Makes 2 quarts

- 1 envelope powdered fruit drink (any flavor)
- 1 cup sugar
- 1 cup water
- 7 cups milk

Combine powdered drink mix, sugar and water. Stir until dissolved. Add mixture to milk and pour into pitcher to serve.

ORANGE FROSTED SHAKE
Serves 2

- 2 cups orange juice
- 4 scoops vanilla ice cream

In blender or with beater in bowl, blend juice and softened ice cream until frothy and ice cream is dissolved.

APPLE TEA COOLER

- 1 cup unsweetened apple juice
- 1 cup sweetened tea, according to own taste
- Ice cubes
- Lemon wedge

"YOUR FLAVOR" JULIUS DRINK

- 1 (6-ounce) can of juice (any flavor)
- 1 cup milk
- ½ cup water
- 15 ice cubes
- 1 egg
- ¼ cup sugar
- 1 teaspoon vanilla

Combine all ingredients in a blender and blend until consistency you desire.

PURPLE COW
Serves 4

- 2 cups milk
- 1 cup bottled grape soda
- 1 pint vanilla ice cream

Combine milk, grape soda and ½ of the ice cream in container of blender. Press high speed button and let mix until thick and foamy. To serve, pour into glasses. Top with remaining ice cream, divided evenly.

TANGY PUNCH
Makes 4 quarts

- 1 (6-ounce) can frozen grapefruit juice
- ½ of 6-ounce can frozen pineapple juice
- 1 (12-ounce) can apricot-pineapple nectar
- 1 cup cranberry juice
- 1 (1.5-liter) bottle rosé wine
- 1 quart club soda

Combine all ingredients and serve in punch bowl with decorated ice ring. Punch can be prepared ahead and refrigerated, adding the club soda just prior to serving.

Brunch
BUFFET

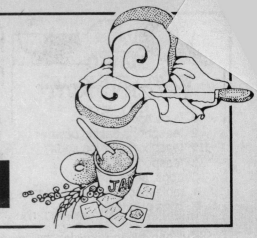

FRUIT DELIGHT

Prepare this ahead of time to allow flavors to develop.

- 1 (20-ounce) can pineapple chunks, juice pack
- 2 (11-ounce) cans mandarin orange sections, drained
- ½ to 1 cup seedless grapes, halved
- 2 kiwis, halved lengthwise and sliced
- ½ cup orange juice
- ¼ cup honey
- 1 tablespoon lemon juice

Drain pineapple; reserve juice. In a large bowl combine pineapple, mandarin oranges, grapes and kiwi. Combine pineapple liquid, orange juice, honey and lemon juice. Pour over fruit. Cover and chill until ready to serve.

QUICK & EASY PUFFY OMELET

- 2 tablespoons bread crumbs
- 3 eggs
- ⅛ teaspoon pepper
- 4 tablespoons milk
- ½ teaspoon salt
- 3 tablespoons butter

Soak bread crumbs in milk.

Separate eggs. Beat yolks until thick and lemon colored. Add crumbs and milk, salt and pepper. Beat egg whites until stiff. Gradually, fold the egg yolk mixture into the whites. Melt butter in the omelet pan or frying pan and allow it to run around the sides of the pan. Pour mixture into the pan and cook slowly for 10 minutes, or until lightly brown underneath. Put pan in a moderate 350-degree oven for 5–10 minutes until it is dry on top. Fold and turn onto a hot platter. Serve at once.

SAUSAGE WEDGES

- ½ pound bulk pork sausage
- 1 cup (4 ounces) shredded cheddar cheese *or* American
- 2 tablespoons diced onion
- ¾ cup milk
- 4 eggs, beaten
- 1 teaspoon dried parsley
- 2 tablespoons butter

Crumble sausage in a 9-inch pie plate. Cover with paper towel and microwave for 3–4 minutes on HIGH. Drain off fat; sprinkle cheese over sausage; stir in onion. In a medium bowl combine milk and eggs; add parsley and butter. Pour over sausage; cover with plastic wrap and microwave 4 minutes on HIGH. Stir; cover and microwave for 6–8 minutes on MEDIUM (50 percent). Let stand, covered, 5 minutes.

GET-UP-AND-GO FRENCH TOAST
Serves 4

- ½ cup creamy peanut butter
- ¼ cup apple butter *or* favorite jelly
- 8 slices white bread
- 1 egg, beaten
- ½ cup milk
- 2 teaspoons sugar
  Dash salt
  Margarine

Make 4 peanut butter and jelly sandwiches. Mix egg, milk, sugar and salt. Melt enough margarine over medium heat to cover bottom of skillet. Dip both sides of sandwiches in egg mixture. Fry until brown on both sides.

COTTAGE CHEESE WAFFLES

- ½ cup sifted flour
- ½ teaspoon salt
- 4 eggs
- ½ cup milk
- ⅓ cup vegetable oil
- 1 teaspoon vanilla
- 1 cup cottage cheese

Sift flour and salt together. Set aside. Beat eggs, milk, vegetable oil and vanilla together. Add cottage cheese and beat until smooth. Combine with flour. Cook as usual.

BASIC WAFFLE RECIPE

2 cups flour
2 teaspoons baking powder
1½ teaspoons baking soda
⅛ teaspoon salt
3 eggs, separated
1 tablespoon melted margarine
2 cups cold milk

Sift flour, baking powder, baking soda and salt together. Set aside. Separate eggs and beat yolks. Gradually add milk and melted margarine, stirring well. Stir in flour mixture. Beat egg whites until stiff and fold into mixture.

Blueberry Waffles:
1 cup blueberries, washed and dried
Basic Waffle Recipe

Fold blueberries into Basic Waffle Recipe and cook in waffle iron.

Strawberry Waffles:
1 cup strawberries, washed and uniformly sliced
Basic Waffle Recipe

Fold sliced strawberries into Basic Waffle Recipe. Cook.
Hint: Both of these recipes taste extra-special when served with a small amount of whipped cream topping!

Cheese Waffles:
1 cup grated cheddar cheese
Basic Waffle Recipe

Fold the grated cheddar cheese into the Basic Waffle Recipe and cook.
Hint: These enticing waffles can be served with creamed tuna fish, ham, chicken or vegetables!

Corn Waffles:
2 cups canned corn, drained
Basic Waffle Recipe

After preparing the Basic Waffle Recipe, mix in the corn and cook in waffle iron.
Hint: These waffles taste great at a barbecue with butter served beside fried chicken or barbecued beef.

TOPPINGS

PINEAPPLE SAUCE

2 tablespoons margarine
1½ cups canned crushed pineapple
1 tablespoon brown sugar

Combine all ingredients in a saucepan and cook until heated through. This can be served hot or cold over waffles along with vanilla ice cream.

CREAM CHEESE TOPPING

1 (8-ounce) package cream cheese
¼ cup milk (or less)
1 cup chopped dates

Beat cream cheese and add milk gradually until desired consistency.

BLUEBERRY TOPPING

1½ cups blueberries, washed and drained
¼ cup sugar
1 tablespoon cornstarch
⅓ cup hot water

Combine blueberries and sugar together. Heat water and cornstarch in a saucepan. Add blueberries and heat slightly. Again, this can be served hot or cold.

NIGHT-BEFORE FRENCH TOAST
Serves 4–6

1 loaf French bread, cut into ¾-inch slices
4 tablespoons butter
⅔ cup brown sugar
4 eggs, beaten
2 cups milk
½ teaspoon cinnamon

The night before serving, melt butter and brown sugar in a small pan, stirring. Pour into a 9 x 13-inch baking dish. Lay bread slices on top of brown sugar mix. Combine eggs with milk and cinnamon. Pour over the bread. Cover with plastic wrap and refrigerate overnight. In the morning preheat oven to 350 degrees and uncover baking dish. Bake for 30 minutes. Serve with syrup, honey or chopped blueberries mixed with 2 tablespoons orange juice.

BREAKFAST HONEY MUFFINS
Makes 9

1 cup sifted all-purpose flour
2 teaspoons baking powder
½ teaspoon salt
½ cup unsifted whole-wheat flour
½ cup milk
1 egg, well-beaten
½ cup honey
½ cup coarsely chopped, cooked prunes
1 teaspoon grated orange peel
¼ cup salad oil *or* melted shorting

Preheat oven to 400 degrees, and lightly grease 9 (2½-inch) muffin pan cups. In large bowl, sift the all-purpose flour with the baking powder and salt. Stir in whole-wheat flour. Combine milk and rest of ingredients in medium bowl. Add, all at once, to flour mixture, stirring only until mixture is moistened. Spoon into cups; bake 20–25 minutes, or until nicely browned. Serve warm.

HAM PANCAKE PIE
Serves 6

- 2 medium sweet potatoes, peeled and thinly sliced
- 3 cups diced, cooked ham
- 3 medium apples, peeled, cored and sliced
- ½ teaspoon salt
- ¼ teaspoon pepper
- 3 tablespoons brown sugar
- ¼ teaspoon curry powder
- ⅓ cup apple juice *or* water
- 1 cup pancake mix
- 1 cup milk
- ½ teaspoon dry mustard
- 2 tablespoons butter, melted

In a 2-quart greased casserole dish, layer half the potatoes, half the ham and half the apples. Combine salt, pepper, brown sugar and curry powder; sprinkle half the mixture over layers in dish. Repeat this process with remaining potatoes, ham, apples and brown sugar mixture. Pour apple juice or water over all. Cover dish and bake at 375 degrees until potatoes are tender, about 40 minutes. Beat together pancake mix, milk, mustard and butter. Remove casserole from oven when potatoes are done; pour pancake batter over top. Bake 20 minutes more, uncovered, or until pancake is puffed and golden.

CHEDDAR EGG BAKE

- 6 eggs, slightly beaten
- 1 cup shredded cheddar cheese (4 ounces)
- ½ cup milk
- 2 tablespoons margarine, softened
- 1 teaspoon prepared mustard
- ½ teaspoon salt
- ¼ teaspoon pepper

Heat oven to 325 degrees. Mix all ingredients. Pour into an ungreased 8 x 8 x 2-inch pan. Bake 25–30 minutes, or until eggs are set. A simple and delicious way to make eggs!

PIMIENTO-CHEESE SOUFFLE

- 6 tablespoons butter
- 6 tablespoons flour
- ⅛ teaspoon dry mustard
  Dash cayenne pepper
- 1½ cups milk
- 6 large eggs, separated
- 1½ cups shredded Swiss cheese
- 1 (4-ounce) jar pimientos, drained and chopped

Heat oven to 350 degrees. Lightly grease a quart soufflé dish. Melt butter in a medium saucepan. Stir in flour, mustard and cayenne. Gradually stir in milk over medium heat until mixture thickens and begins to boil, about 5 minutes. Stir in cheese and pimientos. When cheese is melted, set aside. Beat yolks in a large bowl until light and lemon colored. Stir cheese mixture into beaten yolks. Beat egg whites in a large bowl until soft peaks form. Gently fold beaten whites into cheese-yolk mixture. Pour mixture into soufflé dish. Bake until golden, puffy and a knife inserted comes out clean, approximately 45 minutes.

PUMPKIN FRITTERS
Makes 36

Great for a special breakfast and delicious with pork.

- 2 cups coarsely shredded pumpkin
- 1 teaspoon butter
- 1 large egg
- 1½ cups milk
- 3 tablespoons light brown sugar
- ¼ teaspoon salt
- 1 teaspoon cinnamon
- ½ teaspoon nutmeg
- 1 teaspoon vanilla extract
- 2 cups unsifted all-purpose flour
- 3 teaspoons baking powder

Vegetable oil for frying
Confectioners' sugar

In skillet, sauté shredded pumpkin in butter until no longer raw-looking. Drain. Wash and dry skillet. Add oil to make 2 inches; heat to 350 degrees. In bowl, combine egg, milk, brown sugar, salt, cinnamon, nutmeg, vanilla and pumpkin. Add flour and baking powder to pumpkin mixture; stir until well-combined. Drop fritter batter by heaping teaspoonfuls into hot fat. Fry on all sides for 2–3 minutes. Remove with slotted spoon. Drain on paper toweling. Serve hot, sprinkled with confectioners' sugar.

WINTER BERRY FRENCH TOAST
Serves 4

- ½ cup (canned *or* fresh) whole-berry cranberry sauce
- 1 (10-ounce) package frozen, sliced strawberries in syrup, thawed
- 2 teaspoons orange peel, finely grated
- 4 eggs
- 1¼ cups milk
- 1 tablespoon sugar
- ¼ teaspoon nutmeg
- 8 (1-inch-thick) slices day-old French bread (about 8 ounces)
- 3 tablespoons butter *or* margarine
  Confectioners' sugar

In 1-quart saucepan melt cranberry sauce over low heat, stirring constantly. Mix in strawberries and orange peel. Heat just to boiling; set aside. In shallow bowl beat eggs, milk, sugar and nutmeg to blend thoroughly. Soak bread slices in egg mixture to saturate. Melt some of the butter in large skillet over medium heat. Fry bread slices until browned, about 5 minutes on each side, adding butter to skillet as needed. Transfer to heated platter; dust with confectioners' sugar. Served with warm sauce.

HAM AND MUSHROOM TOAST
Serves 6

3 cups sliced mushrooms
6 tablespoons butter or margarine
2 tablespoons flour
3/4 cup bouillon
1 pint (16 ounces) sour cream
Salt
Pepper
6 slices ham
6 slices hot, buttered toast

Sauté mushrooms in butter (6 tablespoons) for 5 minutes. Add flour, then stir in 3/4 cup bouillon and the sour cream. Cook, stirring, until smooth; season with salt and pepper, and if you wish with chives, tarragon, or dill. Put sliced ham on the hot, buttered toast. Top with mushrooms, and serve at once.

This is a great brunch dish. It is delicious!

OVEN-BAKED APPLE-PECAN PANCAKE

3 cups thin-sliced apples
3/4 cup complete pancake mix
1/2 cup water
1/2 cup margarine
1/4 cup pecans, chopped
1/3 cup sugar
3 eggs
1 teaspoon cinnamon

Preheat oven to 450 degrees. Combine pancake mix, water, eggs, and 1 tablespoon sugar; mix well.

In a 9- or 10-inch ovenproof skillet, sauté apples in melted margarine over medium heat until tender. If an ovenproof skillet is not available, sauté the apples in regular skillet and transfer to pie plate. Remove skillet from heat; sprinkle with nuts. Pour batter evenly over apples and nuts. Mix remaining sugar and cinnamon; sprinkle over batter.

Cover skillet with lid or foil; bake at 450 degrees for 12-14 minutes, or until pancake is puffed and sugar is melted. Loosen sides of pancake from skillet. Cool slightly. Cut into wedges to serve.

THANKSGIVING MORN PUMPKIN COFFEE CAKE
Serves 12

½ cup butter
¾ cup sugar
1¼ teaspoons vanilla extract
3 eggs
2 cups all-purpose flour
1 teaspoon baking powder
1 teaspoon baking soda
½ cup sour cream
1¾ cups solid-pack pumpkin
1 egg, lightly beaten
⅓ cup sugar
1½ teaspoons pumpkin pie spice
Streusel (recipe follows)

Cream butter, ¾ cup sugar and vanilla; add eggs; beat well. Combine dry ingredients; add to butter mixture alternatly with sour cream. Combine pumpkin, beaten egg, ⅓ cup sugar and pie spice. Spoon half of batter into 13 x 9 x 2-inch baking pan; sprinkle half of streusel mixture over batter; spread remaining pumpkin mixture over streusel; sprinkle remaining streusel over top. Bake at 325 degrees for 50–60 minutes, or until tested done in middle.

Streusel:

1 cup brown sugar
⅓ cup butter
2 teaspoons cinnamon
1 cup chopped nuts

Mix all together.

HAM GRIDDLE CAKES
Makes 11

1 cup milk
1 cup quick-cooking oats, uncooked
2 tablespoons vegetable oil
2 eggs, beaten
½ cup all-purpose flour
2 tablespoons sugar
2 teaspoons baking powder
1 cup diced, cooked ham
Maple syrup

Combine milk and oats in a large bowl; let stand 5 minutes. Add oil and eggs, stirring well. Combine flour, sugar and baking powder; add to oat mixture, stirring just until moistened. Stir in ham.

For each pancake, pour about ¼ cup batter onto a hot, lightly greased griddle. Turn pancakes when tops are covered with bubbles and edges look cooked. Serve with maple syrup.

REUBEN BRUNCH CASSEROLE

10 slices rye bread, cubed
1-1/2 pounds cooked corned beef
2-1/2 cups shredded cheese (American, Swiss, or Cheddar, or combination)
6 eggs, lightly beaten
3 cups milk
1/4 teaspoon pepper

Grease 13x9-inch baking dish. Arrange bread cubes on bottom. Coarsely shred corned beef. Layer beef over bread. Sprinkle with cheese. Beat eggs, milk, and pepper until well blended. Pour over corned beef mixture. Cover with foil. Refrigerate several hours or overnight. When ready to bake, preheat oven to 350 degrees; bake covered for 45 minutes, then uncover and bake for 10 additional minutes or until bubbly and puffed.

POACHED EGGS ON CHICKEN MUFFINS
Serves 6

1 (4-3/4 ounce) can chicken spread
1/2 teaspoon ground thyme
3 English muffins, split and toasted
6 eggs, poached
Chopped chives, optional

Mix chicken with thyme; spread on English muffins. Top each muffin half with an egg and sprinkle with chives.

CHOCOLATE-ALMOND ZUCCHINI BREAD

Makes 2 loaves

3 eggs
2 cups sugar
1 cup vegetable oil
2 squares (2 ounces) unsweetened chocolate
1 teaspoon vanilla
2 cups finely grated zucchini
3 cups flour
1 teaspoon salt
1 teaspoon cinnamon
1/4 teaspoon baking powder
1 teaspoon baking soda
1 cup coarsely chopped almonds

Preheat oven to 350 degrees. In small bowl, beat eggs until lemon colored; beat in sugar and oil. Melt chocolate over hot water. In large bowl, add egg mixture, vanilla, and zucchini to chocolate.

Sift together flour, salt, cinnamon, baking powder, and baking soda. Stir into zucchini mixture. Mix in nuts. Pour batter into 2 well-greased 9x5x3 inch loaf pans. Bake 1 hour and 20 minutes or until done. Cool in pans 15-20 minutes. Turn out onto rack. Cool thoroughly before serving.

JIFFY RAISIN LOAF

Makes 1 loaf

3/4 cup golden seedless raisins
Hot water
2 cups prepared biscuit mix
3/4 cup sugar
1 teaspoon cinnamon
1/3 cup chopped nuts
1 egg
3/4 cup milk

Rinse raisins in hot water. Drain. Combine with biscuit mix, sugar, cinnamon, and nuts. Beat egg slightly. Add to milk. Stir into dry ingredients. Pour batter into greased 8-1/2x4-1/4x2-1/2 inch loaf pan. Bake at 350 degrees for 50-60 minutes. Cool on wire rack.

GRANOLA

4 cups uncooked oatmeal
1-1/2 cups wheat germ (raw or toasted)
1 cup grated coconut
1/4 cup powdered milk
1/2 tablespoon cinnamon
1 tablespoon brown sugar
1/3 cup vegetable oil
1/2 cup honey
1 tablespoon vanilla
1/2 cup sesame seeds (optional)
1/2 cup raw nuts, seeds, or raisins, etc. (optional)

In a large bowl, mix dry ingredients. In a saucepan, combine oil, honey, and vanilla; warm. Add these to the dry ingredients; stir until all the particles are coated. Hand mixing works well here. Spread this mixture out in a long, low pan or rimmed baking sheets that have been well greased; bake at either 250 degrees for 1 hour or 300 degrees for 30 minutes. Turn mixture with spatula from time to time. When finished toasting, add dried fruits, such as raisins. Cool and store in an airtight container.

LUSCIOUS BANANA-APRICOT BREAD

Makes 2 loaves

2 cups white flour
1-1/2 cups whole wheat flour
2 teaspoons baking powder
1 teaspoon baking soda
1 teaspoon salt
4 eggs
1 cup sugar
2/3 cup shortening
1/2 cup sour milk
6-7 bananas, mashed
1/4 cup wheat germ
1 cup chopped dried apricots
3 teaspoons black walnut flavoring (or 3 cups chopped nuts)

Mix first 5 ingredients by sifting into bowl. Blend in eggs, sugar, shortening, and sour milk, beating well into dry ingredients. Add bananas, flavoring or nuts, apricots, and wheat germ. Stir well. Bake in greased and floured loaf pans at 350 degrees for 50 minutes.

HAM 'N EGG CREPES

(Serves 4-6)

1 (10-1/2 ounce) can condensed cream of chicken soup
1 cup dairy sour cream
1 cup finely chopped cooked ham
6 hard cooked eggs, chopped
1 tablespoon chives, chopped
1/4 teaspoon dry mustard
1/4 cup milk
1/4 cup grated Parmesan cheese
1 recipe for basic crepes

Mix 1/2 can of soup, sour cream, ham, eggs, chives, and mustard; set aside. Combine remaining soup, milk, and half the cheese; set aside. Put about 1/4 cup ham-egg filling on each crepe and roll up. Arrange filled crepes in greased 13x9x2-inch baking dish. Pour sauce over top and sprinkle with remaining cheese. Bake in preheated 350 degree oven for 30 minutes, or until hot and bubbly.

MEAT BALL PANCAKES

3 egg yolks, lightly beaten
1/2 pound ground beef, browned
1/4 teaspoon baking powder
1/2 teaspoon salt
Dash of pepper
1 tablespoon grated onion
1 teaspoon lemon juice
1 tablespoon parsley
3 egg whites, stiffly beaten

Mix all ingredients, *excluding* egg whites. Blend well. Fold in egg whites. Drop by spoonfuls onto greased hot griddle. When puffed and browned, turn and brown other side. Serve at once, with a mushroom sauce or a creamed vegetable.

MAPLE BUTTER TWISTS

2 Coffee Cakes, Serves 16

3-1/4 - 3-1/2 cups flour
3 tablespoons sugar
1-1/2 teaspoons salt
1 package yeast
3/4 cup milk
1/4 cup butter
2 eggs

Filling:
1/2 cup brown sugar
1/3 cup white sugar
2 tablespoons flour
1/2 teaspoon cinnamon
1/4 cup softened butter
1/4 cup maple syrup
1/2 teaspoon maple extract
1/2 cup chopped nuts

Glaze:
1/2 powered sugar
2-3 teaspoons milk
1/4 teaspoon maple extract

Grease 2 - 8 inch round cake pans. In large bowl, combine 1-1/2 cups flour with the next 3 ingredients. In a small saucepan, heat milk and margarine until very warm. Add with the eggs to the flour mixture. Beat with electric mixer on low speed until moistened, then beat 3 minutes on medium speed. Stir in remaining flour. Place in greased bowl, cover and let rise 1-1/2 hours.

Combine all filling ingredients, except nuts, in small bowl. Beat with electric mixer on medium speed, 2 minutes. Stir in nuts.

Divide dough in half. Roll each half to a 14 x 8 inch rectangle. Spread each with half of filling. Roll up from long side as for jellyroll; seal edges. Cut each roll in half lengthwise. Twist the two halves together and seal ends. Place each twisted roll in a prepared pan circle; flatten with fingertips. Cover; let rise 1 hour.

Heat oven to 350 degrees. Bake 25-30 minutes. Remove from pans immediately. Combine glaze ingredients until smooth and drizzle over coffee cake while still warm.

BAKED CHEESE GRITS

Serves 6

2-2/3 cups water
2/3 cup hominy grits, quick-cooking
2 tablespoons butter or margarine
1-1/2 cups pasteurized process American cheese, shredded
2 eggs, beaten
1/8 teaspoon pepper

Preheat oven to 350 degrees. Grease a 2-quart baking dish. Bring water to a full rolling boil. Add grits; return to boiling point. Cook, stirring constantly, until very thick, about 6 minutes. Remove from heat. Add butter or margarine and mix cheese, eggs, and pepper. Stir into grits. Pour into baking dish and bake 40 minutes or until lightly browned.

CORNMEAL PANCAKES

1/2 cup cornmeal
1/2 cup flour
2 teaspoons baking powder
1/2 teaspoon salt
2 tablespoons sugar
1 egg
1 cup milk
2 tablespoons margarine, melted

Mix first 5 ingredients; stir in egg, milk, and margarine. Blend until smooth. If batter is too thick, thin with additional milk. Cook on a hot, lightly-oiled griddle.

APPLE PECAN CREPES

Serves 8

16 crepes
1 (1-pound, 5-ounce) can apple pie filling
1/2 teaspoon cinnamon
1/2 cup broken pecan pieces
Custard sauce

Combine apple filling, cinnamon, and pecan pieces. Spoon 2-1/2 tablespoons filling down center of each crepe and overlap edges. Place in chafing dish or oven-proof serving dish. Heat through. Serve with custard sauce.

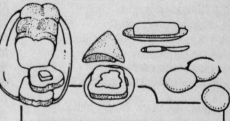

EGGNOG FRENCH TOAST

Loaf of Italian or French bread, cut in 12 3/4-inch slices (day-old bread is best)
1-1/2 cups dairy eggnog
1/4 cup butter
Cinnamon
Confectioners' sugar
Syrup

Place bread in single layer in shallow dish. Pour eggnog over bread. Let stand, turning bread once, until eggnog is absorbed, about 5 minutes.

In large skillet cook slices in butter until golden on both sides. Sprinkle with cinnamon and confectioners' sugar. Serve hot with syrup.

NORWEGIAN COFFEE CAKE

4 cups flour
6 teaspoons baking powder
1 cup sugar
1/2 teaspoon salt
2 eggs
1 cup milk
1 cup butter or margarine

Sift together dry ingredients. Blend in shortening as for pie crust. Beat eggs and milk; add to dry ingredients. Do not mix too much. Grease two 9-inch cake pans and put half of mixture in each pan by putting spoonfuls around the edge. Bake at 400 degrees for about 20 minutes. Frost and add nuts to the top. Great with breakfast!

SURPRISE MUFFINS
Makes 20 small muffins

2 cups sifted flour
1 teaspoon salt
4 teaspoons baking powder
1 tablespoon sugar
4 tablespoons butter
3/4 cup milk
1/4 cup shredded dates
1/4 cup chopped walnuts
20 marshmallows

Sift together flour, salt, baking powder, and sugar into mixing bowl. Cut in butter. Add milk gradually to make a soft dough. Place a teaspoon of the dough in small greased muffin pans. Place over this a marshmallow, some shredded dates, and chopped nuts. Bake in a very hot oven, 450 degrees for 15 minutes, until delicately browned. Serve hot.

BAKED PINEAPPLE TOAST
(Serves 6)

1/4 cup butter or margarine, melted
1/2 cup firmly packed brown sugar
1 (8-ounce) can crushed pineapple, drained
6 white bread slices
2 eggs
1-1/2 cups milk
1/2 teaspoon salt

Combine butter, sugar, and pineapple. Spread on bottom of 13x9-inch baking dish. Top with bread. Beat eggs, milk, and salt together; pour over bread. Bake, uncovered, at 325 degrees for 25 minutes or until golden brown. Cool slightly; invert on heated serving platter.

BAKED EGGS COUNTRY STYLE

1 (10-3/4-ounce) can cream of tomato soup
6 eggs
Salt and pepper to taste
1/8 teaspoon cayenne
1/8 teaspoon nutmeg
1/4 cup Swiss cheese, grated
1/4 cup Parmesan cheese, grated
1/4 cup parsley, chopped
1 teaspoon onion, grated

In a buttered shallow baking dish, pour can of undiluted cream of tomato soup; carefully drop in 6 eggs; sprinkle with salt, pepper, cayenne, nutmeg, and cheeses. Sprinkle parsley mixed with grated onion over all. Bake at 325 degrees for 26 minutes or until eggs are set. Serve immediately over slices of crisp hot toast, or over split toasted English muffins.

BACON AND EGG POCKETS
Serves 2

2 pita bread rounds (whole wheat is better for you)
4 slices bacon
4 eggs
1 tablespoon milk
Salt and pepper to taste
Sliced Cheddar cheese (optional)

Cut pita in half crosswise. Warm in oven as it preheats to about 300 degrees. Meanwhile, in medium skillet, fry bacon until crisp; drain on paper towel. Pour off all grease except what clings to skillet. Whisk eggs with milk, salt and pepper. Pour into skillet; cook, stirring, over medium heat until softly scrambled; crumble in bacon. Stuff pita pockets with cheese, if using, then eggs with bacon.

OATMEAL FLAPJACKS
Makes 12-18

3 cups Basic Campers' Mix
3 tablespoons sugar
2 cups milk
2 eggs

Combine Basic Campers' Mix and sugar. Add milk and eggs; stir until just blended. Pour batter onto hot, lightly greased griddle. Turn pancakes when tops are covered with bubbles and edges look cooked. Turn only once. Serve with butter and syrup.

HASH BROWN OMELET

1/2 pound bacon
Frozen hash brown potatoes, enough to fill bottom of large skillet
6 eggs
1/4 cup milk
1/2 teaspoon salt
1/2 teaspoon pepper
1/4 cup onion, chopped
1 cup grated American cheese
1/4 cup green pepper, mushroom, celery (optional)

Cook bacon until crisp; remove bacon from pan. Cook potatoes in bacon drippings over low heat until thawed. Combine eggs, milk, salt, and pepper; pour over potatoes. Sprinkle bacon, onions, and other vegetables on top of egg mixture. Cover and cook on low heat for 20 minutes or until set. Top with cheese and cover pan until cheese melts. Slice into pie-shaped pieces and serve.

Sausage or shaved ham with mushrooms may be used instead of bacon.

CHOCOLATE WAFFLES

2 cups flour
3 teaspoons baking powder
1/2 teaspoon salt
3 tablespoons cocoa
1/4 cup sugar
2 eggs, separated
1/4 cup melted margarine
1-1/4 cups milk
1 teaspoon vanilla

Sift first 5 ingredients together into a large mixing bowl. Stir in the well-beaten egg yolks, margarine, milk, and vanilla. Beat egg whites until stiff peaks form and fold into flour mixture. Fill the hot waffle iron with batter and close; bake until browned.

If you are a "chocoholic" you'll love these! All my family loves this special breakfast treat.

BLUEBERRY SAUCE

2 cups fresh or frozen blueberries
1/3 cup sugar
1 tablespoon lemon juice
1/4 teaspoon salt
1/2 teaspoon vanilla

Crush blueberries; add sugar, lemon juice, and salt. Mix well. Bring to a boil and boil 1 minute. Add vanilla. Serve over pancakes or blintzes.

CHOCOLATE WAFFLES

1/2 cup melted butter
1 cup sugar
2 squares melted chocolate
3 eggs, well beaten
1 teaspoon salt
1-1/2 cups flour
1 cup milk
1/4 teaspoon vanilla

Cream butter (or margarine) and sugar; add chocolate and eggs. Mix well. Sift in salt and flour; mixing well. Add milk and vanilla. Pour 1/4 cup batter onto greased waffle iron and cook each waffle about 3 minutes.

OATMEAL-RAISIN MUFFINS

1-1/4 cups flour
1 cup rolled oats
1/2 cup raisins
1/4 cup packed dark brown sugar
3 teaspoons baking powder
1/2 teaspoon salt
3/4 teaspoon cinnamon
1 cup milk
1/4 cup oil
1 egg

In large bowl, combine flour, oats, raisins, sugar, baking powder, cinnamon and salt; set aside.

In small bowl, beat remaining ingredients until well blended. Pour into flour mixture and stir just until

moistened (batter will be lumpy). Divide among 12 greased or paper-lined 2-1/2-inch muffin cups. Bake in 400 degree oven for 20-25 minutes, or until toothpick inserted in center of muffin comes out clean. Remove from pan and cool on rack. Wrap in plastic wrap or sandwich bags. Will keep 2 to 3 months when frozen.

SAUSAGE MUFFINS
Makes 1 dozen

1/2 pound bulk pork sausage
Butter or margarine, melted
2 cups all-purpose flour
1 tablespoon baking powder
1/4 teaspoon salt
2 tablespoons sugar
1 egg, slightly beaten
1 cup milk
1/2 cup shredded cheese

Cook sausage over medium heat until browned, stirring to crumble; drain well; reserve drippings. Add butter to drippings to measure 1/4 cup. Set sausage and drippings aside.

Combine flour, baking powder, salt, and sugar in a medium bowl. Mix egg, milk, and 1/4 cup reserved drippings; stir well. Add liquid mixture to dry ingredients, stirring just until moistened. Stir in cheese and sausage. Spoon batter into paper-lined muffin pans, filling 3/4 full. Bake at 375 degrees for 18 minutes. Remove from muffin pan immediately.

OVEN OMELET WITH HAM AND CHEESE
Serves 2

1 cup ham in bite-size pieces
1 tablespoon butter or margarine
4 large eggs
1/2 cup whipping cream
1-1/2 tablespoons flour
1/4 teaspoon salt
Pinch pepper
1/3 cup grated sharp Cheddar cheese

Preheat oven to 450 degrees. Spray 10-inch non-stick skillet with pan release; wrap skillet handle with foil to ovenproof it. (If cheese is in a chunk, grate and set aside to soften.)

Heat butter in skillet until bubbly. Add ham; sauté on medium-low heat until beginning to brown. Meanwhile, in a medium bowl, whisk eggs to blend well. Whisk in cream, flour, salt and pepper. If you have fresh chives, snip some into the egg mixture. Pour over ham. Bake until puffy and golden, about 15 minutes. Sprinkle with cheese. Slip out of skillet onto serving plate.

BRIGHAM YOUNG'S BUTTERMILK DOUGHNUTS

2-1/2 cups sifted flour
1 teaspoon baking soda
3/4 teaspoon salt
3/4 teaspoon grated nutmeg
1/2 teaspoon baking powder
1 cup buttermilk
1/2 cup sugar
1 egg, beaten
1 teaspoon vanilla
2 tablespoons melted butter or shortening
Oil for frying
Confectioners' sugar

Sift together first 5 ingredients. Blend together buttermilk, sugar, egg, and vanilla. Beat buttermilk mixture into dry ingredients and stir in butter or shortening. Chill dough 30 minutes. Roll dough out onto a lightly-floured board to 3/8 to 1/2 inch thickness. Cut with 2-1/2 inch doughnut cutter. Fry in 3 inches of hot oil (375 degrees) until golden on both sides (about 2 minutes total). Drain on paper towels. Dust with confectioners' sugar, if desired. Fry doughnut holes in same manner.

This recipe is adapted from Mrs. Young's Cookbook.

TALLAHASSEE HASH PUPPIES

2 cups cornmeal
2 teaspoons baking powder
1 teaspoon salt
1-1/2 cups sweet milk
1/2 cup water
1 large onion, chopped fine

Sift dry ingredients together. Add milk, water; stir in chopped onion. Add more meal or milk, if necessary, to form a soft dough. Mold with hands. Fry in deep, hot fat until brown.

BAGEL CHIPS

4 bagels
3 tablespoons butter or margarine
3 tablespoons vegetable oil
2 cloves crushed garlic
1/8 teaspoon salt
1/8 teaspoon paprika

Slice each bagel horizontally in 6 pieces. In small pan, saute garlic in 1 tablespoon butter or margarine until lightly browned. Add remaining ingredients; stir until margarine is melted. Spread bagels out on cookie sheet. Brush both sides of bagel slices with mixture. Bake at 375 for 5 minutes on each side. Baking time may vary according to oven and how thin bagels are sliced. After bagels are cooled, place in airtight container. NOTE: Variation-sprinkle with Parmesan cheese the last 2 minutes of baking.

STRAWBERRIES 'N' CREAM BAGEL

2 bagels
1 teaspoon butter or margarine
4 ounces cream cheese
1/2 cup strawberries, mashed
1/2 teaspoon of vanilla
2 tablespoons powdered sugar

1/2 cup sliced strawberries for garnish

Slice bagels in half horizontally. Lightly spread with one teaspoon of butter or margarine; toast lightly. Mix together cream cheese, mashed strawberries, vanilla and powdered sugar. Spread mixture over bagels. Garnish top of each bagel with sliced strawberries.

BREAKFAST BARS
Makes 18 bars

1/4 cup butter or margarine
3 cups miniature marshmallows
1/2 cup peanut butter
1/2 cup nonfat milk
1/4 cup orange - flavored instant breakfast drink
1 cup raisins
3 cups Cheerios cereal

Butter a 9 x 9 x 2 inch pan. Melt butter and marshmallows over low heat, stirring constantly. Stir in milk, breakfast drink, and peanut butter. Fold in raisins and cereal, stirring until coated. With buttered hands, pat evenly in pan. Cool. These are delicious with coffee for breakfast or anytime.

BRUNCH IN A SHELL

1 slice ham, cut 1/4 inch thick
1 unbaked 9 inch pie shell
1/2 can, (10-1/2 ounces) cream of mushroom soup
2/3 cup dairy sour cream
3 eggs
1 to 2 tablespoons chopped chives
1/4 teaspoon salt
Dash pepper

Cut ham slice so it will cover bottom of pie shell evenly. Combine remaining ingredients with rotary beater and pour into ham-lined pie shell. Cover crust edge with 1-1/2 inch aluminum foil. Bake in preheated 425 degree oven for 40-45 minutes, removing protective foil from crust 15 minutes before end of baking time. Pie puffs up near end of baking and sinks back after removal from oven.

BANANA BONANZAS

1 cup sifted flour
3 tablespoons sugar
2-1/2 teaspoons baking powder
1/2 teaspoon salt
1 cup whole bran
1 beaten egg
1/4 cup milk
2 tablespoons oil
1 cup mashed bananas
1/2 cup walnuts (optional)

Sift together flour, sugar, baking powder, and salt. Stir in bran. Combine egg, banana, milk, and oil. Add liquid ingredients all at once, stirring just until flour mixture is moistened. Fill well-greased muffin pans 2/3 full. Bake at 400 degrees for 25 minutes.

OLD-FASHIONED "EGGSPARAGUS"
Serves 4

1 pound fresh asparagus (or use canned)
Boiling salted water
4 eggs, separated
2 tablespoons milk or cream
1 tablespoon butter, melted
Salt and pepper to taste

Trim asparagus; cook in boiling salted water until stalks are tender, about 20 minutes. Drain and arrange in lightly-greased 9 x 13-inch shallow baking dish. Beat egg whites to stiff froth. Fold in beaten egg yolks, milk or cream, butter, salt and pepper to taste. Pour egg-mixture evenly over asparagus. Bake at 325 degrees for about 10 minutes, or until eggs are set.

MONSTER TOAST

1 loaf sliced bread
1 (6 ounce) can frozen concentrated orange juice, thawed, undiluted
Cinnamon

With cookie cutters, cut monster shapes out of bread slices or make a paper pattern and cut out monsters with kitchen scissors.

Dip each cut-out into concentrated orange juice, place on a cookie sheet.

Bake in a 250 degree oven until lightly toasted, about 20 minutes. Sprinkle with cinnamon, if desired.

JURY DUTY WAFFLES
Serves 3

6 eggs
1 cup cottage cheese
1/2 cup flour
1/4 cup milk
1/4 cup oil
Sprinkle of salt
1 teaspoon vanilla

Blend all ingredients together at once, in blender. Only until combined. Do not over-mix. Bake in hot waffle iron. Makes enough for 3 moderate appetites, or 2 big ones. Freeze leftovers and reheat in toaster.

OLD-FASHIONED WAFFLES

1 cup milk
2 eggs, separated
1/4 cup melted margarine or butter
2 teaspoons baking powder
1-1/2 cups flour
Pinch of salt

Beat flour and milk; add margarine; beat. Add well beaten egg yolks; beat again. Add baking powder and pinch of salt; beat very hard for few minutes. Fold in well beaten egg whites. Have waffle iron very hot.

Pile small amount of batter in center of waffle iron. It will spread when cover comes down. Don't use much batter as it will ooze out the sides of the waffle iron.

This recipe has been in our family for decades.

ORANGE GRIDDLE CAKES

1 cup flour
2-1/2 teaspoons baking powder
3/4 teaspoon salt
1 tablespoon sugar
1 egg, well beaten
1-1/4 cups milk
3 tablespoons butter or margarine, melted
1-1/2 cups corn flakes
Grated rind of 1 orange
Sauce:
1/2 cup honey
1/2 cup orange juice

Sift dry ingredients together. Combine egg and milk; add gradually to dry ingredients, mixing only until smooth. Add butter or margarine, corn flakes and rind. Bake on hot griddle. Serve immediately with sauce made by combining honey and orange juice.

MELTAWAY PAN-CAKES
Makes 10 pancakes

3 eggs, separated
1/2 cup sour cream
1/4 cup sifted flour
1/4 teaspoon salt
1 tablespoon sugar

Beat egg yolks well; combine with sour cream. Sift dry ingredients together; stir into egg yolk mixture. Beat egg whites until stiff; fold in. Drop by large spoonfuls onto hot griddle until tops are bubbly; turn and brown on other side.

APPLESAUCE PANCAKES
Makes 16 pancakes

2 cups flour
3 tablespoons sugar
1 teaspoon soda
3/4 teaspoon salt
2 cups buttermilk
2 eggs, slightly beaten
2 tablespoons melted butter
2/3 cup finely chopped apples
Spiced Apple Syrup (recipe below)

Sift flour with sugar, soda and salt. Combine buttermilk, eggs and melted butter; add to dry ingredients. Stir just enough to mix. Fold in chopped apples. Bake on hot, lightly greased griddle or electric skillet until golden brown on both side. Serve with syrup.

Spiced Apple Syrup:
Makes 2 cups
2 apples
1 cup apple cider
3/4 cup brown sugar
1 tablespoon butter or margarine
1/4 teaspoon cinnamon

Peel, core and thinly slice apples. In saucepan, combine apple cider, brown sugar, butter or margarine and cinnamon. Heat to boiling. Add apples; simmer about 10 minutes, or until apples are tender.

This makes a wonderful breakfast with link sausage or crisp bacon.

BASIC CAMPERS' MIX
Makes 7-1/2 cups)

4-1/2 cups sifted flour
3 tablespoons baking powder
2 teaspoons salt
1 cup shortening, soft
1-1/2 cups quick or old fashioned oats, uncooked

Sift together flour, baking powder, and salt into large bowl. Cut in shortening until mixture resembles coarse crumbs. Stir in oats. Store in airtight container in cool dry place until ready to use.

Cakes
TO BAKE

SOUTHERN 7-UP CAKE

- 1 box yellow *or* pineapple cake mix
- 4 eggs
- 1 (4-serving) box vanilla *instant* pudding
- ¾ cup cooking oil
- 1 (12-ounce) can 7-Up, at room temperature

Beat all ingredients together well for 2 minutes with electric mixer. Pour batter into 3 (8-inch) layer pans, or a 15 x 10-inch jelly roll pan that has been greased and floured. Bake at 325 degrees for 25–30 minutes. Cool for 10 minutes, if in layer pans, and remove from pans to cool thoroughly on wire rack. Fill and frost.

Filling:
- 1 cup sugar
- 1 heaping teaspoon cornstarch
- 4 eggs
- ½ cup margarine
- 1 (No. 2) can crushed pineapple
- 1½ cups flaked coconut
- 1 teaspoon vanilla
- 1 cup coarsely broken pecans

Combine first 6 ingredients and cook over medium heat until thick. Remove from heat and add vanilla and pecans. Cool before spreading between layers and over cake. If using 15 x 10-inch pan, leave cake in pan and spread frosting over top. Very moist and delicious!

THREE-LAYER CARROT CAKE
Serves 12–15

- 2½ cups all-purpose flour
- 2 cups granulated sugar
- ½ teaspoon salt
- 2 teaspoons baking soda
- 2 teaspoons ground cinnamon
- 3 cups finely shredded carrots
- 1½ cups cooking oil
- 4 eggs
- 1 cup chopped pecans

Combine flour, sugar, salt, baking soda and cinnamon in a large mixer bowl. Add carrots, oil and eggs. Beat with electric mixer until combined. Stir in pecans. Pour batter into 3 greased and floured (9-inch) round cake pans. Bake in 350-degree oven for 25–30 minutes, or until tests done. Cool on wire racks for 10 minutes, then remove cakes from pans and cool. Frost with Cream Cheese Frosting (recipe follows).

Cream Cheese Frosting:
- 1 (8-ounce) package cream cheese, softened
- ½ cup margarine, softened
- 2 teaspoons vanilla
- 4½ cups sifted confectioners' sugar

Beat together cream cheese, margarine and vanilla until light and fluffy. Gradually add the confectioners' sugar until you have preferred spreading consistency. Frost tops and sides of cake.

RED DEVIL MAGIC MAYONNAISE CAKE

- 2 cups all-purpose flour
- 1 cup real mayonnaise
- 1 cup sugar
- 1 cup cold water (or cold coffee for mocha-flavored cake)
- ⅓ cup cocoa powder
- 2 teaspoons baking soda
- ½ teaspoon salt

Preheat oven to 350 degrees. Combine all cake ingredients in bowl and whisk until very smooth. Pour into 2 greased and floured 8-inch round pans. Bake for 25–30 minutes, until toothpick inserted in center comes out clean. Let cool 5 minutes in pan, then turn out and cool completely on wire racks. Fill and frost top and sides with Devil's Food Fudge Frosting (recipe follows).

Devil's Food Fudge Frosting:
- 3 cups confectioners' sugar
- ½ cup cocoa powder
- ½ cup (1 stick) margarine *or* butter, softened
- 3 tablespoons water *or* cold coffee
- 1 teaspoon vanilla

Combine all ingredients in bowl and beat until smooth and creamy. This novelty cake of the 1950s became a popular conversation-piece dessert. Mayonnaise replaces eggs and oil in the recipe.

HAWAIIAN SPONGE CAKE

2 cups flour
1½ cups sugar
1 teaspoon baking soda
¼ teaspoon salt
1 (20-ounce) can crushed pineapple
2 eggs, lightly beaten

In large bowl, combine flour, sugar, soda and salt. Add undrained pineapple and eggs. Stir until combined. Pour batter into a greased 13 x 9-inch pan. Bake at 350 degrees for 30 minutes, or until done. Cool in pan for 10 minutes. Spread creamy frosting (recipe follows) over hot cake in pan.

Frosting:
¾ cup sugar
¾ cup evaporated milk
½ cup butter
1 teaspoon vanilla extract

Combine all ingredients in a saucepan. Bring to a boil. Boil about 7 minutes, stirring until mixture is thickened. Stir in ½ cup chopped nuts and ½ cup flaked coconut.

LEMON COCONUT CAKE

1 cup shredded coconut
2 tablespoons milk
¾ cup margarine (Fleishmann's)
1¾ cups sugar, minus 1 tablespoonful
3 cups sifted cake flour
½ teaspoon salt
2½ teaspoons baking powder
1 cup water, plus 2 tablespoonfuls
1 teaspoon lemon extract
4 egg whites, stiffly beaten

Soak coconut in milk and set aside. Cream margarine and sugar

until light and fluffy. Sift flour, salt and baking powder together 2 times after measuring flour. Add this flour mixture alternately with water, mixing thoroughly after each addition. Add extract and coconut to mixture. Mix well with wooden spoon or rubber spatula. *Gently* fold in egg whites by hand. Pour into 2 greased and floured pans or flat pan, cutting gently through each way to remove air bubbles. Bake at 350 degrees until light brown and done.

Cream Cheese Frosting:
½ cup margarine
1 small package cream cheese
½ pound confectioners' sugar
Vanilla, lemon juice, *or* lemon extract for flavoring

Cream margarine and cream cheese until light and fluffy. Add confectioners' sugar (½ pound; or enough for spreading consistency); beat together. Flavor with the extract of your choice. This is enough frosting for 2 flat cakes or 1 sheet cake.

E-Z FRUITCAKE
Serves 8–10

1 pound dates
¼ cup flour
2 cans sweetened condensed milk
2 cups flaked coconut
¾ pound candied cherries
2 cups whole pecan halves
1 teaspoon vanilla

Preheat oven to 300 degrees. Generously grease and flour an 8-inch round cake pan; set aside.
Coat dates with flour and chop them finely. Add sweetened condensed milk, coconut, cherries, pecans and vanilla.
Pour batter into prepared pan and bake 1 hour, or until cake holds together. Cool completely before cutting.

ST. PATRICK'S DAY CAKE

1 package white cake mix without pudding
1 (3-ounce) package pistachio *instant* pudding
¾ cup oil
3 large eggs
1 cup lemon-lime carbonated beverage
½ cup chopped pecans
½ cup flake coconut
Frosting (recipe follows)

Combine cake mix, pudding, oil, eggs and carbonated beverage. Grease and flour 2 (9-inch) layer cake pans. Evenly pour in batter; bake at 325 degrees for 30–45 minutes. Cool on rack before frosting.

Frosting:
1 (8-ounce) container whipped topping
1 cup milk
1 (3-ounce) package pistachio instant pudding

Combine ingredients and mix well. Frost layers of cake. Sprinkle nuts and coconut between layers and on top of frosted cake.

QUICK PEANUT CAKE

1 package yellow cake mix
½ cup peanut butter
½ cup light cream
2 cups brown sugar
1 cup flake coconut

Prepare and bake batter from cake mix as directed on package. Blend peanut butter, cream and brown sugar; spread over warm cake. Sprinkle with coconut. Broil 4–5 inches from heat for about 4 minutes, or until frosting is lightly browned. Serve as a coffee cake or, if serving as a dessert, cut into thin slices and top with French vanilla ice cream.

Incredibly rich and good!

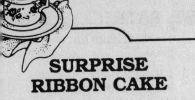

SURPRISE RIBBON CAKE

3 cups cake flour
4 teaspoons baking powder
1 teaspoon salt
2 tablespoons cold water
2 tablespoons cocoa
⅛ teaspoon ground cloves
½ teaspoon cinnamon
⅛ teaspoon baking soda
¾ cup white shortening
2 cups sugar
1¼ cups water
4 egg whites
1 teaspoon vanilla
1 teaspoon almond extract
Few drops red food coloring
Seven-Minute Frosting
(recipe follows)

Sift together 3 times the cake flour, baking powder and salt. Set aside. Mix together and set aside in another bowl the cold water, cocoa, cloves, cinnamon and baking soda. Cream together until soft in third bowl, the shortening and sugar. Add alternately to the creamed mixture, beating constantly, 1¼ cups water and the flour mixture. Then add, all at once, the unbeaten egg whites and continue beating for 2 minutes. Divide batter into 3 equal parts. As each is completed pour into a greased 8-inch layer cake pan. Add to first part, 1 teaspoon vanilla. Add to second part, 1 teaspoon almond extract and a few drops of red food coloring. Add to third part, the cocoa mixture and a few drops of red food coloring. Bake in a preheated oven at 350 degrees for 30 minutes, or until done. Cool cakes. Frost with Seven-Minute Frosting. Put the cake together with the dark layer on the bottom and the pink layer in the middle. Spread the frosting between the layers and frost the cake thoroughly all over. The surprise comes when the white frosting is cut through revealing the pretty tri-colored ribbon slices.

Seven-Minute Frosting:
Makes 2 cups

2 egg whites
1½ cups sugar
⅓ cup water
¼ teaspoon cream of tartar
1 teaspoon vanilla

Combine egg whites, sugar, water and cream of tartar in top of double boiler. Beat with electric mixer at high speed 1 minute. Place over simmering water. Cook 7 minutes, beating constantly with electric mixer at high speed until soft glossy peaks form. Remove from hot water. Stir in vanilla.

MACADAMIA-PINEAPPLE CAKE
Serves 8

3 tablespoons butter *plus* ⅓ cup
½ cup brown sugar
¾ cup crushed pineapple, drained; reserve syrup
¾ cup Macadamia nuts (pieces)
1¼ cups sifted all-purpose flour
½ cup granulated sugar
2 teaspoons baking powder
½ teaspoon salt
½ teaspoon grated lemon peel
2 eggs
1 teaspoon vanilla

Melt 3 tablespoons butter in an 8 x 8-inch square pan. Add ½ cup brown sugar, ¼ cup crushed pineapple and ¼ cup Macadamia nut pieces. Mix and spread evenly in pan.

In bowl, mix ⅓ cup soft butter, 1 ¼ cups sifted all-purpose flour, ½ cup sugar, 2 teaspoons baking powder and ½ teaspoon salt.

Add ¼ cup pineapple syrup, ¼ cup crushed pineapple, ½ teaspoon grated lemon peel, 2 eggs, ½ cup Macadamia nut pieces and 1 teaspoon vanilla.

Mix and beat vigorously for 2 minutes and pour into pan over other mixture. Bake at 350 degrees for 40–45 minutes. Let stand 10 minutes and invert onto plate.

RING-OF-COCONUT FUDGE CAKE

2 cups sugar
1 cup cooking oil
2 eggs
3 cups flour
¾ cup cocoa
2 teaspoons soda
2 teaspoons baking powder
1½ teaspoons salt
1 cup hot coffee
1 cup sour milk
1 teaspoon vanilla
½ cup chopped nuts

Filling:
¼ cup sugar
1 teaspoon vanilla
1 (8-ounce) package cream cheese
1 egg
½ cup coconut
1 cup chocolate chips

Filling: Beat sugar, vanilla, cream cheese and egg until smooth. Stir in coconut and chocolate chips; set aside.

In large bowl combine sugar, oil and eggs. Beat 1 minute at high speed. Add remaining ingredients, *except* nuts and filling. Beat 3 minutes at medium speed. By hand, stir in nuts. Pour half of batter into a greased and floured tube or Bundt pan. Carefully spoon filling over batter in center. Top with remaining batter. Bake at 350 degrees for 70–75 minutes. Cool upright in pan for 15 minutes. Remove from pan. Cool completely; drizzle with Glaze (recipe follows).

Glaze:
1 cup confectioners' sugar
3 tablespoons cocoa
2 tablespoons butter
2 teaspoons vanilla
1–3 tablespoons hot water

Combine ingredients and mix until smooth. This is very good baked in a sheet cake pan without the filling also. In fact, this is one of the best chocolate cakes I have ever tasted!

CHERRY PIE FILLING CAKE

1 package white cake mix
¼ cup oil
½ cup water
2 eggs
1 (16–20-ounce) can
  cherry pie filling
  Confectioners' sugar, optional

Preheat oven to 350 degrees. Pour oil into a 13 x 9 x 2-inch pan. Tilt pan to cover bottom. Put cake mix, eggs and water into pan. Stir with a fork or spoon until blended, about 2 minutes. Scrape sides of pan and spread batter evenly. Spoon pie filling onto batter. Use a fork to fold into batter, just enough to create a marbled effect. Bake at 350 degrees for 30–35 minutes. Insert toothpick into center—when it comes out clean, cake is done. When cool, sprinkle confectioners' sugar on top, if desired. Cover loosely. Also, you could substitute lemon, apple or blackberry pie fillings for cherry, if you prefer.

PEANUT BUTTER SHEET CAKE

Serves 20

2 cups flour
1 teaspoon soda
2 cups sugar
½ teaspoon salt
½ cup oil
1½ sticks margarine
½ cup creamy peanut
  butter
1 cup water
2 eggs
1 teaspoon vanilla
½ cup buttermilk
  Icing (recipe follows)

Mix together in a 2-quart mixing bowl, flour, sugar, soda and salt; set aside. In a 2-quart saucepan bring oil, margarine, peanut butter and water to a boil. Pour over dry ingredients and mix. In a bowl beat eggs, vanilla and buttermilk. Add to mixture; mix until

well-blended. Pour batter into a greased and floured 11 x 15 x 1-inch sheet cake pan. Bake 15–20 minutes in a 350-degree oven.

Icing:

½ cup evaporated milk *or*
  cream
1 cup sugar
1 tablespoon margarine
1 cup peanut butter chips
20 miniature marshmal-
  lows
1 cup chopped, dry-
  roasted peanuts
1 teaspoon vanilla

Bring evaporated milk or cream, sugar and margarine to a boil, cooking 2 minutes. Add chips, marshmallows, vanilla and peanuts. Blend until chips and marshmallows are melted. Spread on warm cake.

ORANGE SLICE CAKE

4½ cups flour
2 sticks butter
2 cups sugar
4 eggs
1 cup sour cream
1 cup buttermilk
½ cup butterscotch pie filling
  mix
1 teaspoon soda
2 teaspoons coconut flavoring
2 cups chopped black walnuts
1 (8-ounce) package chopped
  dates
1 (18-ounce) package orange
  slice candy
  Orange Slice Cake Frosting
  (recipe follows)

Combine flour, soda and butterscotch pie filling mix. Add sugar, butter and sour cream; beat well. Add eggs, 1 at a time, mixing well after each addition. Add buttermilk. Add remaining ingredients: flavoring, chopped dates, walnuts and orange slice candy. Bake in 2 tube

pans for 1½–2 hours at 275 degrees.

Orange Slice Cake Frosting:

1 (6-ounce) can frozen orange
  juice
1 cup brown sugar
2 teaspoons coconut flavor

Cook frosting ingredients until they start to boil. Pour over cake. This cake also freezes well.

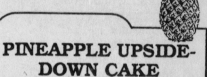

PINEAPPLE UPSIDE-DOWN CAKE

¼ cup butter *or* margarine
1 cup brown sugar, firmly
  packed
½ cup chopped pecans
1 (15¼-ounce) can pineapple
  slices, undrained
3 eggs, separated
1 cup sugar
1 cup all-purpose flour
1 teaspoon baking powder
½ teaspoon salt
6–8 maraschino cherries

Melt butter in a 9-inch cast-iron skillet. Add brown sugar and pecans; stir well. Drain pineapple, reserving ¼ cup *plus* 1 tablespoon pineapple juice; set juice aside. Arrange pineapple slices in a single layer over brown sugar mixture; set skillet aside.

Beat egg yolks with an electric mixer at medium speed until thick and lemon colored; gradually add sugar, beating well. Combine flour, baking powder and salt; add dry mixture to yolk mixture. Stir in reserved pineapple juice.

Beat egg whites (at room temperature) until stiff peaks form; fold egg whites into batter. Spoon batter evenly over pineapple slices. Bake at 350 degrees for 40–45 minutes. Remove cake from oven. Cool cake in skillet for 30 minutes; invert cake onto a serving plate. Place cherries in centers of pineapple rings.

DELICIOUS PUDDING CAKE

- 2 eggs, separated
- ¼ teaspoon cream of tartar
- 1 teaspoon grated lemon peel
- ¼ cup lemon juice
- 1 cup milk
- 1 cup sugar
- ¼ cup all-purpose flour
- ¼ teaspoon salt
- ¼ cup toasted coconut
  Whipped topping
  Maraschino cherries, drained

Beat egg whites and cream of tartar into a 1½-quart bowl until stiff peaks form; set aside. Beat egg yolks slightly. Beat in lemon peel, lemon juice and milk. Add sugar, flour and salt; beat until smooth. Fold into beaten egg whites. Pour into 1-quart microwavable casserole; sprinkle with coconut. Pour 1 cup very hot water into 1½-quart casserole. Carefully set casserole of pudding mixture into 1½-quart casserole. Microwave, uncovered, on MEDIUM-HIGH until wooden pick inserted in center comes out clean, 10–12 minutes. Garnish with whipped topping and Maraschino cherries.

BLACK-AND-WHITE CUPCAKES
Makes 4 dozen

- 1 (8-ounce) package cream cheese
- 1 egg, unbeaten
- ½ cup sugar
- ¼ teaspoon salt
- 1 (6-ounce) package semisweet chocolate chips
- 1½ cups flour
- 1 cup sugar
- ¼ cup cocoa
- 1 teaspoon baking soda
- ½ teaspoon salt
- 1 cup cold water
- ½ cup cooking oil
- 1 tablespoon vinegar
- 1 teaspoon vanilla

In a small mixing bowl, combine cream cheese, egg, ½ cup sugar and ¼ teaspoon salt; stir in chocolate chips and set aside.

Sift in large mixing bowl flour, 1 cup sugar, cocoa, baking soda and ½ teaspoon salt. Add to sifted ingredients cold water, cooking oil, vinegar and vanilla. Beat well.

Fill mini muffin pans (lined with cups) ⅓ full with chocolate batter. Top each with 1 teaspoon of cream cheese mixture. Bake at 350 degrees for 20–25 minutes.

IRRESISTIBLE CAKE
Makes 1 (8-inch) layer cake

- ⅔ cup *plus* 1 tablespoon finely diced pecans
- ¾ cup butter, softened
- 1 cup sugar
- 3 eggs
- 1 tablespoon freshly grated orange peel
- 1½ cups flour
- 1½ teaspoons baking soda
- ½ cup sour cream
- ¼ cup Grand Marnier liqueur
- 1 cup orange marmalade

Glaze:
- 4 ounces semisweet chocolate
- 3 ounces sweet butter

Preheat oven to 350 degrees. Prepare 2 (8-inch) cake pans by generously buttering, then lightly flouring; set aside. Cream butter and sugar until creamy. Add eggs; beat well. Stir in orange peel. Sift together flour and baking soda. Alternately add flour mixture and sour cream to butter mixture, mixing well after each addition. By hand, fold in the ⅔ cup pecans, mixing well. Reserve 1 tablespoon of pecans for garnish. Pour into prepared pans evenly. Bake for 30 minutes, or until edges pull from sides of pan, and a toothpick inserted in center comes out clean. Cool for 5 minutes in pan, then turn onto a rack to finish cooling.

Glaze:

Melt chocolate and butter over hot water. Split cooled layers and brush liqueur on cut surface of layers, repeating until all has absorbed. Place layers on plate, top side down; spread with marmalade. Repeat the marmalade for the next 2 layers. Drizzle with chocolate glaze. Garnish with 1 tablespoon of nuts.

SO-EASY BLACK MAGIC CAKE

- 1¾ cups all-purpose flour, unsifted
- 2 cups sugar
- ¾ cup cocoa
- 2 teaspoons soda
- 1 teaspoon baking powder
- 1 teaspoon salt
- 2 eggs
- 1 cup strong black coffee
- 1 cup buttermilk *or* 1 tablespoon vinegar *plus* milk to equal 1 cup
- ½ cup vegetable oil
- 1 teaspoon vanilla

Combine flour, sugar, cocoa, soda, baking powder and salt in large mixing bowl. Add eggs, coffee, buttermilk, oil and vanilla; beat 2 minutes on medium speed (batter will be thin).

Pour into greased and floured 13 x 9 x 2-inch pan or 2 (9-inch) layer pans. Bake at 350 degrees for 35–40 minutes for oblong pan, or 30–35 minutes for layer pans. Cool 10 minutes; remove from pans and cool completely before frosting.

Mocha Frosting:
- 6 tablespoons cocoa
- 6 tablespoons hot coffee
- 6 tablespoons margarine
- 1 teaspoon vanilla
- 3 cups sifted confectioners' sugar

Combine cocoa and coffee; add margarine and vanilla. Beat until smooth; add sugar gradually, until of spreading consistency. This frosts sides and tops of 2 (9-inch) layers. If using the oblong pan, halve the recipe for frosting.

LOW-FAT CARROT CAKE

Serves 9–12

- 1 cup coarsely grated carrots
- 1 cup raisins
- 1 cup water
- 1 cup sugar
- 2 tablespoons vegetable oil
- 1 teaspoon cinnamon
- ½ teaspoon ground cloves
- 2 cups all-purpose flour
- 1 teaspoon baking soda
- ½ cup chopped walnuts

Combine first 7 ingredients in saucepan and boil slowly for 8 minutes. Cool to room temperature. Add remaining ingredients. Blend well. Bake in a greased 9-inch square pan for 45 minutes.

Recipe may be doubled and baked in 13 x 9 x 2-inch pan for 50 minutes. This eggless cake keeps well and may be frozen. If other fruit is added such as apricots or pineapple, add ½ teaspoon more of baking soda. When cake cools dust with confectioners' sugar.

RAINBOW CAKE

- 1 yellow cake mix
- 1 cup sour cream
- ¼ cup water
- 2 eggs
- 1 (3-ounce) package raspberry-flavor gelatin
  Confectioners' sugar

Combine cake mix, sour cream, water and eggs. Blend, then beat at medium speed 2 minutes until creamy. Spoon ⅓ of batter into a well-greased and floured 10-inch, fluted tube pan. Sprinkle with half of the gelatin. Repeat layers. Spread remaining batter over gelatin to cover. Bake at 350 degrees for 45–50 minutes, or until

cake springs back when lightly pressed. Cool in pan for 5 minutes. Remove from pan and cool on rack. Sprinkle with confectioners' sugar.

WATERMELON RAISIN CAKE

- 1½ cups sugar
- ½ cup shortening
- 3 eggs, beaten
- 1 cup cold water
- 1 teaspoon vanilla
- 2 cups flour
- 2 teaspoons baking powder
  Few drops of red food coloring
- ¾ cup raisins

Soak raisins in boiling water for 15 minutes. Drain well. Dust with flour and set aside. Cream together the sugar and shortening. Add beaten eggs, water and vanilla; beat well. Add sifted flour and baking powder. Add a few drops of red food coloring, enough to make a pink batter. Fold in the floured raisins. Pour batter into 2 greased and floured, 9-inch round cake pans. Bake in a 375-degree oven for 20–25 minutes. Frost with green confectioners' sugar icing. This cake resembles a watermelon.

FRESH APPLE CAKE

- 3 cups chopped, raw apples
- 2 cups flour
- 2 cups sugar
- ½ cup shortening
- 2 eggs
- ½ teaspoon salt
- 1 teaspoon baking soda
- 2 teaspoons vanilla
- ½ teaspoon nutmeg
- ½ teaspoon cinnamon
- 1 cup chopped nuts

Mix all ingredients together. Bake in greased and floured 13 x 9-inch pan. Bake at 350 degrees for 45 minutes.

CHOCOLATE CHIP FILLED CUPCAKES

Makes 3–4 dozen

Filling:
- 1 (8-ounce) package cream cheese
- 1 egg
- ⅓ cup sugar
- ⅛ teaspoon salt
- 1 cup chocolate chips

Mix together and set aside.

Cupcakes:
- 3 cups flour
- 2 cups sugar
- ½ cup cocoa
- 2 teaspoons soda
- 1 teaspoon salt
- 2 cups water
- ⅔ cup oil
- 2 teaspoons vanilla
- 2 tablespoons vinegar

Preheat oven at 375 degrees. Mix cupcake ingredients together and pour into paper-lined cupcake pan. Drop the filling in teaspoonfuls into the center and bake at 375 degrees for 15–20 minutes.

GRAHAM CRACKER CAKE

- 1 cup sugar
- ½ cup butter, creamed
- ¾ cup milk
- 3 eggs, beaten
- 1 cup nuts, chopped
- 1 cup dates, chopped
- 1½ cups ground graham crackers
- 2 teaspoons baking powder
- 2 teaspoons flour

Cream sugar and butter; add beaten eggs. Mix and add milk, graham crackers and baking powder. Flour dates and nuts; add. Bake in 2 layers at 350 degrees for 30–35 minutes. Spread with a cream filling of your choice and frost with your favorite chocolate icing.

CHAMPAGNE CAKE

1 (1-layer) package cake mix (your flavor choice)
1 (8-ounce) package cream cheese, softened
1 (3-ounce) box instant pudding (complementary flavor to cake)
1 (20-ounce) can crushed pineapple, drained
1 1/2 cups milk
Whipped topping

Prepare cake mix as directed on package, but pour batter into a 9 x 13-inch pan. Bake for 15 minutes at suggested temperature. Let cool. Beat cream cheese until very soft. Blend cream cheese, pudding mix and milk. Spread over top of cooled cake. Spread drained pineapple over cake. Top with whipped topping.

LEMON CREAM-CHEESE POUND CAKE

3 cups sugar
1 1/4 cups butter, softened
1 (8-ounce) package cream cheese, softened
1 tablespoon lemon juice
2 teaspoons vanilla
1 teaspoon lemon extract
1/2 teaspoon orange extract
1/8 teaspoon salt
6 eggs
3 cups cake flour

Glaze:

1 cup confectioners' sugar
1 tablespoon butter, softened
2 teaspoons grated lemon peel
2–3 tablespoons lemon juice

For Cake:

Beat sugar, butter and cream cheese until fluffy. Beat in lemon juice, vanilla, lemon extract, orange extract and salt. Add eggs, 1 at a time, beating after each addition. Add flour; beat until smooth. Spread batter into greased and floured tube pan or Bundt pan. Bake at 325 degrees for 1 1/2 hours, or until golden brown. Cool 10 minutes. Remove from pan and cool completely.

Glaze:

Mix all ingredients until smooth. Spread glaze over cooled cake, allowing some to drizzle down sides.

14-KARAT CAKE

Mix:

2 cups flour
2 teaspoons baking powder
1 teaspoon baking soda

Blend:

1-1/2 cups cooking oil
1-2/3 cups sugar
4 eggs
4 teaspoons cinnamon
1 teaspoon salt

Add:

2 cups grated raw carrots
1 small flat can crushed pineapple (reserve 3 tablespoons for frosting)
1 cup chopped walnuts or pecans

Mix all ingredients together and blend well. Pour into 3 layer cake pans. Bake 25 minutes at 350 degrees. Cool on wire racks.

Frosting:

1 pound confectioners' sugar, sifted
1/2 pound (2 sticks) butter
8 ounces cream cheese
3 tablespoons crushed pineapple
1 teaspoon lemon extract

Blend together confectioners' sugar and softened butter. Add softened cream cheese, crushed pineapple, and lemon extract. Blend thoroughly and spread between layers, on top and sides of cooled cake.

APPLESAUCE LOAF CAKE

1/2 cup shortening
1 cup sugar
1 egg
1 cup unsweetened applesauce
1-3/4 cups sifted flour
1 teaspoon baking soda
1-1/2 teaspoons cinnamon
1 teaspoon allspice
1 teaspoon nutmeg
1/4 teaspoon cloves
1/2 teaspoon salt

Cream shortening and sugar until fluffy; add egg; beat well. Add applesauce. Sift remaining ingredients and mix. Bake in greased and floured 8x5x3 or 11x4-1/2x2-1/2 inch pan. Bake at 350 degrees for 1 hour. Frost with butter frosting. Decorate with whole walnuts. Delicious!!

BANANA WALNUT CAKE
Serves 8–10

2/3 cup mashed banana (mash ripe banana with fork)
1/2 cup butter, softened
3 large eggs
3/4 cup water
2 cups flour
2 teaspoons baking powder
1 teaspoon baking soda
1 teaspoon cinnamon
1 cup chopped walnuts, or use 1/2 cup nuts and 1/2 cup raisins

In mixing bowl beat together banana and butter until creamy. Add eggs and water; beat well. Stir in flour, baking powder, baking soda and cinnamon. Beat until smooth. Add nuts. Spoon batter into an oiled and floured 9 x 13-inch baking pan. Spread batter evenly in pan. Bake in 350-degree oven for 20–25 minutes. Cool and cut into squares.

I am a diabetic and enjoy this scrumptious cake.

PINEAPPLE-CHERRY CAKE

1 large can crushed pineapple, undrained
1 can cherry pie filling
1 box cake mix, yellow *or* butter-pecan
1 cup chopped pecans *or* walnuts
1 cup flaked coconut
1½ sticks margarine

Pour undrained pineapple into a 9 x 13-inch cake pan. Pour cherry pie filling over this and sprinkle cake mix over top of cherry pie filling. Sprinkle with nuts and coconut. Pour melted margarine over cake top. Bake in a 350-degree oven for 45 minutes, or until done.

REJOICE CAKE

2 cups flour
2-1/2 teaspoons baking soda
2 teaspoons cinnamon
1 teaspoon salt
1 cup cooking oil
2 cups sugar
3 eggs
1 (8-ounce) can crushed pineapple in juice
2 cups grated carrots
1-1/3 cups flaked coconut
1/2 cup chopped walnuts
1 (3-ounce) package cream cheese
1/4 cup margarine
3 cups sifted powdered sugar
1 tablespoon milk
1/2 teaspoon vanilla

Mix flour, soda, cinnamon, salt. Beat oil, sugar, and eggs thoroughly. Add flour mixture. Beat until smooth. Add pineapple, carrots, 1/3 cup coconut, and walnuts. Pour into greased 9 x 13-inch pan. Bake at 350 degrees

for 50-60 minutes. Cool 10 minutes, then remove from pan and cool on rack.

Frosting:

Toast 1 cup coconut, cool. Cream together cream cheese and margarine. Add powdered sugar, milk, and vanilla. Beat until smooth. Add 1/2 of the coconut. Frost cake and top with remaining coconut.

AUTUMN APPLE CAKE

3 medium-size apples, peeled, cored and chopped
1 cup sugar
1½ cups cake flour
1 teaspoon baking soda
½ teaspoon salt
½ teaspoon nutmeg
½ teaspoon allspice
½ cup butter *or* margarine, melted
1 egg

Peel and core apples. Coarsely chop and measure 1¾ cups apples into a large bowl. Add sugar; let stand 10 minutes. Sift flour; measure. Add soda and spices; mix together. Blend butter and egg into apple mixture. Add flour mixture; mix just until blended. Bake in a greased 8-inch square pan at 350 degrees for 45 minutes, or until toothpick comes out clean after testing. Cool on cake rack. Sprinkle top with confectioners' sugar, if desired.

APPLE-RAISIN CAKE

1 yellow cake mix
½ cup margarine, melted
¾ cup raisins
½ cup sugar
1 teaspoon cinnamon
4 apples, pared and thinly sliced

1 egg, beaten
1 cup sour cream
1 teaspoon cinnamon

Melt margarine and cool slightly. Add to cake mix; mix well. Stir in 1 teaspoon cinnamon and raisins. Pour batter into a greased and floured 9 x 13-inch baking pan. Lay sliced apples over batter.

In bowl, beat together egg, sour cream and sugar. Pour over apples. Sprinkle with 1 teaspoon cinnamon. Bake at 350 degrees for 30 minutes.

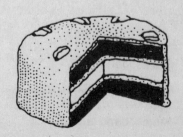

APPLE ORANGE CAKE
Serves 12

2½ cups canned apple slices
¼ cup butter
1 cup light brown sugar
Dash of cinnamon
1 package yellow cake mix
Orange juice
Grated orange rind
Whipped cream
Nutmeg

Drain apples. Melt butter in 12 x 8 x 2-inch pan. Sprinkle with brown sugar and cinnamon. Arrange apples in rows on sugar mixture. Prepare cake mix according to directions on package, substituting orange juice for the liquid called for in the recipe. Add grated orange rind. Pour batter over apples in pan. Bake in preheated oven of 375 degrees for 40 minutes. Cool 15 minutes in pan. Turn upside down on serving platter. Serve hot or cold with whipped cream sprinkled with dash of nutmeg.

NO-COOK FROSTING

1/4 teaspoon salt
2 egg whites
3/4 cup sugar
3/4 cup Karo syrup, red or blue label
1-1/4 teaspoons vanilla

Beat salt and egg whites until mixture peaks. Add sugar, 1 tablespoon at a time, beating until smooth and glossy. Continue beating and add Karo syrup gradually, until frosting peaks. Fold in vanilla. Add vegetable coloring, if desired; frost top and sides of two 9 inch layers.

APPLE BUTTER CAKE

1/2 cup shortening
1 cup sugar
3 eggs
1 cup apple butter
2-1/2 cups sifted cake flour
3 teaspoons baking powder
1/2 teaspoon baking soda
1/2 teaspoon salt
1/2 teaspoon cinnamon
1/4 teaspoon nutmeg
1/2 cup apple butter
1 cup sour milk

Cream together shortening and sugar. Beat in eggs, one at a time; beat until light and fluffy. Stir in 1 cup apple butter. Sift together flour, baking powder, soda, salt, cinnamon, and nutmeg. Add dry ingredients to creamed mixture, alternately with sour milk. Turn into 2 greased and floured 9 inch cake pans. Bake at 350 degrees for 30-35 minutes. Cool thoroughly. Spread bottom layer of cake with 1/4 cup of remaining apple butter. Top with frosting. Cover with top cake layer. Frost top and sides with any marshmallow frosting. Swirl remaining apple butter on top for marbled effect.

DUTCH APPLE CAKE
Makes 1 13 x 9-inch cake

1 (18-1/2 ounce) package spice cake mix
1/2 cup butter or margarine, melted
2 eggs
1 (21 ounce) can apple pie filling
3/4 cup brown sugar, firmly packed
1 teaspoon cinnamon
1/4 cup butter or margarine, softened
1/2 cup chopped nuts

In large bowl, combine dry cake mix, melted butter, and eggs. Blend well. Spread on bottom of 13 x 9 inch baking pan. Spoon pie filling evenly over batter. In small bowl combine brown sugar and cinnamon; cut in softened butter; stir in nuts. Sprinkle over pie filling. Bake at 350 degrees for 50 minutes or until cake springs back when lightly touched.

APPLESAUCE CAKE

1 stick (1/2 cup) butter or margarine, softened
1 cup sugar
1 large egg
1-1/2 cups applesauce
2 cups all-purpose flour
2 teaspoons baking soda
1 teaspoon cinnamon
1 teaspoon nutmeg
1/4 teaspoon ground cloves
1 cup chopped, pitted dates
1/2 cup chopped walnuts

In a large bowl cream the butter, add the sugar, a little at a time. Beat the mixture until light and fluffy. Beat in the egg and add the applesauce. Into a bowl sift together the flour, soda, and spices, gently stir the mixture into the applesauce mixture with the dates and walnuts. Transfer the batter into a well greased baking pan, 12 x 8 x 2 inches, and bake in a preheated oven 350 degrees for approximately 45 minutes. Let the cake cool in pan on a rack. Frost if desired.

Very moist cake. Raisins may be used instead of dates.

APPLESAUCE LAYER CAKE

2 eggs
1-1/2 cups sugar
1-1/2 cups applesauce
1/2 cup butter or shortening
1 teaspoon soda
1 teaspoon salt
1 teaspoon cinnamon
1 teaspoon nutmeg
1/2 cup nut meats
2 cups flour
1 cup raisins (if desired)

Cream together the shortening and sugar. Add eggs, applesauce; and then sift the flour, soda, salt, and spices together. Add to creamed mixture; stir in raisins.

Grease (2) 8-inch round cake pans or use typing paper cut to fit inside pans. Pour batter into pans and bake at 325 degrees for 40 minutes or until cake tests done.

This cake is especially tasty with a mocha or caramel frosting.

SAUCY APPLE SWIRL CAKE
Serves 16

1/4 cup sugar
1 teaspoon cinnamon
1 package yellow cake mix (Pillsbury Plus best)
1 (15 ounce) jar (1-1/2 cups) applesauce
3 eggs

Heat oven to 350 degrees. Grease and flour 12-cup fluted pan or 10-inch tube pan. In small bowl, combine sugar and cinnamon; set aside. In large bowl, blend cake mix, applesauce, and eggs until moistened. Beat 2 minutes at high speed. Pour 1/2 of batter into prepared pan. Sprinkle with sugar mix. Cover with remaining batter. Bake 35-45 minutes until toothpick comes out of center clean. Cool upright in pan 25 minutes; turn onto serving plate. Cool completely. Dust with powdered sugar.

"500" CAKE

1/2 cup butter
1 cup sugar
2 eggs
1/2 cup sour cream
1 cup mashed bananas
2 cups flour
1/2 teaspoon salt
1 teaspoon baking soda
1 teaspoon baking powder
1/2 cup chopped dates
1/2 cup chopped nuts
1 teaspoon vanilla

Cream butter and sugar. Add eggs. Add sour cream and mashed bananas alternately with sifted dry ingredients. Fold in nuts and dates which have been dusted with a little of the flour. Add vanilla. Pour into greased cake pans or cupcake tins. Bake at 350 degrees for 30 minutes.
Note: Buttermilk may be used instead of sour cream.

ORANGE PEANUT–BUTTER CAKE
Serves 12

2 oranges
1 (18-ounce) package yellow cake mix with pudding
1-1/4 cups water
3 eggs
1/2 cup peanut butter
1 teaspoon ground cinnamon
1/3 cup packed brown sugar

Grate peeling from oranges; reserve. Peel oranges and cut into bite–size pieces; drain well. In large bowl, combine cake mix, water, eggs, peanut butter, and cinnamon; mix according to package directions. Stir in orange peel and pieces. Pour batter into greased and floured 13x9x2-inch cake pan. Sprinkle brown sugar over top of batter. Bake at 350 degrees for 35-40 minutes or until done. Serve warm or cool.

CHOCOLATE SUNDAE CAKE

1 package devil's food cake mix
1 cup brown sugar
1/3 cup cocoa
2 cups water
2 cups miniature marshmallows
1 cup pecans, chopped

Combine brown sugar, cocoa, and water. Mix well. Pour into a 13x9-inch pan. Place marshmallows evenly on top.
Make cake batter following package directions. Pour into pan. Top with nuts. Bake at 350 degrees for 30 minutes. Cool in pan on wire rack. Cut into bars or squares to serve.

COOKIES 'N CREAM CAKE

1 package white cake mix
1-1/4 cups water
1/3 cup oil
3 egg whites
1 cup crushed, creme-filled chocolate sandwich cookies
10 whole cookies

Frosting:
3 cups powdered sugar
3/4 cup shortening
1 teaspoon vanilla
2 egg whites

Heat oven to 350 degrees. Grease and flour 2 round cake pans. In large bowl, combine all cake ingredients, except cookies. Mix at low speed until moistened. Beat 2 minutes at high speed. Stir in crushed creme-filled chocolate cookies. Bake at 350 degrees for 25-35 minutes or until it tests done. Cool layers.
In small bowl combine 1/2 cup of the powdered sugar, shortening, vanilla, and egg whites. Blend well. Beat in remaining sugar until frosting is smooth. Fill and frost cake. Arrange whole cookies on end and on top of frosted cake.

SOUR CREAM CAKE

1/2 cup chopped pecans
1/2 cup sugar
1 teaspoon cinnamon
4 eggs
1 package yellow cake mix
1 package instant vanilla pudding mix
1/2 cup oil
1 cup sour cream

Combine pecans, sugar, and cinnamon; set aside. Combine remaining ingredients; beat for 4 minutes. Spoon half the batter into well-greased and floured bundt or spring pan. Sprinkle half of the pecan mixture over batter, then add remaining batter and remaining pecan mixture over top. Bake in a preheated 350-degree oven for 1 hour. Cake may be glazed with thin icing or dusted with confectioners' sugar.

PRALINE CHEESECAKE
Serves 12

Crust:
1-1/2 cups graham cracker crumbs
6 tablespoons butter, melted
1/4 cup sugar
2 tablespoons pecans, finely chopped

Filling:
1-1/2 pounds cream cheese
1 cup dark brown sugar
2 tablespoons flour
3 eggs
1/2 teaspoon vanilla
1/4 cup pecans, finely chopped

Combine all crust ingredients. Press on bottom and up sides of 9-inch springform pan.
For filling beat together cheese and sugar until creamy. Add flour, then eggs. Blend in vanilla and pecans. Pour into crust. Bake at 350 degrees for 50 minutes. Allow to cool. Chill in refrigerator before serving.

CHOCOLATE CHERRY UPSIDE-DOWN CAKE

2-1/4 cups flour
1-1/2 cups sugar
3/4 cup cocoa
1-1/2 teaspoons baking soda
3/4 teaspoon salt
1-1/2 cups water
1/2 cup cooking oil
1/4 cup vinegar
1-1/2 teaspoons vanilla
1 can cherry pie filling

Spread pie filling in a greased 9x13-inch pan. In a large bowl mix flour, sugar, cocoa, soda, and salt. In another bowl, mix water, oil, vinegar, and vanilla. Add liquid mixture to dry mixture and stir just to moisten. Pour batter over cherries. Bake 350 degrees for 35 minutes. Cool 10 minutes in the pan. Invert on large platter. Serve with ice cream or whipped topping.

CHOCOLATE CHIP CAKE

2 cups all purpose flour
1 cup packed brown sugar
1/2 cup granulated sugar
3 teaspoons baking powder
1 teaspoon salt
1/2 teaspoon baking soda
1/2 cup shortening
1-1/4 cups milk
3 eggs
1/2 cup semi-sweet chocolate chips finely chopped or
1/2 cup miniature semi-sweet chocolate chips
1-1/2 teaspoons vanilla

Heat oven to 350 degrees. Grease and flour oblong pan, 13 x 9 x 2 inches or 2 round layer pans, 8 or 9 inch x 1-1/2 inches. Beat all ingredients in large mixer bowl on low speed, scraping bowl constantly, 30 seconds. Beat on high speed, scraping bowl occasionally, 3 minutes. Pour into pans. Bake in a 350 degree oven for 40-50 minutes. Bake until wooden pick inserted in center comes out clean. While cake is cooling, prepare Chocolate Butter Frosting.

CHOCOLATE ECLAIR CAKE
Serves 15

1 cup flour
1 stick (1/2 cup) butter or margarine
1/4 teaspoon salt
1 cup water
4 eggs (best at room temperature)
2 packages instant French vanilla pudding
2-1/2 cups cold milk
8 ounces cream cheese, softened
12 ounces (large container) Cool Whip or other whipped topping
3 ounces chocolate chips (1/2 of 6-ounce bag)
2 tablespoons butter or margarine
1 cup confectioners' sugar
3 to 4 tablespoons milk

Bring water and butter to a boil until all butter is melted. All at once add flour and salt; beat until mixture forms a ball that leaves the sides of saucepan; cool slightly. Add eggs one at a time, beating thoroughly after each addition. Spread pastry mixture into ungreased jelly roll pan (15 x 10 x 1-inch). Bake at 400 degrees for 35 minutes. Remove from oven; pierce bubbles with fork while hot. Cool completely.

Mix instant pudding with milk; add softened cream cheese, beat together thoroughly. Spread whipped topping over pudding mixture. Melt chocolate chips and butter over low heat, mix to add confectioners' sugar and milk, alternately until thin glaze forms. Pour or drizzle chocolate glaze over whipped topping. Refrigerate at least 1 hour or longer. Cut into squares to serve.

APPLE CAKE WITH TOPPING

3 cups flour
2 cups sugar
1-1/2 teaspoons soda
1 teaspoon salt
3/4 cup cooking oil
2 eggs, beaten
1 teaspoon vanilla
1 cup chopped walnuts
3 cups chopped apples (unpeeled)

Mix oil, sugar, and eggs. Add dry ingredients and vanilla by hand. Add nuts and apples. Bake at 350 degrees for 1 hour in a well-greased tube or bundt pan. Remove from oven and pour topping over cake. Return cake to oven and bake 15 minutes more. Slide knife around cake to loosen.

Topping:
1 cup light brown sugar
1 stick butter or margarine
1/4 cup orange juice

Cook over low heat for 3 minutes after the mixture starts boiling. Pour over cake as directed above.

POPPY SEED CAKE
Serves 10-12

1 (18-1/2–ounce) package yellow cake mix
1 (3-3/4-ounce) package instant vanilla pudding mix
4 eggs
1 cup sour cream
1/2 cup (1 stick) melted butter
1/2 cup cream sherry
1/3 cup poppy seeds

Preheat oven to 350 degrees. Grease bundt cake pan and flour lightly, shaking out excess. Combine all ingredients in large bowl and beat 5 minutes with electric mixer. Pour batter into pan. Bake until tester in center comes out clean, about 1 hour. Let cool completely in pan. Invert onto platter and serve. Garnish each serving with sliced fruit.

LEMON CRACKLE CAKE

20 soda crackers (2" squares)
3/4 cup brown sugar
1 cup flour
1 teaspoon baking soda
1/2 cup butter or oleo
1 cup coconut

Crush crackers in bowl; add brown sugar, flour and soda. Work in butter; add coconut. Pat 3/4 of mixture into greased and floured 8 or 9-inch baking pan. Carefully spread on filling; cover with rest of crumb mixture. Bake at 350 degrees for 30 to 35 minutes or until slightly brown.

Lemon Filling:

1 cup sugar
2 tablespoons cornstarch
1 cup cold water
2 eggs, beaten
Juice of 2 lemons or 1/2 cup lemon juice
1/4 cup butter
1 teaspoons vanilla

In sauce pan, combine sugar and cornstarch. Gradually stir in water. Add remaining ingredients. Cook over medium heat until thickened. Cool before adding to cake.

ORANGE - KISS ME CAKE

Serves 12

1-6 ounce can (3/4 cup) frozen orange juice concentrate, (thawed)
2 cups flour
1 cup sugar
1 teaspoon baking soda
1 teaspoon salt
1/2 cup shortening
1/2 cup milk
2 eggs
1 cup raisins
1/3 cup chopped walnuts

Grease and flour bottom of 13 x 9 inch pan. Combine 1/2 cup orange juice concentrate with remaining ingredients in large mixer bowl. Blend at lowest speed of mixer for 30 seconds. Beat 3 minutes at medium speed. Pour into pan. Bake at 350 degrees for 40-45 minutes. Drizzle remaining orange juice concentrate over warm cake; sprinkle with sugar-nut topping (recipe follows).

Sugar-Nut Topping:

1/3 cup sugar
1/4 cup chopped walnuts
1 teaspoon cinnamon

Combine all ingredients in small bowl.

CREAM CHEESE TOPPED PINEAPPLE CAKE

2 eggs
2 cups sugar
2 cups all-purpose flour
1 (20-ounce) can crushed pineapple packed in own juice, undrained
1/2 cup chopped pecans
2 teaspoons baking soda
1 teaspoon vanilla

Preheat oven to 350 degrees. Lightly grease 9 x 13-inch baking pan. Beat eggs in large bowl until light and fluffy. Add sugar and beat until thick. Stir in flour, pineapple, pecans, baking soda, and vanilla; mix thoroughly. Pour into pan and bake until tester inserted in center comes out clean. Bake 40-45 minutes. Let cake cool in pan on rack.

Cream Cheese Frosting:

2 cups powdered sugar

1 (8-ounce) cream cheese (room temperature)
1/4 cup (1/2 stick) butter (room temperature)
1 teaspoon vanilla
Additional chopped pecans for garnish

Combine powdered sugar, cream cheese, butter, and vanilla; mix until fluffy. Spread over cooled cake and sprinkle with chopped nuts. Cut into squares to serve.

This is a quick and easy cake to make and is delicious!

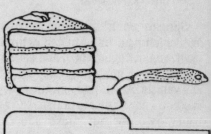

PINEAPPLE UPSIDE DOWN CAKE

1/2 cup packed brown sugar
1/4 cup butter
1 - can sliced pineapple (drained - reserve 1 tablespoon juice)
Maraschino cherries, halved
1 - 16 ounce container frozen pancake batter, thawed
1/4 cup granulated sugar

Heat oven to 350 degrees. Melt butter and put in glass pie plate. Add brown sugar and stir till smooth. Cut pineapple slices in half and arrange pineapple and cherries on sugar mixture in a decorative manner. Open top of pancake batter container completely. Add granulated sugar and reserve pineapple juice. Stir well. Pour over pineapple. Bake 30-35 minutes until golden brown and toothpick inserted in center comes out clean. Cool 5 minutes. Loosen edges of cake with small knife. Invert cake on serving platter.

This is a delicious and unusual way to make an upside-down cake. If pineapple is arranged pinwheel fashion, with a half-cherry in each curve, you get a lot more fruit on your cake.

OATMEAL CAKE

1 cup quick oatmeal
1 1/4 cups boiling water
1 stick butter or margarine
2 eggs, beaten
1 cup white sugar
1 cup brown sugar
1 1/2 cups flour
1 teaspoon soda
1 teaspoon cinnamon
1/2 teaspoon salt
1 teaspoon vanilla

Stir together the oatmeal, boiling water and butter until butter melts. Let cool. Add the eggs and beat, then add sugar and beat mixture again. Sift together the flour, soda, cinnamon and salt and add to cake mixture with the vanilla. Beat all well.

Pour into greased and floured 9x13" pan. Bake at 350-degrees for about 32 minutes.

When done and still hot, spread with the following topping. Mix together in heavy pan 3/4 cup brown sugar, 3/4 cup pecan pieces (or other chopped nuts), 6 tablespoons butter and 1/2 cup condensed milk (1/2 cup coconut, optional). Cream and cook until thick (but not too long). Evenly place mixture on cake. Place cake under broiler until topping becomes bubbly.

$100 CHOCOLATE CAKE

1/2 cup butter
2 cups sugar
4 ounces semi-sweet chocolate, melted
2 eggs, beaten
2 cups sifted cake flour
1/4 teaspoon salt
2 teaspoons baking powder
1-1/2 cups sweet milk
1 teaspoon vanilla
1 cup chopped nuts

Cream butter and sugar. Add melted chocolate. Add beaten eggs. Add flour, salt, baking powder mixture, and vanilla, alternately with milk. Beat with hand beater, not mixer, after addition. Put in 2 (9-inch) cake pans. Bake in 350 degree oven for 45 minutes. Batter is thin.

Frosting:
1/2 cup butter
2 ounces semi-sweet chocolate, melted
1 egg, beaten
1/4 teaspoon salt
1 teaspoon lemon juice
1 teaspoon vanilla
1-1/2 cups confectioners' sugar
1 cup chopped nuts

Mix first 6 ingredients, then stir in confectioners' sugar. Beat until thick enough to spread. (Beat by hand.) Sprinkle chopped nuts on top.

ORANGE KISS ME CAKE

1 (6-ounce) can frozen orange juice, (3/4 cup thawed)
2 cups flour
1 cup sugar
1 teaspoon soda
1 teaspoon salt
1/2 cup shortening
1/2 cup milk
2 eggs
1 cup raisins
1/3 cup chopped walnuts

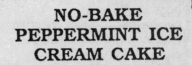

Preheat oven to 350 degrees. Grease and flour bottom of 9x13-inch pan. Combine 1/2 cup orange juice with remaining ingredients in large bowl. Blend at lowest speed of mixer for 30 seconds. Beat 3 minutes at medium speed. Bake 40-45 minutes. Drizzle remaining orange juice over warm cake and sprinkle with topping (recipe follows).

Topping:
1/3 cup sugar
1/4 cup chopped walnuts
1 teaspoon cinnamon
Combine in a bowl.

SUNSHINE CAKE

7 egg yolks
1 teaspoon lemon extract
1-1/2 cups powdered sugar
10 egg whites
1 teaspoon cream of tartar
1 cup cake flour
1/4 teaspoon salt

Preheat oven to 325 degrees. Line bottom of a 10-inch tube pan with wax paper; cut to fit. Beat egg yolks; add lemon extract and 1 cup of the powdered sugar. Beat until thick and pale; set aside. Beat egg whites until foamy; add the cream of tartar, and beat until whites form soft peaks. Gradually, add remaining 1/2 cup powdered sugar and beat until stiff. Stir a fourth of the whites into the yolk mixture. Spoon remaining whites on top of the yolk mixture and sift flour and salt over them. Carefully fold until blended. Spoon into pan and bake for 50-60 minutes, until a toothpick comes out clean. Invert pan on a rack and let cake cool completely before removing from the pan. Frost with your favorite icing.

NO-BAKE PEPPERMINT ICE CREAM CAKE

10-inch angel food cake
6 chocolate peppermint patties
1/2 cup nuts
1/8 teaspoon peppermint extract
1 quart vanilla ice cream

Cut cake in 4 layers. Chop patties and nuts. Soften ice cream slightly. Stir in candy, nuts, and extract. Spread thick layer of ice cream mixture between cake layers and rebuild the cake. Cover top with ice cream mixture. Keep in freezer; no thawing necessary.

ZUCCHINI PINEAPPLE CAKE

3 eggs
2 cups sugar
2 teaspoons vanilla
1 cup cooking oil
2 cups zucchini, peeled and grated
3 cups flour
1 teaspoon baking powder
1/2 cup raisins
1 teaspoon salt
1 teaspoon nuts
1 cup crushed pineapple, drained

Beat eggs until fluffy; add sugar, vanilla, oil, and zucchini. Blend well. Add dry ingredients and mix well. Stir in pineapple, raisins, and nuts.

Bake in one large greased and floured loaf pan or two small loaf pans. Bake in 325-degree oven for 1 hour. Cool in pan on wire rack. When cool wrap in foil to store.

HAZELNUT CHEESECAKE

1-1/2 pounds cream cheese, at room temperature
1 cup sugar
3 eggs
1 cup hazelnuts, finely chopped
1 teaspoon vanilla extract
1 cup heavy cream
2 tablespoons rum
Bread crumbs

Preheat oven to 375 degrees. In bowl of electric mixer, combine cream cheese, sugar, eggs, hazelnuts, vanilla extract, heavy cream, and rum. Butter a 10x3-inch deep layer-cake or springform pan and coat with bread crumbs. Pour batter into pan. Put pan with the cheesecake batter into a deep pan. Fill outside pan with water until water reaches halfway up sides of cheesecake pan. Bake for 45 minutes. Cool and serve.

ELEGANT APPLE CHEESECAKE

2 (8-ounce) packages cream cheese, softened
1 (16-ounce) carton cream-style cottage cheese
1-1/2 cups sugar
4 eggs
3 tablespoons cornstarch
1-1/2 tablespoons lemon juice
1 tablespoon vanilla
1/4 pound butter, melted and cooled
2 cups dairy sour cream
1 (21-ounce) can apple pie filling

Lightly butter a 9-inch springform pan. In a large mixing bowl, combine cheeses; beat until light and fluffy. Add sugar; blend well. Add eggs, one at a time, beating well after each addition. Add cornstarch, lemon juice, vanilla, and butter; blend until smooth. Blend in sour cream. Pour batter into prepared pan. Bake at 325 degrees for 1 hour and 10 minutes, or until center is set. Turn oven off. Let cheesecake stand in oven, with the door closed, for 2 hours. Cool completely. Chill 6 hours. Spoon apple pie filling over the top.

APRICOT NECTAR CAKE

1 (46-ounce) can apricot nectar
7 tablespoons cornstarch
1-1/2 cups sugar
1 large angel food cake

Combine the first three ingredients and cook over medium heat until mixture becomes clear and bubbly. Watch closely, stirring constantly. Take off heat and pour over a large angel food cake, which has been torn into small pieces and placed in a greased 9x13 glass baking dish. Cover and allow it to chill 24 hours in refrigerator. Serve with a scoop of whipped topping. This is a quick and easy cake that is absolutely delicious!!

CRANBERRY CAKE

3 cups sifted flour
1-1/2 cups sugar
1 teaspoon soda
1 teaspoon salt
1 cup mayonnaise
1 cup chopped nuts
3/4 cup whole cranberry sauce
2 tablespoons orange peel
1/3 cup orange juice

Sift dry ingredients. Add remaining ingredients. Pour into greased 9x13-inch pan. Bake at 350 degrees for 45 minutes.

Icing:
2 tablespoons butter
2 cups sifted confectioners' sugar
1/4 cup whole cranberry sauce

Combine ingredients and spread on hot cake.

ORANGE HONEY CAKE

2 cups sifted cake flour
3-1/2 teaspoons baking powder
3/4 teaspoon salt
1/2 cup butter or shortening
1/2 cup sugar
2/3 cup honey
2 egg yolks
1/2 cup orange juice
2 egg whites, stiffly beaten

Sift flour; measure; add baking powder and salt; sift 3 times. Cream butter thoroughly; add sugar gradually; cream until light and fluffy. Add honey; blend. Add egg yolks and beat thoroughly. Add flour alternately with orange juice, a small amount at a time, beating well after each addition until smooth. Fold in egg whites. Bake in 2 greased 9-inch layer pans in 350-degree oven for 30-35 minutes.

CARROT CAKE

2 cup oil
cup sugar
eggs, well beaten
2 cup grated carrots, packed
2 cup crushed pineapple
1/2 cups sifted flour
2 teaspoon salt
2 teaspoon baking soda
2 teaspoon baking powder
2 teaspoon cinnamon
teaspoon vanilla
2 cup chopped walnuts

Combine oil and sugar; add well-beaten eggs, carrots, and crushed pineapple. Mix just to combine. Sift flour, salt, baking soda, baking powder, and cinnamon. Stir into oil mixture. Add vanilla and nuts. Mix to combine. Pour batter into a greased and floured 9x13-inch pan. Bake at 350 degrees for 30 minutes or until done. Cool.

Icing:

(3 ounce) cream cheese
ounces margarine
-1/2 cups powdered sugar
teaspoon walnuts, chopped fine
teaspoon crushed pineapple

Mix together cream cheese, margarine, and powdered sugar. Beat until light and fluffy. Add nuts and pineapple. Ice cooled cake.

NO-FUSS FRUITCAKE

3/4 cup brown sugar
1/2 cup margarine or butter
1 egg
2-1/2 cups all-purpose flour
1 teaspoon baking soda
1/4 teaspoon *each* nutmeg and cloves
1/2 teaspoon cinnamon
1/4 cup orange or pineapple juice
1 cup applesauce, unsweetened or diced
2 cups chopped candied fruit
1 cup *each* raisins and chopped walnuts

In large bowl cream sugar and margarine or butter; add egg; beat well. Mix flour with spices and soda; stir into creamed mixture alternately with applesauce and juice. Fold in fruits, raisins, and nuts. Pour into two greased, floured 7-1/2 x 3-1/2 x 2 inch loaf pans. Bake for 1 hour at 325 degrees or until tests done with toothpick. Remove from pans; cool. Lightly glaze tops with mixture of confectioners' sugar and enough fruit juice or water to spread thinly. When glaze is set, press halved candied cherries over the top. Wrap in foil; store in cool place or freeze until needed.

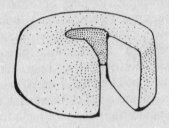

GRAPEFRUIT CHIFFON CAKE

2 cups all-purpose flour
1-1/2 cups sugar
3 teaspoons baking powder
1/2 teaspoon salt
1/2 cup oil
6 egg yolks
3 teaspoons grated grapefruit peel
2/3 cup grapefruit juice
6-7 egg whites
1/4 teaspoon cream of tartar

In a small mixer bowl stir together flour, sugar, baking powder, and salt. Make a well in center; in order add oil, egg yolks, peel, and juice. Beat smooth with an electric mixer. Wash beaters and in large bowl beat egg whites with the cream of tartar until stiff.

Gradually pour flour mixture (it will be thick) in a thin stream over surface and fold in gently. Bake in a 10-inch ungreased tube pan for 55 minutes at 350 degrees or until it tests done when lightly touched with the finger the cake springs back. Invert. Cool completely on cake cooling rack, loosen edges, and remove to cake plate. Glaze with the following:

2 cups sifted powdered sugar
3 teaspoons grapefruit peel, grated
1 teaspoon vanilla
2-3 tablespoons grapefruit juice

Mix all ingredients together using enough grapefruit juice to make it spread easily and drizzle down the sides when spread on top of cake.

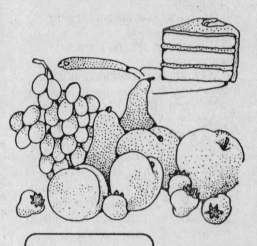

HAWAIIAN CAKE

1 package yellow cake mix
1-6 ounce package instant vanilla pudding mix
1-1/4 cups cold milk
1-8 ounce package cream cheese
1-8 or 9 ounce container frozen whipped topping
1-20 ounce can crushed pineapple, well drained
1/2 cup chopped pecans
1/2 cup flaked coconut
1/2 cup Maraschino cherries, drained and chopped

Prepare cake according to directions on package. Pour into greased 10 x 15 jelly roll pan. Bake in preheated oven 350 degrees 15-20 minutes, or until done. Cool in pan.

Blend pudding mix with milk, beat in cream cheese (room temperature); then fold in frozen whipped topping. Spread on cooled cake. Sprinkle drained pineapple over pudding, then cherries, nuts, and coconut. Refrigerate until ready to cut. Can be made a day ahead. This not only makes a big beautiful cake but is very delicious. I've taken this to a lot of potlucks and someone always wants the recipe.

CHOCOLATE ANGEL FOOD CAKE

1/4 cup cocoa
1 cup cake flour
1-3/4 cups sugar
1-1/2 cups egg whites
3/4 teaspoon salt
1-1/2 teaspoons cream of tartar
1 teaspoon vanilla
1/4 teaspoon almond extract

Sift cocoa, cake flour, and 3/4 cup sugar together four times. Beat egg whites and salt until foamy. Sprinkle cream of tartar over egg whites; continue beating until stiff, but not dry. *Fold* in remaining sugar, one tablespoon at a time. Add vanilla and almond extract. *Fold* in dry ingredients, a little at a time. Pour into ungreased 10 inch tube pan. Bake 60-70 minutes at 325 degrees. Frost, if desired, although it is delicious plain.

OLD-FASHIONED TRIPLE FUDGE CAKE

1 package devil's food cake mix
1/2 cup chopped nuts
1/2 cup semi-sweet chocolate pieces
1 (12 ounce) jar thick fudge ice cream topping
Ice cream, whipped topping, or whipped cream

Mix cake as directed on package. Stir in nuts; spread batter in a greased and floured 13 x 9 x 2 inch pan. Sprinkle chocolate-pieces evenly over batter; bake as directed on package. Immediately after baking, poke deep holes through top of hot cake (still in pan), space holes about 1 inch apart. Spoon fudge topping evenly over cake. Topping will melt into holes. Serve when completely cool. Top with ice cream or whipped cream.

OREO COOKIE CAKE

1 pound oreo cookies
1 cup melted margarine
8 ounce soft cream cheese
2 - 8 ounce containers whipped topping
1 cup powdered sugar
1 large package instant chocolate pudding

Crush cookies and (set aside 1/2 cup). Mix crumbs with butter, and press into 9 ix 13 pan. Refrigerate 1 hour. Mix cream cheese, sugar, 1 carton whipped topping. Spread over cookie crust. Refrigerate 1 hour. Prepare pudding mix by directions on package. Spread over cheese mixture. Refrigerate 1 hour. Top with whipped topping, sprinkle with rest of cookie crumbs. Garnish with maraschino cherries.

TURTLE CAKE

1 package German chocolate cake mix
1 (14-ounce) package caramels
1/2 cup evaporated milk
6 tablespoons margarine
1 cup chopped pecans
1 cup chocolate chips

Prepare cake mix according to directions. Pour 1/2 batter into greased and floured 9 x 13 inch pan. Set other batter aside. Bake at 350 degrees for 18 minutes. Melt caramels and milk together, then stir in pecans. Sprinkle baked part of cake with chocolate chips, and pour caramel mix over that. Pour remaining batter over top. Return pan to oven and bake 20 minutes. Cut into squares to serve.

BUTTERMILK COFFEE CAKE
9 Servings

2 cups sifted flour

1 cup sugar
1/2 teaspoon ground cinnamon
1/4 teaspoon baking powder
1/4 teaspoon salt
1/2 cup butter or margarine
1 teaspoon ground cinnamon
1/2 teaspoon baking soda
3/4 cup buttermilk
1 teaspoon vanilla

Sift together flour, sugar, 1/2 teaspoon cinnamon, baking powder and salt into bowl. Cut in butter with pastry blender or two knives until mixture is crumbly. Reserve 1/2 cup crumb mixture. Combine reserved crumbs with 1 teaspoon cinnamon, set aside. Dissolve baking soda in buttermilk. Add buttermilk mixture and vanilla to remaining crumb mixture, stirring just enough to moisten. Spread batter in greased 8 inch square pan. Sprinkle with reserved crumbs. Bake in 375 degree oven 35 minutes or until done. Cut into squares and serve warm. If you love cinnamon you will love this coffee cake.

BLUEBERRY COFFEE CAKE

2 cups flour
1 cup sugar
3 teaspoons baking powder
1/4 teaspoon salt
1/2 cup butter or margarine
2 eggs, beaten
1 cup milk
1-1/2 cups blueberries
1/2 cup coconut
1/2 cup chopped nuts

Mix flour, sugar, baking powder, and salt; cut in butter until mixture resembles cornmeal. Combine beaten eggs and milk; stir in dry ingredients. Stir only until dry mixture is well moistened. Do not overmix! Fold in blueberries. Grease a 9 x 12-inch pan and pour cake batter into pan. Sprinkle with coconut and chopped nuts. Bake in a 350 degree oven for 25-30 minutes. "Great for breakfast."

RHUBARB DESSERT CAKE

Serves 16-20

? cups half and half
? cups sugar
? cups diced rhubarb
? box yellow cake mix

Mix cake as directed on box. Pour into greased 9x13 inch pan. Mix cream, sugar, and rhubarb together. Pour over cake. Bake at 350 degrees for 1 hour. May be served with whipped cream.

FOURTH OF JULY WATERMELON CAKE

3 cups sifted flour
3 teaspoons baking powder
1/4 teaspoon salt
1/2 cup shortening
1-1/2 cups sugar
3 egg whites, stiffly beaten
1 cup milk
1 teaspoon vanilla
1/2 teaspoon red food coloring
1/2 cup raisins

Sift together flour, baking powder, and salt. Cream shortening. Add sugar gradually and cream together. Add flour alternately with milk, beating until smooth. Add vanilla and fold in egg whites. Divide batter into 2 parts. To one part, add food coloring and floured raisins. Put layer of white batter in bottom of greased melon mold. Place layer of red batter in center and a layer of white on top. Bake in a 350 degree oven for about 30 minutes. Frost with green-tinted icing.

Pour into greased 13x9x2 inch pan. Sprinkle with 1/2 cup chopped nuts. Bake in preheated oven at 350 degrees for 40 to 45 minutes or until pick comes out clean. Cool in pan on rack. Cut in bars.

**Optional if desired: sprinkle with powdered sugar or drizzle with powdered sugar frosting.

EASY PUMPKIN CHEESECAKE

Serves 8

10-1/2 or 12-1/8 package no-bake cheese cake mix
1 teaspoon ground cinnamon
1/2 teaspoon ground nutmeg
1/4 teaspoon cloves
3/4 cup milk
3/4 cup canned pumpkin
1/2 teaspoon vanilla
Whipped cream
Ground cinnamon

Prepare graham cracker crust in the cheesecake mix according to package direction; press into 9-inch pie plate. Chill in freezer while preparing pie filling. In small mixer bowl, combine cheesecake filling mix, teaspoon cinnamon, nutmeg and cloves. Add milk, pumpkin and vanilla. Beat at low speed of electric mixer until blended; beat 3 minutes at medium speed. Pour mixture into crust. Chill at least 1 hour. Garnish with whipped cream and additional cinnamon, if desired.

For easy serving, let stand at room temperature for five minutes before slicing.

CARROT - CREAM CHEESE CAKE

12-16 Servings

4 eggs
1-1/2 cup vegetable oil
1 - 8 ounce package cream cheese, softened
3 cups grated carrots
1 cup chopped nuts
2 cups sugar
2 cups flour
2 teaspoons soda
1 teaspoon salt
1-1/2 teaspoon cinnamon
1 teaspoon vanilla

Beat cheese and sugar together at medium speed of mixer until smooth and creamy. Add eggs and oil; blend well. Gradually add remaining ingredients and blend well. Pour batter into a greased and floured 13 x 9 x 2 inch pan and bake at 350 degrees, 45-55 minutes. Cool. Dust with powdered sugar. Cut into squares and serve with dollops of whipped cream.

DELLA ROBIA CHEESECAKE

Makes 9-inch cheesecake

Crust and Filling:

1-3/4 cups graham cracker crumbs
1-1/4 cups sugar (divided)
1/3 cup shortening, melted
3 (8 ounce) packages cream cheese, softened
2 teaspoons vanilla
3 eggs
1 cup dairy sour cream
Assorted fruits (fresh or canned, well drained)

Glaze:

3 tablespoons cornstarch
2 tablespoons sugar
2/3 cup apple, orange, or pineapple juice
1/2 cup apple or currant jelly

Preheat oven to 350 degrees. For crust, combine crumbs, 1/4 cup sugar, and melted shortening. Press firmly in bottom and up side of ungreased 9 inch springform pan. Set aside. For filling, beat cream cheese in large bowl at low speed of electric mixer, just until smooth. Gradually add remaining 1 cup sugar and vanilla. Beat in eggs, one at a time. Blend in sour cream. Pour into prepared pan. Bake 1 hour, or 1 hour and 10 minutes, or until set. Turn off oven. Open door slightly. Leave cheesecake in oven 1 hour. Chill 4 hours or overnight. Top with fruit and glaze 1-2 hours before serving.

For glaze, combine cornstarch and sugar in small saucepan. Stir in juice; add jelly. Cook and stir until mixture is smooth and thickened. Cook about 2 minutes; cool slightly. Spoon 1/3 cup over top of cheesecake. Arrange fruit in circles on top of glaze. Gently spoon and spread remaining glaze in thin layer over top of fruit. Chill until serving time.

QUICK COFFEE-CHOCOLATE CAKE

1 package yellow cake mix
1/2 cup brewed coffee
1 teaspoon flavoring

Prepare cake mix according to package directions, using coffee as part of the liquid and add vanilla. Bake according to package directions.

Topping:
3 tablespoons butter or margarine, room temperature
1/2 box confectioners' sugar
1 square unsweetened chocolate, room temperature
Brewed coffee
1 teaspoon vanilla flavoring
1 teaspoon chocolate flavoring (optional)

In a saucepan, brown the butter or margarine. Add chocolate and stir until melted. Pour over confectioners' sugar in bowl and mix, adding enough coffee until spreading consistency. Add flavoring and spread on cake.

SNICKERDOODLE COFFEE CAKE

1 cup flour
1 cup sugar
1 teaspoon baking powder
1/2 teaspoon salt
1 tablespoon ground cinnamon
1/2 cup milk
1/4 cup melted margarine
1 egg

Mix together the flour, sugar, baking powder, salt, cinnamon, milk, margarine and egg. Pour into a greased and floured 8 or 9 inch square pan. Sprinkle top heavily with sugar (this gives a crusty top). Bake at 400 degrees for 25 minutes. Best when served warm.

ORANGE BUTTERSCOTCH COFFEE CAKE

Batter:
1/2 cup butter or margarine
1 cup granulated sugar
1 egg
1 teaspoon vanilla
1-1/2 cups sifted all-purpose flour
1-1/2 teaspoons baking powder
1/2 teaspoon cinnamon
1/2 teaspoon salt
1 cup milk
3/4 cup uncooked oats

Topping:
1/4 cup firmly packed brown sugar
1 tablespoon all-purpose flour
1 tablespoon butter or margarine, melted
2 teaspoons grated orange peel

Beat together butter and sugar until light and fluffy; add egg and vanilla; blend well. Sift together flour, baking powder, cinnamon and salt; add to creamed mixture alternately with milk; stir in oats. Pour batter into greased and floured 8 inch square baking pan. Combine all topping ingredients and sprinkle evenly over batter. Bake in preheated 350 degree oven for 40 to 45 minutes. Cool in pan 15 minutes before serving.

ALMOND POUND CAKE

3 cups sugar
2 sticks (1/2 pound) butter or margarine
1/2 cup shortening
5 large eggs
1/4 teaspoon salt
3 cups flour
1 small can evaporated milk (3/4 cup) plus water to make 1 cup liquid
2 teaspoons almond extract

Cream sugar and shortening. Add eggs and salt, cream well. Add remaining ingredients. Pour into a very lightly greased 12 cup bundt pan. Put into cold oven; set temperature at 320 degrees. Bake 1 hour and 30 minutes. Cool 15 minutes and remove from pan.

CHERRY NUT BROWNIE CAKE

1/2 cup maraschino cherries
3/4 cup flour, spooned lightly into cup
1/2 teaspoon baking powder
1/4 teaspoon salt
1/2 cup butter or margarine, softened
1 cup sugar
2 large eggs
2 envelopes Choc-bake (or 2 squares unsweetened chocolate, melted)
1 teaspoon vanilla
1/2 cup chopped walnuts or pecans

Quarter cherries with scissors; place on paper towel to drain; set aside. Measure flour, baking powder and salt into small bowl; whisk to blend; set aside.

In large bowl, beat butter or margarine briefly; beat in sugar. Beat in eggs one at a time; beat in chocolate and vanilla. By hand or on lowest mixer speed, beat in dry ingredients. Stir in cherries and nuts. Spread in greased and floured or foil-lined 8-inch squares pan. Bake at 350 degrees until firm in center, about 35 minutes. Cool on rack. Ice as directed below. Freeze leftovers in serving size units.

Chocolate Icing:
Looks and tastes like fudge icing.
2 tablespoons cocoa
2 tablespoons water
2 tablespoons butter or margarine
1 teaspoon maraschino cherry juice
1-1/8 cups unsifted confectioners' sugar (1/8 cup is 2 tablespoons)

Measure cocoa, water, butter and cherry juice into medium saucepan. Heat, stirring, just until smooth. Remove from heat; whisk in sugar. Icing should be just thin enough to pour. Add a little more sugar if necessary. Pour over cool cake; spread to edges. Allow icing to set before cutting cake.

CHOCOLATE YOGURT CAKE

cups unsifted all-purpose flour
-1/2 cups sugar
/2 cup unsweetened cocoa
teaspoons baking soda
teaspoon salt
cup plain yogurt
eggs
/3 cup oil
-1/2 teaspoons vanilla

Preheat oven to 350 degrees. Grease and flour two 9-inch round layer pans. Set aside. Mix flour, sugar, cocoa, baking soda and salt in large mixing bowl. Add yogurt, eggs, oil, and vanilla. Beat with electric mixer at low speed until ingredients are moistened; scraping bowl constantly. Beat at medium speed 2 minutes; scraping bowl occasionally. Pour into prepared pans. Bake at 350 degrees, 30-35 minutes, or until wooden pick inserted in center comes out clean. Cool 10 minutes. Remove from pans. Cool completely on wire rack.

Frosting:
1 package (6 ounces) semi-sweet
  chocolate chips
1/4 cup butter or margarine
2/3 cup plain yogurt
1/2 teaspoon vanilla
1/8 teaspoon salt
2-1/2 - 3 cups confectioners sugar

Combine chocolate chips and butter in small saucepan. Cook over low heat; stirring constantly, until melted. Transfer mixture to medium mixing bowl. Cool slightly. Blend in yogurt, vanilla and salt. Stir in enough confectioners sugar until frosting is thick enough to spread. Frost the layers of the cooled cake.

FUDGE SURPRISE CAKE

1 cup butter or margarine

1/4 cup cocoa
1 cup water
1/2 cup buttermilk
2 eggs, beaten
2 cups sugar
2 cups flour
1 teaspoon baking soda
1 teaspoon vanilla

In saucepan, combine the butter, cocoa, water, buttermilk, and eggs. Stir constantly over low heat until mixture bubbles. In large bowl, mix together the sugar, flour, and baking soda. Stir in the hot cocoa mixture, beat until smooth. Stir in vanilla, spread evenly in a greased and floured 9 x 13 pan. Bake 25-30 minutes at 350 degrees, until firm to the touch in center. Cool.

Filling:
In bowl, mix 1 cup creamy peanut butter with 1 tablespoon oil, until smooth. Spread over the cooled cake.

Frosting:
1/2 cup butter or margarine
1/4 cup cocoa
6 tablespoons buttermilk
1 pound powdered sugar
1 teaspoon vanilla

In saucepan, heat butter, cocoa, and buttermilk until bubbly. Place sugar in bowl, beat in hot mixture until smooth. Stir in vanilla. Spread mixture over the peanut butter layer. . . .Enjoy!

GERMAN CHOCOLATE CAKE

2 cups sugar
1/2 cup shortening
1/2 cup pure butter (1 stick)
4 eggs
1 teaspoon vanilla
4 tablespoons cold black coffee
1/4 teaspoon salt
1 teaspoon baking soda
4 tablespoons cocoa
2 1/2 cups flour
1 cup buttermilk

Cream shortening, butter and sugar together; add eggs one at a time. Sift dry ingredients together. Add to creamed mixture, alternately with buttermilk one half at a time. Add coffee and vanilla. Bake in three 9-inch round cake pans at 350 degrees for 35 minutes.

Filling and Icing:
1 cup cream (half & half)
3 egg yolks
1/4 pound butter (1 stick)
1 cup chopped pecans
1 cup sugar
1 teaspoon vanilla
1 cup coconut

Place cream, sugar, egg yolks, vanilla and butter in saucepan. Cook together for 10 minutes, stirring constantly. Add coconut and nuts. Cool. Spread and cool cake.

INSIDE-OUT CHOCOLATE BUNDT CAKE

4-1/2-ounce package instant chocolate flavor pudding
2-layer size chocolate or Devil's Food cake mix
12 ounces chocolate chips
1-3/4 cups milk
2 eggs

Combine pudding mix, cake mix, chips, milk and eggs in bowl. Mix by hand until well blended, about 2 minutes. Pour into greased and floured 12-cup tube or Bundt pan. Bake at 350 degrees for 50 to 55 minutes, or until cake springs back when lightly pressed with fingers. Do not overbake. Cool 15 minutes in pan, remove and continue cooling on rack.

If you love chocolate, this is for you. It's moist and easy to make, and doesn't need frosting. However, if you like, you can sift confectioners' sugar on top.

DUTCH HUSTLE CAKE

1-1/2 cups flour
1/4 cup sugar
1/2 teaspoon salt
1 package active dry yeast
2 tablespoons soft butter
1/2 cup very hot tap water
1-1/2 cups drained cooked apple slices
2 tablespoons brown sugar
1/4 teaspoon ground cinnamon
1/4 teaspoon ground nutmeg
2 tablespoons butter
Confectioners' sugar glaze (use own recipe)

In large bowl, mix 1/2 cup flour, sugar, salt, yeast and butter. Gradually add water. Beat at high speed in mixer 2 minutes, scraping often. Add 1/2 cup more flour and beat again. Add another 1/2 cup flour (1-1/2 cups in all) and beat until very thick batter is formed. Spread batter evenly in buttered 9-inch square pan. Toss apples with cinnamon, nutmeg and sugar. Arrange on top of batter. Dot with butter. Cover; let rise in warm place, free from drafts, until doubled in bulk, about 1 hour. Bake in 400 degree oven about 25 minutes or until done. Drizzle with confectioners' sugar glaze. Let stand on wire rack about 10 minutes before removing from pan.

ROOT BEER CAKE

1 cup sugar
½ cup butter
½ teaspoon vanilla
2 eggs
2 cups flour
1 tablespoon baking powder
1 teaspoon salt
⅔ cup A & W Root Beer

Combine all ingredients in large mixer bowl. Blend at low speed; beat 3 minutes at medium speed. Pour into a greased and floured 12 x 8-inch pan. Bake at 375 degrees for

30–35 minutes.

Frosting:
1 pound confectioners' sugar
1 cup chilled root beer

Combine in mixer bowl and blend well. Beat until thick and fluffy.

PEEK-A-BOO CAKE

1/2 pound margarine
2 cups sugar
4 eggs, add and beat one at a time
1 teaspoon vanilla extract
Dash of salt
1 cup pie filling (your favorite)
3 cups flour

In a large bowl, mix together margarine, sugar, eggs, vanilla, salt, and flour. Grease a 13 x 9 x 2-inch pan. Spread half of batter in pan, then spoon pie filling over the batter. Drop remaining batter over pie filling. Bake at 350 degrees for 40 minutes.

POUND CAKE

2/3 cup shortening
1-1/4 cups sugar
2/3 cup milk
1 teaspoon lemon extract
2 cups sifted flour
1 teaspoon salt
1/2 teaspoon baking powder
3 eggs

Preheat oven to 325 degrees. Grease and flour 9 x 5 x 3-inch loaf pan. Cream shortening and sugar until light and fluffy. Add milk and lemon extract; blend. Sift dry ingredients; add to creamed mixture. Beat until smooth. Add eggs, one at a time and beat well after each addition. Beat entire mixture well before pouring into loaf pan. Bake for 75 - 80 minutes.

"PRETTY POSY EASTER CAKE"

1 - 18-1/4 ounce box yellow cake mix
2 egg whites, unbeaten

1-1/4 cups granulated sugar
Dash of salt
1/3 cup water
2 teaspoons light corn syrup
1 teaspoon vanilla extract
2 cups shredded coconut
18 colored jelly beans

Bake in two 8" cake pans according to directions; cool on rack. Combine next 6 ingredients beating well until thick. Spread between layers and on top and sides of cooled cake. Sprinkle coconut generously on top and sides. Place 3 jelly beans together 6 times around top of cake to form posies (flowers).

TREASURE TOFFEE CAKE

Serves 16

1/4 cup sugar
1 teaspoon cinnamon
2 cups flour
1 cup sugar
1-1/2 teaspoons baking powder
1 teaspoon baking soda
1/4 teaspoon salt
1 teaspoon vanilla
1 cup sour cream
1/2 cup butter, softened
2 eggs
1/4 cup chopped nuts
3 - 1 1/8 ounce chocolate Toffee bars, coarsely crushed
1/4 cup melted butter
Confectioners' sugar

Combine cinnamon and 1/4 cup sugar. Combine remaining ingredients except nuts, candy, and melted butter.

Blend at low speed with electric mixer until moistened. Beat at medium speed for 3 minutes. Spoon half of the batter into greased and floured 10-inch bundt pan. Sprinkle with 2 tablespoons cinnamon-sugar mixture. Spoon remaining batter into pan. Top with remaining cinnamon-sugar mixture, nuts, and candy. Pour melted butter over top. Bake in a 325 degree oven for 45 minutes. Cool 15 minutes. Remove from pan; dust with confectioners' sugar.

CINNAMON PULL-APART COFFEE CAKE
Serves 8-10

1 cup Frosted Rice Crispies, crushed to 1/2 cup
2-1/3 cups all-purpose flour
1 tablespoon baking powder
1/2 teaspoon salt
1/4 cup shortening
1/2 cup milk
1/4 cup butter, melted
1/2 cup sugar
1 teaspoon cinnamon

Stir together Rice Crispies cereal, flour, baking powder, and salt. Cut in shortening until mixture resembles coarse crumbs. Add milk; stir with a fork until dough leaves sides of bowl. Shape dough into balls, about 1 inch in size. Roll dough balls in melted butter, then in sugar-cinnamon mixture. Arrange in single layer on ungreased 8-inch round cake pan. Bake at 425 degrees for 18-20 minutes. Serve warm.

CHERRY CRUMB COFFEE CAKE

1/4 cup margarine
1 cup sugar
2 eggs
1 cup low fat plain yogurt
1/4 cup milk
2 cups flour
1/2 teaspoon baking soda
1/4 teaspoon vanilla
1/4 teaspoon almond extract
1 (21 ounce) can cherry pie filling

Topping:
1/2 cup flour
1/4 cup brown sugar
1 teaspoon cinnamon
3 tablespoons margarine
1/2 cup chopped pecans

In mixing bowl, cream together margarine and sugar. Add eggs, one at a time. Mix well. Add remaining cake ingredients, except cherry pie filling. Beat well. Spread 1/2 of the batter in a greased 9x13-inch baking pan. Spread cherry filling over batter and cover with remaining batter.

For topping, combine all ingredients, except butter and nuts, into a small mixing bowl. Cut in butter and stir in nuts. Sprinkle topping over batter. Bake at 350 degrees for 45 minutes until cake springs back when lightly touched with fingers.

COFFEE CAN CAKE

3-1/2 cups flour
2 teaspoons baking soda
1 teaspoon salt
1 teaspoon cinnamon
1 teaspoon nutmeg
3 cups sugar
4 eggs
2 cups pumpkin (fresh is preferred, but if not available, use canned)
2/3 cup water
1 cup vegetable oil
1 cup raisins
1 cup nuts
1 cup candied cherries

Sift flour, baking soda, salt, cinnamon and nutmeg together in a bowl. In separate bowl, mix eggs, pumpkin, water and oil. Slowly stir in dry ingredients. When all ingredients are mixed, add raisins, nuts and cherries. Pour mixture into large, well-greased coffee cans. Fill only halfway to allow room to rise. Bake at 350 degrees for about 1 hour. Cool in cans on wire rack before removing from cans. This cake resembles fruit cake and is delicious served with hard sauce or a wine-flavored sauce.

FRUIT FILLED SOUR CREAM COFFEE CAKE

1/2 cup butter or margarine
1 cup sugar
2 eggs
1 cup sour cream
2 cups flour
1-1/2 teaspoons baking powder
1/2 teaspoon baking soda
1/2 teaspoon salt
1 teaspoon vanilla
1 can fruit pie filling (any kind)

Grease and flour 9 x 13 inch pan. Mix dry ingredients together. Cream butter and sugar. Add eggs and vanilla. Add sour cream alternately with dry ingredients. Pour 1/2 batter into pan. Smooth pie filling gently over this. Add remaining batter, spread over filling. Bake in 350 degree oven for 45 - 50 minutes or until tested done.

Topping:
2 tablespoons butter or margarine
1/2 cup sugar
2 tablespoons flour
1/2 cup chopped nuts
1 teaspoon cinnamon

Melt butter. Mix together remaining ingredients, add melted butter and mix. Add to the top of the cake about half way through the baking time.

HEATH COFFEE CAKE

1/4 pound butter (1 stick)
1/2 cup white sugar
1 cup brown sugar
1 egg
1 teaspoon soda
2 cups flour
1 teaspoon vanilla
1 cup buttermilk

Blend flour, sugars, and butter. Take out 1/2 cup of crumb mixture. To rest of mixture, add buttermilk, soda, egg, and vanilla. Blend well; pour into greased and floured 10 x 14 x 2-inch pan.

Sprinkle on topping of:
3/4 cup chopped Heath bars
1/4 cup nuts
1/2 cup mixture (reserved earlier)

Bake 350 degrees for 30 minutes. This is a great coffee cake, so tasty and very moist!!

EDMONTON SPICE CAKE

1 cup water
1 cup sugar
1 teaspoon nutmeg
1 teaspoon cinnamon
1 cup raisins
1/3 cup cooking oil
1/2 teaspoon cloves
1/2 teaspoon salt

Boil all above ingredients in saucepan for 3 minutes. Let cool well.

2 cups flour
1 teaspoon baking powder
1/2 teaspoon baking soda

Sift flour, baking powder, and soda together; add to first mixture and stir well. Bake on 9 x 15 x 2-inch shallow pan or jelly roll pan, at 375 degrees for approximately 15 minutes. Good with whipped topping.

FAVORITE SPICE CAKE

No milk, butter or eggs

2 cups brown or white sugar
2 cups water
1 cup raisins
2/3 cup lard
1/4 teaspoon salt
2 teaspoons cinnamon
1/2 teaspoon nutmeg
1 teaspoon ground cloves
2 teaspoons baking soda mixed with
    1/3 cup water or cold coffee
4 cups flour sifted with 1 teaspoon
    baking powder
1 cup nuts chopped (optional)
Whole or half nuts (optional)

Preheat oven to 350 degrees. Boil sugar, water, lard, raisins, salt and spices for 5 minutes. Let cool; add baking soda and flour mixture. Mix thoroughly (batter should be quite stiff); add chopped nuts. Pour into greased and floured rectangular or square pan. Decorate with nut halves. Bake 350 degrees for 30 to 35 minutes or until knife inserted comes out clean.

1917 WAR CAKE

Very popular in 1917 when sugar and butter were scarce and eggs too costly for luxuries such as cake. My mother used it for years.

1 cup corn syrup
1 cut cold water
1 teaspoon salt
1/2 teaspoon cloves
1 teaspoon cinnamon
1/2 teaspoon nutmeg
1 tablespoon Crisco
1 teaspoon soda
2 cups flour
1/2 teaspoon baking power

Put first 6 ingredients in saucepan; cook 3 minutes after reaching boiling point. Add Crisco. When cool, add soda dissolved in a little hot water; add flour and baking powder. Stir; pour into greased tube pan. Bake for one hour at 325 degrees.

BLUE RIBBON POPPY SEED BUNDT CAKE

1/4 cup poppy seeds
1 cup buttermilk
1 cup butter
1-1/2 cups sugar
4 eggs
1 teaspoon vanilla
2-1/2 cups flour
1/2 teaspoon salt
1 teaspoon soda

2 teaspoons cinnamon
1/3 cup sugar

Soak poppy seeds for 2 hours in buttermilk. Cream together butter and sugar. Add eggs one at a time, beating well after each; add vanilla. Sift together flour, salt and soda. Add buttermilk-poppy seed mixture and flour mixture, alternately to butter-sugar mixture. Grease well 12-cup bundt pan; spoon in 1/3 of batter; top with half cinnamon-sugar mix; spoon in 1/3 more batter, cinnamon-sugar mix, and end with batter. Bake at 350 degrees for 50 minutes. Let cool in pan 5 minutes before turning onto rack to finish cooling.

Cinnamon-sugar mixture:
2 tablespoons cinnamon
1/3 cup sugar

Mix cinnamon and sugar together. Super to have on hand in the freezer. Just pop into the oven and warm a bit, serve with apricot butter and coffee or tea!

BUTTERMILK NUTMEG CAKE

1/2 cup butter
1-1/2 cups sugar
3 eggs, beaten
2 cups sifted all-purpose flour
1/4 teaspoon salt
1 teaspoon baking powder
1/4 teaspoon baking soda
2 teaspoons nutmeg
1 cup buttermilk

Preheat oven to 350 degrees. Cream butter; add sugar gradually; cream well. Add eggs; stir. Sift together flour, salt, baking powder, soda, and nutmeg. Add to sugar-butter mixture, alternately, with buttermilk; mix well. Pour batter into two 9-inch layer pans. Sprinkle top of cake batter with sugar and nutmeg before baking. Bake at 350 degrees for 35 minutes or until done. No frosting is necessary; the sugar and nutmeg make a sweet topping.

PECAN CAKE WITH PRALINE GLAZE

Makes 1 (10-inch) cake

1 cup raisins
1/2 cup bourbon
1 cup butter or margarine, softened
2-1/4 cups sugar
5 eggs
3-1/4 cups all-purpose flour
1 teaspoon baking powder
1/2 teaspoon baking soda
1-1/2 teaspoons ground nutmeg
1 cup buttermilk
2 cups coarsely-chopped pecans
Praline Glaze (recipe follows)

Combine raisins and bourbon, stirring well. Cover and refrigerate at least 1 hour. Cream butter; gradually add sugar, beating well. Add eggs, one at a time, beating well after each addition. Combine flour, baking powder, soda, and nutmeg; add to creamed mixture alternately with buttermilk, beginning and ending with flour mixture. Mix well after each addition. Fold in pecans and reserved raisin mixture. Mix well to thoroughly blend.

Pour batter into greased and floured 10-inch tube pan. Bake at 325 degrees for 1 hour and 30 minutes or until wooden pick inserted in center comes out clean. Cool in pan 10 minutes; remove to wire rack, and drizzle Praline Glaze over cake. Cool completely.

Praline Glaze:

1/2 cup firmly-packed brown sugar
1/4 cup sugar
1/4 cup butter or margarine
1/4 cup whipping cream
1/2 cup pecan halves

Combine first 4 ingredients in a heavy saucepan. Cook over low heat, stirring constantly, until mixture reaches soft ball stage (240 degrees). Remove from heat and stir in pecans. Makes about 1 cup glaze.

NUTTY PRETZEL BUNDT CAKE

1 cup vegetable shortening

2 cups sugar
6 eggs
1/2 cup milk
1-1/2 cups very finely crushed pretzels (a blender can be used)
1-1/2 cups sifted all-purpose flour
3 tablespoons baking powder
2 teaspoons cinnamon
1 cup raisins
1 cup chopped nuts

Cream shortening and sugar in large bowl. Beat with electric mixer until fluffy. Add eggs, one at a time, beating until smooth after each addition. Beat in milk. Fold in pretzels, along with flour, baking powder, and cinnamon. Blend thoroughly. Add raisins and chopped nuts gradually, mixing well after each addition.

Pour batter into a well-oiled and lightly floured Bundt pan. Bake in pre-heated oven of 350 degrees 45-50 minutes, or until cake tests done. Cool in pan on wire rack 10 minutes. Turn out and complete cooling.

Glaze:

1-1/2 cups confectioners' sugar
2-3 tablespoons fresh lemon juice

Combine confectioners' sugar with lemon juice until well blended and drizzle over the cooled cake.

BUTTERSCOTCH SPICE CAKE

1 cup brown sugar
1/2 cup sugar
1/2 cup corn oil
1-1/2 cups flour
1-1/2 teaspoons baking soda
1 teaspoon cinnamon
1/2 teaspoon nutmeg
2 eggs
2 tablespoons molasses
1 cup quick cooking oatmeal
1 cup water
3/4 teaspoon salt
1 teaspoon vanilla

Cream sugars and oil. Add eggs and beat. Add molasses, oatmeal, and water. Beat together. Add the rest of the ingredients; beat. Pour into a 13 x 9 inch pan, which has been greased and floured. Bake in a 350 degree oven for approximately 25-28 minutes. Cool and frost.

Creamy Frosting:

1/4 cup butter, softened
1 cup powdered sugar
2 tablespoons cream
1 teaspoon vanilla

Whip for 4 minutes with electric mixer.

SPICY NUT SPONGE CAKE

5 eggs, separated
3 tablespoons Sucaryl
1 tablespoon lemon juice
1/2 cup water
2-1/2 cups sifted cake flour
1/4 teaspoon salt
1/2 teaspoon baking powder
1 teaspoon cinnamon
1/2 teaspoon nutmeg
1/2 teaspoon cloves
1/2 teaspoon allspice
3/4 teaspoon cream of tartar
1/2 cup finely chopped nuts

Beat egg yolks until thick and lemon colored. Add Sucaryl, lemon juice and water. Beat on high speed of mixer until thick, about 10 minutes. Sift together flour, salt, baking powder and spices. Sift a little at a time over egg yolk mixture, folding in gently but thoroughly. Beat egg whites until foamy. Add cream of tartar and beat until stiff peaks are formed. Fold egg yolk mixture gently into whites. Add chopped nuts. Pour into 9-inch ungreased tube pan. Bake 45 to 50 minutes at 350 degrees. Invert and let hang until cold.

Casseroles
CREATIVE

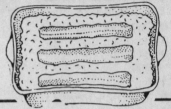

HAMBURGER STROGANOFF
Serves 4–6

1 pound ground beef
1 medium onion, chopped (¹/₂ cup)
¹/₄ cup butter *or* margarine
2 tablespoons flour
1 teaspoon salt
1 teaspoon garlic salt *or* 1 clove garlic, minced
¹/₄ teaspoon pepper
1 (8-ounce) can mushroom stems and pieces, drained
1 (10¹/₂-ounce) can condensed cream of chicken soup
1 cup dairy sour cream
2 cups hot cooked noodles
Snipped parsley

In large skillet, cook and stir beef and onion in butter until onion is tender. Stir in flour, salt, garlic salt, pepper and mushrooms. Cook 5 minutes, stirring constantly. Remove from heat. Stir in soup; simmer, uncovered, for 10 minutes. Stir in sour cream; heat through. Serve over noodles. Sprinkle with parsley.

PIZZA CASSEROLE

3 cups all-purpose flour
3 cups instant mashed potatoes
1¼ cups milk
1 cup margarine, melted
1 pound ground beef
1 pound bulk sausage

1 large onion, chopped
1 (8-ounce) can tomato sauce
1 (6-ounce) can pitted ripe olives, drained
1 (6-ounce) can tomato paste
½ package sloppy joe seasoning mix
¼ teaspoon garlic powder
1¼ cups shredded mozzarella cheese

For crust, combine flour, potatoes, milk and margarine. Set aside. For filling, in a 12-inch skillet, cook beef, sausage and onion until onion is tender and meat is no longer pink. Drain off fat. Stir in tomato sauce, olives, tomato paste, seasoning mix and garlic powder.

Press half of crust into 13 x 9 x 2-inch baking pan. Spread filling over crust. Sprinkle with cheese. Roll remaining crust and put on top of filling. Bake at 425 degrees for 30–35 minutes, or until crust is golden. Let stand 5 minutes.

ROMAN RICE

1 (2¼-ounce) can sliced black olives, drained
1 (11-ounce) can Green Giant Delicorn, drained
1 (15-ounce) can red kidney beans, drained
6 slices bacon strips
1 cup uncooked regular rice
1 small onion, chopped
1 teaspoon salt
⅛ teaspoon pepper

1½ cups water
½ cup chicken broth
¼ cup ketchup
Dash minced garlic
1 (16-ounce) can tomatoes, undrained and cut up
½ cup mozzarella cheese, shredded
½ cup Monterey Jack cheese, shredded
¼ cup mixture Parmesan and Romano cheese, grated
1 tablespoon sugar

Fry bacon, saving 2 tablespoon of drippings. Cook rice and onion i it until onion is tender. Add draine Delicorn, beans, olives, seasoning and tomatoes. Stir well. Add grate cheese mixture, ketchup, water an broth. Cover and simmer for 30–4 minutes. Sprinkle shredded cheese on top.

ONION LOVERS' CASSEROLE
Serves 4–6

1 pound ground beef
3 large onions, sliced
1 large green pepper, chopped
1 (1-pound) can tomatoes
½ cup uncooked regular rice
1 teaspoon chili powder
1 teaspoon salt

Heat oven to 350 degrees. In larg skillet, cook and stir ground bee until light brown; drain off fat. Ad onions and green pepper; cook an stir until onion is tender. Stir i tomatoes, rice, chili powder and sa Pour into an ungreased 2-qua casserole. Cover; bake 1 hour.

TUNA BAKE
Serves 6–8

1 (1-pound, 1-ounce) can green peas
1½ cups diced potatoes
1 cup diced carrots
½ cup chopped onion
4 tablespoons butter
4 tablespoons flour
Milk
1 teaspoon salt
⅛ teaspoon pepper
2 teaspoons soy sauce
2 (7-ounce) cans tuna, drained

Drain peas; reserve liquid. Cook potatoes, carrots and onions in reserved liquid for 8–10 minutes. Drain; save liquid. Melt butter in saucepan; stir in flour to make a smooth paste. Add milk to vegetable liquid to make 2 cups. Add to butter mixture. Cook over low heat; stir until mixture thickens. Add seasonings. Combine vegetables and tuna in buttered 2-quart casserole. Pour sauce over all (may be refrigerated overnight). To serve, bake covered in 325-degree oven for 1 hour.

MEXICAN DINNER PRONTO
Serves 4

2 tablespoons vegetable oil
1 onion, chopped
1 (15-ounce) can tamales in chili gravy
1 (15-ounce) can chili without beans
1 (15-ounce) can chili with beans
¼ teaspoon oregano
½ cup Monterey Jack cheese, shredded

In a skillet heat oil; sauté onion until tender; transfer to ovenproof baking dish. Unwrap tamales; arrange ½ over onions. Add the 2 cans of chili; sprinkle with oregano; top with remaining tamales. Bake at 350 degrees for 30 minutes, or until bubbling hot. Remove from oven; sprinkle with cheese; bake 15 minutes longer, or until cheese has melted.

PORK CHOW MEIN
Serves 6

1 pound pork steak
3 tablespoons cooking oil
1 cup sliced onion
1 cup sliced celery
1 (8-ounce) can mushrooms
1 (8-ounce) can water chestnuts, drained and sliced
1 (13¾-ounce) can chicken broth
¼ cup soy sauce
1 (16-ounce) can chop suey vegetables, undrained
5–6 tablespoons cornstarch
1 chicken bouillon cube
Hot cooked rice

Boil celery and onion in ½ cup water. Add 1 chicken bouillon cube. Cook until tender. Set aside. Slice partially frozen pork in thin, bite-size slices, across the grain. Preheat a large skillet or wok. Add cooking oil. Stir-fry pork for 2–3 minutes. Add bouillon mixture, mushrooms, water chestnuts, chicken broth, soy sauce and chop suey vegetables. Cook to a boil. Add cornstarch. Stir after each tablespoon of cornstarch. Serve over rice. Enjoy!! It is my favorite!.

HAM & RICE CASSEROLE
Serves 6

2 cups Spam, cut up in small squares
3 cups cooked rice *or* 2 cups uncooked rice
1 cup peas, drained
1 teaspoon salt
1 teaspoon prepared mustard
¼ teaspoon pepper
1 cup grated cheddar cheese
1 (10-ounce) can cheddar cheese soup, undiluted
¼ cup milk

Preheat oven to 350 degrees. Grease a 3-quart casserole. Combine ham, rice, peas, salt, mustard, pepper, ½ cup cheddar cheese, cheddar cheese soup and milk. Turn into casserole. Top with remaining ½ cup cheese. Bake 30 minutes, until bubbly. If chilled before baking, bake 1 hour.

CHICKEN CASSEROLE SUPREME

3 cups cooked chicken, deboned
1 (6-ounce) package Uncle Ben's rice, cooked
1 can cream of celery soup, undiluted
1 can cream of chicken soup, undiluted
1 can French-style green beans, drained
1 medium jar pimientos, sliced
1 cup mayonnaise
1 small can water chestnuts, sliced
Salt and pepper to taste

Mix all ingredients together and pour into 3-quart casserole. Bake 25–30 minutes at 350 degrees.

FAMILY GOULASH
Serves 4

4 ounces noodles
1 pound ground beef
1 medium onion, chopped
2 cups sliced celery
½ cup ketchup
1 (2½-ounce) jar sliced mushrooms
1 (14½-ounce) can tomatoes
1 teaspoon salt

Cook noodles as directed on package. While noodles cook, cook and stir ground beef and onion in large skillet until meat is brown and onion tender. Drain off fat. Stir in drained noodles, celery, ketchup, mushrooms (with liquid), tomatoes and salt. Cover; simmer 30–45 minutes.

THREE-CHEESES SPINACH PASTA
Serves 5

1 pound thin spaghetti
⅓ cup creamy cottage cheese
3 ounces cream cheese
½ cup sour cream
1 (junior-size) jar baby food spinach
¼ cup white wine
4 green onions, finely chopped
Salt and pepper to taste
½ teaspoon nutmeg
3 tablespoons Parmesan cheese, grated
2 tablespoons butter *or* margarine

Cook spaghetti; drain; set aside. In a bowl, mix the next 9 ingredients. Butter a shallow, ovenproof casserole; place spaghetti in it; pour cheese mixture over all. Sprinkle with Parmesan cheese; dot with butter. Bake at 350 degrees for 30 minutes; serve hot.

SPRING CASSEROLE

1 can asparagus
Milk
1 can cream of mushroom soup
2 cups cooked rice
1 large can white tuna
1 (8-ounce) carton sour cream
1 (16-ounce) carton cottage cheese
1 teaspoon onion, chopped
12 to 14 green stuffed olives, sliced
1 teaspoon salt
1 whole green stuffed olive
Buttered bread crumbs

Drain asparagus; reserve juice. Set aside 4 asparagus spears. Combine reserved asparagus juice and enough milk to make 1 cup liquid. Combine liquid, soup, rice, tuna and asparagus. Stir in sour cream, cottage cheese, onion, sliced olives and salt. Place in buttered casserole. Arrange reserved asparagus spears on top in spoke fashion; place whole olive in middle. Sprinkle with bread crumbs. Bake at 350 degrees for 1 hour.

RANCHO SAUSAGE SUPPER
Serves 6

1 pound pork sausage
1 cup chopped onions
1 green pepper, chopped
2 cups stewed tomatoes
2 cups dairy sour cream
1 cup uncooked elbow macaroni
1 teaspoon chili powder
1 teaspoon salt
1 tablespoon sugar

In a large skillet fry sausage until pink color disappears. Drain. Add onions and green pepper; cook slowly for 5 minutes. Stir in tomatoes, sour cream, macaroni, chili powder, salt and sugar. Cover. Simmer 30 minutes, stirring frequently, until macaroni is done. Serve hot.

Serve with a green salad and hard rolls.

MACARONI HOT DISH
Serves 6

2 cups warm, cooked macaroni
1-1/2 cups grated cheese
1-1/2 cups bread crumbs
1 green pepper, diced
3 eggs, beaten
1 onion, diced
2 tablespoons margarine, melted
Pepper and salt to taste
1-1/2 cups milk
1 can mushroom soup

Mix all ingredients, except mushroom soup, and place in pan set in hot water. Bake at 350 degrees fo minutes. Cut in squares and then over undiluted mushroom soup w has been heated.

NO-FUSS SHORTC PAELLA
Serves 6

2 cups cooked chicken, cut into inch pieces
1-1/2 cups chicken broth
10 ounces shrimp, shelled
1 (8-1/2-ounce) can peas, draine
2 cups rice
1 (3-ounce) can mushrooms, sli and drained
1 envelope onion soup mix
1 teaspoon paprika

Combine chicken, chicken b shrimp, peas, rice, mushrooms, o soup mix and paprika. Pour int quart casserole; bake at 350 deg covered, for 1-1/4 hours until ri tender.

DRIED BEEF CASSEROLE
Serves 4–6

1 cup uncooked elbow macaroni
1 (10½-ounce) can condens cream of mushroom soup
½ cup milk
1 cup shredded cheddar cheese
3 tablespoons finely choppe onion
¼ pound dried beef, cut into bite-size pieces
2 hard-cooked eggs, sliced

Heat oven to 350 degrees. Co macaroni according to packa directions. Blend soup and milk. in cheese, onion, drained macar and dried beef; fold in eggs. Po into an ungreased 1½-quart cas role. Cover; bake 30 minutes, until heated through.

PASTA PRIMAVERA
Makes 4-6 servings

8 ounces uncooked spaghetti
1 cup tender green beans, cut in
    1-inch pieces
2 small zucchini, sliced
2 small yellow squash, sliced
1 cup thinly sliced carrot
1 cup cauliflower flowerets
1 tablespoon olive oil
2 garlic cloves, minced
1/8 teaspoon crushed red pepper
    flakes
1/4 cup chicken broth
1/4 cup lightly packed fresh basil
    leaves, chopped
1/4 cup oil-packed, sun-dried
    tomatoes
3 tablespoons grated Parmesan
    cheese
1/4 cup chopped fresh parsley

Cook spaghetti according to package directions, drain and set aside. Steam vegetables only until crisp-tender, drain and chill. Sauté garlic in olive oil until light brown. Add crushed red pepper, stir; then add chicken broth and simmer 1 minute. Add chopped basil, spaghetti and vegetables; toss. Arrange on platter. Garnish with sun-dried tomatoes, Parmesan cheese and parsley. Serve at room temperature.

BAKED MACARONI AND CHEESE WITH SOUR CREAM
Serves 2

3/4 cup macaroni, uncooked
1/3 cup sour cream
1 cup grated sharp Cheddar cheese
1/3 cup milk
Paprika

Preheat oven to 325 degrees. Cook macaroni in boiling, salted water according to package directions until barely tender. Drain well. Return to saucepan. Add sour cream, cheese, and milk; mix well. Turn into a small greased baking dish; sprinkle on paprika. Bake at 325 degrees for about 25 minutes.

HARVEST SWEET POTATO CASSEROLE
Serves 6

1 (23-ounce) can sweet potatoes or
    yams, drained, or
1 (18-ounce) can vacuum-packed
    sweet potatoes
7 tablespoons butter, melted
1 apple, cored and thinly sliced

Topping:
1/4 cup firmly packed brown sugar
1 tablespoon all-purpose flour
1/4 teaspoon cardamom
1 tablespoon cold butter
2 tablespoons chopped pecans

Preheat oven to 350 degrees. In 1-quart round casserole, mash sweet potatoes until smooth. Stir in the 7 tablespoons melted butter. In small bowl cut 1 tablespoon cold butter into brown sugar, flour, and cardamom. Stir in pecans and sprinkle one-half of the mixture over potatoes. Arrange apple slices on top. Sprinkle with remaining mixture. Bake for 35-40 minutes or until apples are crisp/tender.

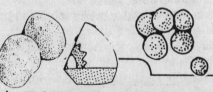

POTATO AND HAM CASSEROLE
Serves 6-8

1 (5-1/2 ounce) package au gratin
    potatoes
2-1/2 cups diced cooked ham
1 cup canned or frozen peas
1 small onion, chopped
1 small green pepper, chopped
1/3 cup chopped celery
1 cup shredded Cheddar cheese

Preheat oven to 400 degrees. Mix potatoes as directed on package in a 2-quart ovenproof dish. Mix together ham, peas, onion, green pepper, celery, and add to casserole. Sprinkle cheese on top.
Bake 30 minutes and serve hot.

REUBEN CASSEROLE

1 can corned beef—or 1 pound deli
1/2 cup thousand island dressing
1 can sauerkraut, drained
6 slices rye bread, cut in cubes or
    crumbled
1/2 pound Swiss cheese, grated
1/2 cup margarine, melted

Crumble corned beef into well-greased 12x8-inch glass dish. Spread dressing, then sauerkraut. Cover with cheese. Toss crumbled bread with melted margarine; sprinkle on top. Bake at 350 degrees for 30 minutes or until hot and bubbly.

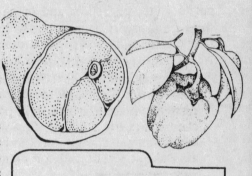

SAUCY SAUSAGE SUPPER
Serves 4

1 (16-ounce) can applesauce (2
    cups)
1 (16-ounce) can sauerkraut,
    drained and snipped (2 cups)
1/3 cup water
2 tablespoons brown sugar, packed
1/2 teaspoon salt
4 small onions, quartered
4 small potatoes, peeled and
    quartered
1 (12-ounce) Polish sausage, cut
    diagonally to desired lengths
Snipped parsley

In a 3-quart saucepan, combine applesauce, sauerkraut, water, brown sugar, and salt; add onions and potatoes. Cover and simmer 20 minutes, stirring occasionally. Add sausage; simmer, covered about 20 minutes longer, stirring occasionally. To serve, spoon sauerkraut mixture onto a platter and top with sausage. Sprinkle with parsley.

LADIES' LUNCHEON LAYERED DISH

1 cup crushed potato chips
4 hard-cooked eggs, sliced
1 onion, sliced thin and separated
　into rings
1/3 cup parsley, chopped
1 (10-1/2-ounce) can cream of
　mushroom soup
1/4 cup sour cream
3/4 cup milk
1/2 teaspoon paprika

Spread 1/3 of potato chips in bottom of a greased 1-1/2 quart ovenproof baking dish. Cover with 1/3 of the egg slices, 1/3 of the onion rings and chopped parsley. Repeat layers until potato chips, egg slices and onion rings are all used. Combine soup with sour cream, milk, and paprika; mix well; pour over all; cover. Bake 350 degrees for 30 minutes; uncover, bake 10 minutes longer until hot, bubbly, and golden.

BAKED RICE WITH HERBS
Serves 4-6

2 tablespoons butter
1 green onion, minced
1/4 cup parsley, chopped fine
1/4 teaspoon thyme
1/4 teaspoon sage
Salt and pepper to taste
1 cup brown rice
2-1/2 cups water
1/2 teaspoon garlic powder

Preheat oven to 350 degrees. Place butter in ovenproof baking dish with lid. Heat butter and sauté green onion until golden. Add parsley, thyme, and sage. Sprinkle with salt and pepper; add rice. Pour 2-1/2 cups water over rice and then stir in garlic powder. Bring to a boil for about 45 minutes or until liquid is absorbed and rice is tender.

This rice goes well with turkey, goose, or duck.

LASAGNA SURPRISE
Serves 6-8

3/4 cup chopped onion
2 cloves garlic, finely chopped
2 tablespoons vegetable oil
2 (26-ounce) jars prepared spa-
　ghetti/pasta sauce or prepare
　about 2 quarts of your own
　tomato-based spaghetti/
　lasagna sauce recipe (add
　ground meat or sausage, if
　desired)
1 (15- or 16-ounce) container
　ricotta or cottage cheese
1 (10-ounce) package frozen
　chopped spinach, thawed and
　well-drained
1 pound mozzarella cheese,
　shredded
1/2 cup grated Parmesan cheese
2 eggs
1 (1-pound) package lasagna
　noodles, cooked according to
　package directions

In a large pan, cook onion and garlic in oil. Add prepared pasta sauce. (If you cook your own sauce, it may not be necessary to add more onion and garlic.) Simmer 15 minutes. In bowl, mix ricotta, spinach, and *1 cup* mozzarella, all the Parmesan, and eggs. In 15x9-inch baking dish (or smaller dishes as needed), layer *2 cups* sauce, half the lasagna, half the remaining sauce, all the spinach mixture, half the mozzarella, remaining lasagna and sauce. Cover; bake at 350 degrees for 45 minutes or until hot. Uncover; top with remaining mozzarella. Bake 15 minutes. Let stand 15 minutes before serving.

PORK PAGODA

1 cup diced cooked pork
1/2 cup sliced celery
1 cup cooked bean sprouts
1/2 cup sliced mushrooms
1/2 cup sliced carrots
1/4 cup sliced green onions
2 tablespoons oil

1 (10-ounce) can condensed cream
　of asparagus soup
1/4 cup water
2 teaspoons soy sauce
1 (10-ounce) box frozen chopped
　spinach, thawed and squeezed
　dry.

In large skillet, sauté pork and all the vegetables in oil until meat is brown and vegetables are tender. Blend in soup, water, soy sauce, and spinach. Heat, stirring occasionally. Serve hot over chow mein noodles. I have substituted beef for the pork and any other creamed soup, also.

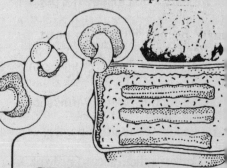

CROWD PLEASER CASSEROLE
Serves 10-12

1 (20-ounce) package frozen
　broccoli flowerets
1 (20-ounce) package frozen
　cauliflower flowerets
4 tablespoons butter or margarine
3 tablespoons flour
3 cups milk
6 ounces (or 1-1/2 cups) shredded
　cheddar cheese
1 cup Parmesan cheese, shredded
　or grated
1/2 teaspoon salt
3 cups chopped ham
3 cups fresh bread crumbs tossed
　with 4 tablespoons butter

Cook broccoli and cauliflower in slightly salted water. Cook slightly underdone. Drain; set aside. Melt 4 tablespoons butter in a 1-quart saucepan; add flour; blend well. Add milk, stirring constantly, until thickened. Add cheddar, Parmesan, and salt. Stir over low heat until cheese melts. Place vegetables in an ungreased 4-quart casserole. Sprinkle with chopped ham. Pour cheese sauce mixture over ham. Make a border of buttered bread crumbs around edge of casserole. Bake uncovered at 350 degrees for 30 minutes.

WINTER SQUASH CASSEROLE
Serves 2

cup mashed squash, thawed if frozen
or 2 slices bacon (use two if you can afford the calories)
/4 cup chopped onion
/3 cup grated Cheddar cheese
/4 teaspoon salt
)ash Tabasco or use black pepper
/4 cup buttered bread crumbs

Grease or spray with pan release a mall baking dish, one quart or maller. Put squash into medium bowl. ry bacon until crisp; crumble into quash. Leave about 1 tablespoon lrippings in skillet. Fry onions in lrippings until transparent; add to quash. Add cheese (I grate it directly nto the bowl, estimating the measre). Add salt and Tabasco or pepper; nix well. Transfer to prepared baking lish; top with bread crumbs.

Bake at 325 or 350 degrees (deending on what else may be cooking n the oven) until heated through and crumbs begin to brown, 25 to 30 ninutes.

TAGLIARINA

1 pound hamburger
1 onion, chopped
2 tablespoons butter
1 (8-ounce) can tomato sauce
1-1/2 cups water
2 cups uncooked noodles
1 (1-cup) can corn
1 large jar whole mushrooms
1 (No. 2) can pitted ripe olives
1 cup Parmesan cheese
Salt to taste

Mince and brown onion in butter in large skillet. Add meat and brown. Add tomato sauce, water and noodles; stir until noodles are tender. Add more water, if needed. Add salt and rest of ingredients. Pour into 11x11x2-inch glass baking dish and sprinkle with Parmesan cheese. Bake 45 minutes in 350 degree oven. Let stand in oven with door open for 15 minutes before serving.

MOCK OYSTER CASSEROLE

1 medium eggplant
1 stick margarine
1-1/2 cups Ritz cracker crumbs
1 egg, beaten
1 (6-1/2 ounce) can minced clams, drained (reserve liquid)
Salt, pepper, Tabasco sauce to taste

Peel eggplant; cut into 1-inch cubes and parboil 3 minutes. Drain well; set aside. Melt margarine and add Ritz crackers; mix well. Reserve 1/3 cup cracker crumb mixture for topping.

Gently mix beaten eggs, drained clams, and eggplant. Add crumbs, salt, pepper, and Tabasco sauce. Then add enough clam liquid to make quite moist, but not soupy. Pour into buttered casserole. Top with remaining crumbs and bake at 350 degrees for 45 minutes.

LUNCHMEAT AND NOODLE CASSEROLE

1/4 cup margarine
1/4 cup all-purpose flour
1/2 teaspoon salt
Dash of pepper
2-1/2 cups milk
1 can lunch meat, cubed
2 cups cooked noodles
1 teaspoon mustard
3/4 cup bread crumbs
2 tablespoons melted margarine
1 (16-ounce) can peas and carrots

Preheat oven to 375 degrees. Melt margarine in a skillet. Blend in flour, salt, pepper, and gradually stir in milk. Cook over medium heat, stirring constantly, until mixture is smooth and thick.

Add meat, noodles, mustard, and peas and carrots. Mix well. Spoon into a greased 1-1/2 quart casserole. Combine crumbs and melted butter; sprinkle over noodles. Bake 25 minutes.

CORNED BEEF SCALLOP CASSEROLE

1 (3-ounce) package potato soup mix
1-1/2 cups milk
1 cup water
1 cup American cheese, grated
1/2 teaspoon Worcestershire sauce
1 (12-ounce) can corned beef, shredded
3/4 cup carrots, sliced and cooked
1/2 cup celery, sliced and cooked
1/4 cup green peas, cooked
2 tablespoons pimiento, chopped
1 teaspoon parsley, chopped
3/4 cup soft bread crumbs

Empty potato soup mix into saucepan; add milk and water; stir constantly until blended. Cook until mixture comes to a boil; remove from heat. Add cheese and Worcestershire sauce; mix well. Stir in corned beef shreds, carrots, celery, green peas, and pimiento. Turn into a well-greased 1-1/2 quart ovenproof casserole. Sprinkle parsley over the top, then bread crumbs; cover. Bake 350 degrees for 20 minutes; uncover; bake 12 minutes longer until top is golden.

MAIN DISH NOODLES
Serves 2

2-1/2 cups uncooked medium noodles
2 tablespoons butter or margarine
2 tablespoons half-and-half or cream
2 tablespoons Parmesan cheese
1 (6-ounce) can boneless salmon or tuna

Cook noodles in boiling, salted water according to directions on package.

Meanwhile, in a medium saucepan, melt butter. Stir in half-and-half and cheese; leave over low heat. Drain fish; break into lumps; add to butter mixture. Drain cooked noodles; immediately add to saucepan; toss to mix. Serve with additional Parmesan cheese.

HAM, POTATO, AND ONION CASSEROLE
Serves 8-10

6 tablespoons ham drippings or butter
6 tablespoons enriched flour
3 cups milk
2 teaspoons salt
1/4 teaspoon pepper
1/4 pound Cheddar cheese, grated
1 pound diced cooked ham
4 cups cubed cooked potatoes
12 small cooked onions
1/2 cup buttered bread crumbs

Melt drippings or butter. Blend in flour and add milk, stirring constantly. Cook mixture until thickened, boiling about 3 minutes. Add seasonings and grated cheese. Cook slowly until cheese melts. Add cooked ham, potatoes, and onions. Pour mixture into a greased casserole. Sprinkle with buttered bread crumbs. Bake, uncovered, in a 350 degree oven for 30-40 minutes or until crumbs are lightly browned.

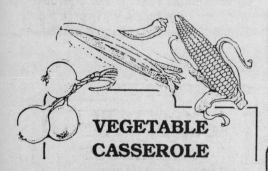

VEGETABLE CASSEROLE

1 can whole kernel corn, drained
1 can French green beans, drained
1 cup finely chopped celery
1 cup finely chopped onion
1/2 cup green pepper, finely chopped
4 cups grated sharp cheese
1 container sour cream
1 can cream of celery soup

Mix well and pour into a very large casserole.

Topping:
3/4 box Cheese-It crackers, crumbled into 3/4 stick melted margarine. You may add a can of slivered almonds. Bake at 350 degrees for 45 minutes. This makes a large amount. Great for a covered-dish supper!!

CHICKEN-PASTA HOT DISH
Serves 6-8

1/2 pound elbow or spiral pasta (2 cups uncooked)
1/4 cup butter or margarine
1/4 cup finely chopped onion
3 tablespoons all-purpose flour
1-1/2 teaspoons salt
1/8 teaspoon pepper
3 cups milk
3 cups shredded cheddar cheese
2 cups diced cooked chicken or turkey
1 (9-ounce) package frozen Italian-cut green beans, thawed and drained
1 (2-ounce) jar diced pimiento, drained
3 tablespoons cornflake crumbs

Cook pasta according to package directions; drain. In large saucepan, melt butter; add onion and cook until tender. Stir in flour, salt, and pepper. Blend in milk. Cook, stirring constantly, until thickened and bubbly. Add cheese; stir until melted. Combine pasta, cheese sauce, chicken, green beans, and pimiento; mix well. Pour into a 3-quart casserole. Top with cornflake crumbs. Bake in a 350-degree oven until hot, about 30 minutes. Refrigerate leftovers.

ONE-POT TUNA PASTA
Serves 4

3-1/2 cups water
4 chicken bouillon cubes
1/8 teaspoon pepper
1 teaspoon basil leaves
2 cups (8 ounces) elbow pasta or spiral pasta
1 (4-ounce) jar pimiento
1 (9-ounce) package frozen cut green beans
2 cups milk
1 cup (4 ounces) process American cheese
1 (7-ounce) can tuna, drained and broken into chunks
1/4 cup chopped parsley

Bring water, bouillon cubes, pepper and basil leaves to a boil in a quart pot. Gradually add uncooked pasta so that water continues to boil. Cover and simmer for 7 minutes, stirring occasionally.

Meanwhile, dice pimiento. Stir diced pimiento, beans, and milk in pot; cover and simmer 6 to 8 minutes longer or until pasta and beans are tender. Stir in cheese, tuna, and parsley until cheese is melted. Serve from pot or turn into serving dish. Serve immediately.

ONION CASSEROLE
Serves 2

2 large or 3 medium onions
1/4 teaspoon salt
Dash of pepper
2 or 3 tablespoons whipping cream (see directions)
1/3 cup buttered bread crumbs
Garlic powder (optional)

Grease or spray with pan release a small baking dish, about 2-cup capacity

Peel onions; cut in half lengthwise; place cut-side down on board; cut in 1/4-inch slices. Use your hands to separate layers. Drop into saucepan of cold salted water. Bring to boil over high heat; boil until onions are transparent but barely fork tender, about 3 minutes. Drain thoroughly. (If doing ahead, set aside.) Return to pan. Sprinkle on salt and pepper. Add 2 tablespoons cream; toss to mix; if onions seem dry, add another tablespoon cream (this depends on how well drained onions were). Spread evenly in prepared dish. Top with crumbs; sprinkle crumbs lightly with garlic powder, if desired.

Bake at 325 or 350 degrees (depending on what else may be cooking in the oven) until heated through and crumbs are golden. 20 to 25 minutes.

STEAK AND POTATO CASSEROLE

2-1/2 pounds round steak, 1/2 - 3/4 inch thick
1/4 cup flour
4 teaspoons salt
1/2 teaspoon pepper
1/4 cup oil
3-1/2 cups water
8 medium carrots, thinly sliced diagonally
8 medium potatoes, thinly sliced
1-3/8-ounce envelope onion soup mix
Chopped parsley for garnish

Preheat oven to 325 degrees. Cut meat into 6 - 8 serving pieces, trimming fat and bone. On wooden board or waxed paper, using meat mallet or edge of heavy saucer, pound mixture of flour, salt and pepper into meat.

In heavy skillet over medium heat, brown meat well on both sides in hot oil. Do not crowd pieces. Arrange browned meat in 3-quart casserole. Place carrots and potato slices on top. Sprinkle with onion soup mix and pour over 3-1/2 cups water. Bake, covered 2 hours or until tender. Skim excess fat. If you wish, thicken with 2 tablespoons flour mixed with 1 tablespoon butter; form into balls and drop into casserole. Return to oven 10 minutes. Sprinkle with parsley and serve.

CHINESE TUNA CASSEROLE
Serves 4

14 ounce can Chinese vegetables, drained
10 3/4 ounce can cream of mushroom soup
9 1/4 ounce can tuna fish, drained and flaked
3/4 cup celery, thinly sliced
1 tablespoon soy sauce
1/4 teaspoon pepper
3 ounce can Chinese noodles

Preheat oven to 350 degrees. Mix all ingredients, except noodles, in ungreased 1-1/2 quart casserole. Sprinkle with noodles. Bake uncovered until contents are bubbly and noodles golden brown, about 40 to 45 minutes. Serve with hot rolls and salad.

SHRIMP AND ASPARAGUS CASSEROLE
Serves 6 to 8

1 cup rice, cooked
1 pound fresh asparagus, cut up and cooked, (or 1 package frozen cut-up asparagus, cooked)
3 cans (4-1/2 ounces each) shrimp
2 tablespoons butter
2 tablespoons flour
1-1/4 cups milk
1/2 pound sharp Cheddar cheese, grated
Salt and paprika

Heat oven to 350 degrees (moderate). Spread rice in buttered baking dish, 11-1/2 x 7-1/2 x 1-1/2". Spread asparagus over rice. Cover with shrimp. Melt butter, stir in flour; cook over low heat, stirring until mixture is smooth, bubbly. Remove from heat. Stir in milk and cheese. Bring to boil; boil 1 minute, stirring constantly. Season to taste with salt and paprika. Pour sauce over shrimp in baking dish. Sprinkle with paprika. Bake 20 minutes.

CHICKEN AND HAM CASSEROLE

7 slices white meat of chicken, uniform size
3 slices boiled ham, cut same size
1/2 small Bermuda onion, finely minced
1/4 cup butter
1/2 cup sliced mushrooms
1 teaspoon paprika
1 teaspoon salt
1/4 teaspoon nutmeg
3/4 cup cream
3-4 tablespoons grated Parmesan cheese

Cook the onion in butter for 5 minutes, stirring constantly and do not let it brown. Add the sliced mushrooms and seasonings and let simmer for 15 minutes. Turn the mixture into an oblong baking dish and arrange chicken and ham on the top. Add enough hot cream to cover the meat. Let simmer in a hot 400 degree oven for 10 minutes. Cover with Parmesan cheese; let remain in oven until cheese is browned.

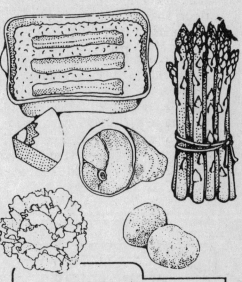

"SOUPER" CHICKEN CASSEROLE

2 cups diced, cooked chicken
1 (16-ounce) bag frozen broccoli, carrots, and cauliflower (thawed and drained)
1 can cream of mushroom soup
1 cup shredded Swiss cheese
1/3 cup sour cream
1/4 teaspoon pepper
1 can French fried onions

Combine all ingredients *except* the cheese and onions. Add one-half of the cheese, and one-half of the onions. Pour into casserole; bake uncovered, in a 350 degree oven for 30 minutes. Top with remaining onions and cheese; bake uncovered 5 minutes longer.

CHEESY SPAGHETTI

1 (12-ounce) package thin spaghetti
1/4 pound bacon, cut in small pieces
1 large onion, chopped
1 pound ground beef
2 cups (2 8-ounce cans) tomato sauce
1 (4-ounce) can sliced mushrooms, drained
1 teaspoon salt
1/2 teaspoon Italian seasoning
1/2 teaspoon garlic salt
1/8 teaspoon pepper
1 cup (4 ounces) shredded cheese
1/2 cup shredded Provolone cheese

Cook spaghetti; drain. Fry bacon slowly until browned. Drain off grease. Add onion and beef; cook until meat is brown; mix in tomato sauce and seasonings. Simmer 15 minutes. In large bowl, combine sauce and spaghetti. Place half of mixture in a buttered 2 quart casserole. Top with half of the Cheddar and half of the Provolone cheese. Repeat layers. Bake in pre-heated 375 degree oven for 20-25 minutes.

PORK CHOP CASSEROLE

6 pork chops
1 cup uncooked brown rice
6 slices onion
6 tomato slices
6 green pepper rings
1 teaspoon salt
1/8 teaspoon pepper
2 cups tomato juice

Spray 12-inch skillet with vegetable cooking spray. Brown pork chops on each side. Transfer to plate.
Place rice over bottom of skillet. Arrange chops on top. Stack slices of onion, tomato, and green pepper on top of each chop. Sprinkle with salt and pepper. Pour tomato juice over chops. Cover; simmer 45 minutes or until chops are tender.

BACON AND RICE CREOLE

1 pound bacon
1 green pepper, diced
3 small onions, chopped
2-1/2 teaspoons salt
1/8 teaspoon pepper
2 cups canned tomatoes
1 cup raw rice (not quick-cooking)

Simmer vegetables and spices in a sauce pan. At the same time, fry the bacon. When bacon is done, remove from pan and crumble into small pieces. Drain off all but 3 tablespoons of fat, to which add the raw rice. Let rice brown lightly. Add the vegetables and bacon; let simmer over very low heat for 30 minutes. Check after 20 minutes to see if it is drying out, if so, add more tomatoes, or some water, or a combination of both.

FIESTA CORN CASSEROLE
Serves 4-6

3 tablespoons butter
3 cups corn flakes
1 pound lean ground beef
3/4 teaspoon seasoned salt
1 (8-ounce) can tomato sauce
1 (1-1/4 ounce) package Lawry's Taco Seasoning Mix
1 (17-ounce) can whole kernel corn, drained (save 1/4 cup liquid)
2 cups grated Cheddar cheese.

Combine butter and 2 cups corn flakes in bottom of a shallow 1-1/2 quart baking dish. Crush remaining corn flakes; set aside. In skillet, brown beef until crumbly; drain. Add seasoned salt, tomato sauce, taco seasoning mix, and reserved liquid from corn; mix well. Layer 1/2 each; corn, meat mixture, and cheese over buttered corn flakes in baking dish; repeat layers. Sprinkle crushed corn flakes over top in diagonal strips.

CHICKEN ALMOND CASSEROLE

5 cups diced, cooked chicken breasts
2 cups diced celery
3 cups cooked rice
1 (8-ounce) can sliced water chestnuts
2 cans cream of chicken soup
1/2 cup sour cream
1/2 cup mayonnaise
2 tablespoons chopped onion
2 tablespoons lemon juice
1 tablespoon salt
3/4 teaspoon white pepper
1 cup sliced almonds

Mix above ingredients and put in buttered 9x13 inch baking dish.

Topping:
1/2 cup sliced almonds
3 cups crumbled corn flakes
2/3 cup butter

Mix above ingredients and sprinkle on top of casserole. Bake at 350 degrees for 35-45 minutes. Can be prepared ahead and refrigerated until baking.

GERMAN SUPPER
Serves 4-5

5-6 potatoes, scrubbed (not peeled)
1/4 cup chopped onion
1/4 teaspoon garlic powder
1/2 teaspoon salt
1/3 teaspoon pepper
3 cups cubed beef Hillshire Farms sausage or Eckrich smoked sausage
1 (7-ounce) can sauerkraut

Cut potatoes into thumb-size pieces. Add onion, garlic powder, salt, and pepper. Brown in a small amount of oil for 25 minutes until tender. Add sausage; heat; stir occasionally. Drain kraut and spread on top surface. Do not stir. Cover and heat.

FRESH CORN CASEROLE

Preheat oven to 350 degrees. Generously butter a 2-quart rectangular baking dish. In blender puree:

1 cup corn (fresh or frozen, thawed)
1/2 cup butter, softened
2 eggs

Pour into bowl; blend in:

1 cup corn
4-ounce can green chilies; drained, seeded, and chopped
1 cup sour cream
1 cup diced Monterey Jack cheese
1/2 cup cornmeal
1-1/2 teaspoons salt

Spread above ingredients in baking dish. Bake 50 - 60 minutes. Serve with sliced tomatoes. This is delicious and very light!

STUFFED SHELLS
Serves 8-10

1 (12-ounce) package jumbo shells for stuffing
2 tablespoons butter
1 clove garlic, crushed
1/2 cup finely-chopped onion
2 beaten eggs
2 pounds Ricotta cheese
1/2 cup Parmesan and Romano cheese, mixed
1/3 cup parsley flakes
1/8 teaspoon nutmeg
1 cup shredded Mozzarella cheese (4 ounces)
2-3 pounds Italian meat sauce
1/2 cup Parmesan and Romano, mixed for topping

Preheat oven to 350 degrees. Cook shells according to package directions. Rinse with cold water; drain. Melt butter; sauté garlic and onion until soft. Mix together onion, garlic, eggs, ricotta, Parmesan, Romano, parsley, and nutmeg. Stir in Mozzarella, stuff shells with filling. (At this point, the shells may be frozen for future use).
Cover the bottoms of two 13x9x2-inch baking dishes with meat sauce.

Place shells on top of sauce and sprinkle with Parmesan and Romano. Bake, covered with foil, at 350 degrees for 30-40 minutes or until hot and bubbly.
This is a dish that is easy to prepare; and receives many compliments at potluck dinners.

DEVILED HAM AND RICE CASSEROLE
Serves 6

1 medium onion, chopped
1/2 medium green pepper, chopped
1/2 cup finely diced celery
2 tablespoons butter or margarine
1 cup raw rice
2 chicken bouillon cubes
2 (4-1/2 ounce) cans deviled ham
3 cups boiling water
Chopped parsley

Sauté first 3 ingredients in butter for 2-3 minutes. Place mixture in 1-1/2 quart casserole with remaining ingredients, except parsley. Mix with fork. Cover and bake for 45 minutes in pre-heated moderate oven at 350 degrees, stirring twice at 15-minute intervals, or until rice is tender. Sprinkle with parsley.

ANOTHER HAMBURGER CASSEROLE

1 pound hamburger
1 green pepper, chopped
1 (8-ounce) package of 1/4 inch noodles, cooked
1 can cream of mushroom soup
1 can evaporated milk

Fry hamburger with green pepper, then blend in soup and milk. Combine with cooked noodles and bake 45-60 minutes at 350 degrees. Do not alter any of these ingredients. It takes this combination for the special flavor.

CHICKEN LIVER CASSEROLE
Serves 5-6

2 (10-ounce) packages frozen French-style green beans
4 slices bacon, diced
1 pound chicken livers, cut in half
1/2 teaspoon seasoning salt
2 tablespoons sherry
1 (10-ounce) can cream of mushroom soup
1/2 cup sour cream
3/4 cup crushed barbecue potato chips

Cook green beans according to directions. Drain and spread in greased 9x6 or 8x8 inch baking dish. Sauté bacon until crisp; scatter over beans. Stir-fry chicken livers in bacon fat until pinkness disappears. Add next 4 ingredients, as soon as heated; pour over bacon. Top with potato chips. Bake at 375 degrees for 15 minutes, or until bubbly.
This is a very tasty dish and easy to make!

ZUCCHINI CASSEROLE
Serves 12

2 cups bread crumbs
1/4 cup butter or margarine, melted
1/4 teaspoon Italian seasonings
1/4 cup Parmesan cheese
2 pounds zucchini; sliced, parboiled, and drained
1 medium carrot, shredded
10-1/2-ounce can cream of chicken soup
1 cup sour cream
1/4 cup chopped green onion

Combine crumbs, butter, seasonings, and cheese; spread half in bottom of 13 x 9 x 2-inch pan. Combine zucchini and carrot; spread over crumbs. Mix soup, sour cream, and onion; pour over vegetables. Top with remaining crumbs. Bake at 350 degrees for 1 hour.

AMISH-STYLE YUM-A-SETTA
Serves 6–8

2 pounds hamburger
  Salt and pepper to taste
2 tablespoons brown sugar
¼ cup chopped onion
1 (10¾-ounce) can tomato soup, undiluted
1 (10¾-ounce) can chicken soup, undiluted
1 (16-ounce) package egg noodles
1 (8-ounce) package processed cheese, such as Kraft or Velveeta

Brown hamburger with salt, pepper, brown sugar and onion. Add tomato soup. Cook egg noodles according to package; drain. Add cream of chicken soup. Layer hamburger mixture and noodle mixture in 9 x 12-inch casserole with processed cheese between layers. Bake at 350 degrees for 30 minutes.

This is a great recipe to make for a potluck dinner, for a reunion, or to use up staples around the house. Can easily be made the day before.

MACARONI AND SAUSAGE BAKE
Serves 6

1 pound bulk pork sausage
1/2 cup chopped onion
1 cup elbow macaroni
1 (10-1/2 ounce) can cream of celery soup
2/3 cup milk
3 beaten eggs
1-1/2 cups shredded processed American cheese

Cook macaroni according to package directions. Cook sausage and onion until browned. Drain off excess fat. Combine sausage mixture, macaroni, soup, milk, eggs, and cheese. Place in 2-quart casserole. Bake at 350 degrees for 40-45 minutes.

BROCCOLI CASSEROLE
Serves 8

1/4 cup chopped onion
6 tablespoons butter or margarine
1/2 cup water
2 tablespoons flour
8 ounces processed cheese spread
2 packages frozen chopped broccoli, thawed and drained
3 eggs, well beaten
1/2 cup cracker crumbs

Sauté onion in 4 tablespoons butter until soft; stir in flour and add water. Cook over low heat, stirring, until mixture thickens and comes to a boil. Blend in cheese. Combine sauce and broccoli. Add eggs; mix gently until blended. Turn into a 1-1/2 quart casserole; cover with crumbs and dot with remaining butter. Bake at 325 degrees for 30 minutes.

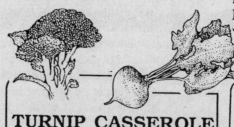

TURNIP CASSEROLE
Serves 4

1 1/2 lbs. turnips, peeled and thinly sliced
2 tablespoons butter
1 onion, thinly sliced
2/3 cup chopped celery
2 tablespoons flour
1 cup milk
1/2 cup grated sharp cheese
  Salt and pepper to taste
3 tbsps. bread crumbs

Cook turnips in boiling, salted water to cover until just tender. Drain. Sauté in butter the oinion, green pepper, and celery until tender. Sprinkle with flour and cook 1 minute. Add milk and stir until thickened. Stir in cheese, salt and pepper. Combine cheese sauce with turnips, place in baking dish and top with curmbs. Brown under broiler. May be prepared ahead and place-dunder broiler just before serving.

YELLOW SQUASH CASSEROLE

2 pounds yellow squash
1 large onion
1 can cream of chicken soup
1 jar pimientos (optional)
1 cup sour cream
1 teaspoon salt
1/4 teaspoon pepper
1 stick margarine
1 (8-ounce) package Pepperidg Farms herbal dressing

Boil squash until tender; drain an mash. Chop onion; sauté in a ha stick margarine until tender. Ac soup, chopped pimiento, sour crear salt, and pepper. Melt the remainir margarine and add to dressin crumbs. Put half of dressing in botto of baking dish. Mix all ingredients to gether. Pour on dressing. Sprea remaining half of the dressing on to Bake at 350 degrees for approx mately 1 hour.

PARSNIP CASSEROLE

2 pounds parsnips
2 tablespoons butter
1/4 teaspoon fresh or dried rosemary
2 tablespoons flour
1/4 cup grated Parmesan cheese
2 cups light cream or half-and-half
1/2 cup cracker crumbs
1/4 cup melted butter

Peel parsnips. Cook in boiling, salted water until tender. Drain; cut each in half lengthwise, or slice in rounds, if parsnips are large. Arrange half the parsnips in bottom of greased 1-1/2 quart baking dish. Dot with half the butter; sprinkle with half the rosemary, flour, and cheese. Drizzle with half the cream. Repeat layers. Mix cracker crumbs with melted butter; sprinkle over casserole. Bake, uncovered, in 400 degree oven for 20 minutes.

SUNSHINE TORTILLA PIE
Serves 7

1½ pounds ground beef
1 onion, chopped
1 green pepper, chopped
½ cup flour
½ teaspoon salt
1¼ teaspoons chili powder
1 (16-ounce) can tomato sauce
1 cup water
½ cup pimiento-stuffed olives, chopped
12 tortillas
3½ cups sharp cheddar cheese, grated
6 hard-cooked eggs, divided

Sauté meat; add onion and green pepper; cook 5 minutes. Sprinkle vegetables and meat with flour, salt and chili powder. Stir in tomato sauce, water and olives; simmer 5 minutes. In ovenproof dish alternate layers of tortillas, cheese, 3 sliced eggs and sauce over all. Finely chop or sieve remaining 3 eggs; sprinkle on top of sauce.

QUICK AND EASY MACARONI AND CHEESE

1 (7-ounce) package Creamettes macaroni (2 cups)
1 pound lean ground beef
½ cup chopped onion
½ cup sliced celery
2 (8-ounce) cans Hunt's tomato sauce with mushrooms
1 teaspoon salt
¼ teaspoon pepper
1 (8-ounce) package shredded cheddar cheese (2 cups)

Cook macaroni as directed on package; drain. Brown ground beef, onion and celery in skillet. Pour off excess fat. Stir in tomato sauce with mushrooms, salt and pepper. Combine meat mixture with Creamettes macaroni. Pour into a 2-quart casserole and stir in a portion of the cheese; sprinkle top with additional cheese. Bake at 350 degrees for about 25 minutes, or until cheese melts.

Very good with a lettuce salad and Italian bread.

MEXICALI CASSEROLE
Serves 8

1/2 cup chopped onion
1 tablespoon shortening, melted
1 (16-ounce) can tomatoes, chopped and drained
1 (17-ounce) can whole-kernel corn, drained
2 (15-ounce) cans chili with beans
1 (8-ounce) package corn muffin mix
1 cup (4 ounces) shredded cheddar cheese

Heat oven to 350 degrees. In skillet, cook onion in shortening for 10 minutes. Add tomatoes, corn and chili; mix until well-blended. Pour into 12 x 8-inch baking dish. Prepare corn muffin mix according to package directions; stir cheese into batter. Spoon batter mixture around edge of baking dish. Bake 30 minutes. This is great with jalapeño pepper cheese, as well as with cheddar cheese.

LASAGNA-STYLE CASSEROLE
Serves 6

6 ounces large bow-tie pasta (2-1/4 cups)
1 pound ground beef or pork
1 (15-ounce) can pizza sauce
1 teaspoon minced dry onion
1/2 teaspoon dry basil, crushed
1 egg, beaten
1 cup ricotta cheese or cottage cheese
1/4 cup grated Parmesan cheese
1 cup shredded mozzarella cheese

Cook pasta until tender; drain. Fry meat until browned; drain off fat. Add pizza sauce, onion, and basil to meat and mix well. In a bowl, combine egg and cottage cheese or ricotta. In a greased 12x9-1/2x2-inch baking dish, layer half of the pasta.

Spoon cheese mixture over pasta. Sprinkle with Parmesan cheese. Layer remaining pasta, meat, and mozzarella cheese. Bake, covered, at 425 degrees for 15 minutes. Uncover and bake 5-8 minutes longer, or until heated through.

MANDARIN ORANGE CASHEW CASSEROLE
Serves 5

1 pound ground beef
1/4 cup celery, cut diagonally
1/2 cup green onion, cut diagonally in 1-inch pieces
1/4 cup green pepper, chopped
1 1/2 teaspoons garlic, minced
1 cup water
1/4 teaspoon toasted sesame oil
2 tablespoons cornstarch
1 teaspoon sugar
1/4 teaspoon 5-Spice Powder
1/4 teaspoon ginger root, minced
1/4 cup soy sauce
2 tablespoons water
1 (16-ounce) can chop suey vegetables, drained
1 (10-ounce) package frozen peas
1 (3-ounce) can chow mein noodles
1 cup cashew halves

In a skillet cook beef, celery, green onion, green pepper, garlic; drain. Add the water and sesame oil; bring to a boil. Combine cornstarch, sugar, 5-Spice Powder, ginger root, soy sauce and water. Add to beef mixture in skillet; cook until thickened and bubbly. Stir in the drained chop suey vegetables; add frozen peas. Turn into 2-quart casserole; bake, covered, at 375 degrees for 1 1/2 hours; uncover and bake 10 minutes more.

To serve: Sprinkle each individual serving with chow mein noodles; scatter the cashew halves over top surface.

Cookies
& BARS

QUICK AND EASY BROWNIES

½ cup shortening
2 eggs
2 squares bitter chocolate
½ teaspoon baking powder
1 cup sugar
½ teaspoon salt
1 cup nuts, chopped
¼ cup flour
1 teaspoon vanilla

Melt chocolate and shortening together over hot water. Add sugar and eggs; beat thoroughly. Add vanilla and nuts. Mix baking powder and salt with the flour. Add to first mixture. Mix thoroughly. Pour into a greased 8 x 12-inch baking pan and bake 25 minutes in a moderate 350-degree oven.

MINT BROWNIES

¾ cup plus 2 tablespoons sifted cake flour
1 cup sugar
7 tablespoons cocoa
½ teaspoon baking powder
¾ teaspoon salt
⅔ cup shortening
2 eggs
1 teaspoon vanilla
1 tablespoon light corn syrup
1 cup walnuts, coarsely chopped

In large bowl, beat all ingredients together at low speed, except walnuts;

stir in walnuts with spoon. Pour battter into greased 8-inch square pan. Bake at 350 degrees about 40 minutes or until toothpick inserted near center comes out clean. Cool and frost.

Mint Frosting:

1 tablespoon shortening
1 tablespoon butter
2½ tablespoons scalded hot cream
2 cups powdered sugar
¼ teaspoon salt
½ teaspoon vanilla
¼ teaspoon peppermint extract
Green food coloring
1 ounce semisweet chocolate
1 teaspoon shortening

Melt 1 tablespoon shortening and 1 tablespoon butter in hot cream. Pour over powdered sugar and salt; stir well. Add vanilla and peppermint extract, beat until thick enough to spread. Add enough food coloring to tint a pastel mint green. Spread brownies with frosting. Melt chocolate and shortening together. Cool and drizzle over frosting in thin stream from teaspoon. Cut into squares.

CHOCOLATE BROWNIES

2 cups sugar
2 cups flour
1 teaspoon soda
2 eggs, beaten
1 cup buttermilk
¼ pound margarine *or* butter
½ cup shortening
¼ cup cocoa
1 cup water

Sift flour, sugar and soda together large bowl. Bring margarine, wate cocoa and shortening to a boil. Pou over flour and sugar, mix well. Ad remaining ingredients. Pour into grease 15½ x 10½ x 1-inch pan. Bake at 35 degrees for 20–30 minutes, or unt done.

Brownie Icing:

1 stick margarine *or* butter
¼ cup cocoa
6 tablespoons milk
4 cups confectioners' sugar, sifted
1 teaspoon vanilla
1 cup nuts, chopped

Mix first 5 ingredients well wit mixer; fold in chopped nuts, and sprea on brownies while hot. The icing melt a bit, but firms up again as it all cools Brownies stay moist and are delicious!

GOLD RUSH BROWNIES

2 cups graham cracker crumbs
1 can sweetened condensed milk
1 (6-ounce) package chocolate chips
½ cup chopped pecans

Mix together and put into an 8 x 8-inch pan (well-greased). Bake at 350 degrees for 30 minutes. Let brownies cool 10 minutes. Cut into squares and remove from pan.

DELUXE FUDGY BROWNIES

4 squares unsweetened chocolate
½ cup butter *or* margarine
4 eggs
2 cups sugar
1 cup sifted flour
1 teaspoon vanilla
1 cup coarsely chopped nuts

Melt chocolate and butter together over hot water. Cool slightly. Beat eggs until foamy; gradually add sugar, beating thoroughly after each addition. Add chocolate mixture and blend. Stir in flour. Then add vanilla and nuts. Spread in greased 9 x 9 x 2-inch pan. Bake at 325 degrees for 40–50 minutes. Cool in pan, then cut into squares or bars. Will have crunchy top and bottom crust with a center almost like chocolate cream. Delicious served straight from the freezer.

BABY RUTH CANDY BROWNIES

⅔ cup margarine
1 cup brown sugar
¼ cup light corn syrup
¼ cup smooth peanut butter
1 teaspoon vanilla
1 cup quick oatmeal

Topping:
1 (12-ounce) package chocolate chips
1 (6-ounce) package butterscotch chips
⅔ cup smooth peanut butter
1 cup salted Spanish peanuts

Combine margarine, sugar and syrup in saucepan. Stir over low heat until margarine melts and sugar dissolves. Add peanut butter and vanilla. Pour over oatmeal; mix well. Press into a greased 13 x 9-inch pan and bake at 375 degrees for 12 minutes. Melt chocolate and butterscotch bits. Add peanut butter and peanuts. Pour over baked mixture. Cool and cut into squares.

APPLE BROWNIES

½ cup butter
¼ teaspoon salt
1 egg, beaten
1 cup sugar
3 medium apples, pared and diced *or* ½ cup applesauce
½ cup chopped walnuts
1 cup flour
½ teaspoon baking powder
½ teaspoon baking soda
½ teaspoon cinnamon

Preheat oven to 350 degrees. Cream together butter and salt, then add the egg and sugar; beat well. Stir in apples, nuts and dry ingredients. Blend well. Pour mixture into a greased and floured 8-inch square pan. Bake for 40 minutes. When cool, cut into squares.

CANDY COOKIES
Makes 4–5 dozen

1 (12-ounce) bag chocolate chips
1 (12-ounce) bag butterscotch chips
1 (10-ounce) bag miniature marshmallows
1 cup coarsely chopped walnuts
1 cup peanut butter

Melt both bags of chips in a large pan. Stir in peanut butter. Let cool completely. Add nuts and marshmallows; stir so they are covered with chocolate mixture. Drop the mixture from a spoon onto cookie sheets that are covered with waxed paper. Put into refrigerator until set and cool. Then place in containers and store in refrigerator.

PECAN BUTTER-SCOTCH BROWNIES
Makes 24 squares

¼ cup vegetable oil
1 tablespoon dark molasses
½ cup brown sugar, firmly packed
½ cup pecans, chopped
2 cups all-purpose flour
2 eggs
2 teaspoons vanilla
¼ teaspoon salt
½ cup milk
½ teaspoon baking powder

Combine all ingredients; spread in a greased 8 x 8 x 2-inch pan. Bake at 350 degrees for 30 minutes; turn out of pan; cut into squares or bars while hot; place a whole pecan on each square.

TOFFEE SQUARES
Makes 40

1 cup butter, softened to room temperature
1 cup brown sugar
1 egg yolk
2 teaspoons vanilla extract
1⅞ cups all-purpose flour
6 milk chocolate bars (1.65 ounces each)
1 cup chopped, toasted almonds *or* pecans

In mixing bowl, cream together butter and brown sugar until light-colored and fluffy. Add egg yolk and vanilla; gradually beat in flour until smooth and blended. (Dough will be thick.) Spread evenly on ungreased 16 x 14 x 1-inch baking pan. Bake at 350 degrees for 15 minutes, or until crust is golden brown and puffy. Remove from oven. Arrange unwrapped chocolate bars evenly over surface of crust; let stand for 5 minutes to soften. Spread chocolate evenly over crust; sprinkle with chopped nuts. Cool; cut into squares.

SIMPLY DELICIOUS EASY BROWNIES

Makes 25–30 bars

Grease a 9 x 13-inch baking pan. In large bowl, combine in order given:

- 1 cup butter *or* margarine
- 2 cups sugar
- 4 eggs (beating after each addition)
- 2 teaspoons vanilla
- 1½ cups all-purpose flour
- ½ cup plus 1 tablespoon cocoa
- 1 teaspoon salt

Mix well and add 1 cup chopped nuts, if desired. Put in pan; bake at 350 degrees for 30 minutes. Check at 25 minutes, if you like brownies chewy. Frost, if desired.

WHOLE-WHEAT SNICKERDOODLES

Makes 30

- ½ cup margarine
- ¾ cup brown sugar, firmly packed
- 1 egg
- 1 teaspoon vanilla
- 1½ cups whole-wheat flour
- ½ teaspoon baking soda
- ½ teaspoon cream of tartar
- ¼ teaspoon salt
- 2 tablespoons sugar
- ½ teaspoon cinnamon

Preheat oven to 375 degrees. In a small mixer bowl beat margarine with electric mixer on medium speed until softened (about 30 seconds). Add brown sugar and beat until fluffy. Add egg and vanilla. Beat well. In a medium bowl stir together flour, baking soda, cream of tartar and salt. With mixer on low speed, gradually add flour mixture to butter mixture, beating until well-mixed. Stir together sugar and cinnamon. Shape dough into 1-inch balls. Roll the balls in sugar-cinnamon mixture. Place about 2 inches apart on ungreased cookie sheet. Flatten slightly with bottom of drinking glass. Bake in 325-degree oven for 8–10 minutes, or until edges are firm. Cool on rack.

PINWHEEL COOKIES

- 6 cups sifted flour
- ½ teaspoon salt
- 2 cups butter
- 2 cups sugar
- 12 tablespoons milk
- 4 teaspoons vanilla
- 2 teaspoons double-acting baking powder
- 4 egg yolks, well-beaten
- 3 squares unsweetened chocolate, melted

Sift flour, baking powder and salt together. Cream butter with sugar until fluffy. Add egg yolks and vanilla. Beat well. Add flour alternately with milk, mixing well after each addition. Divide dough into 2 parts. To 1 part, add chocolate and blend. Roll each half into a rectangular sheet, about ⅛-inch thick. Top with other sheet. Roll as for jelly roll. Chill until firm enough to slice. Slice into ⅛-inch slices. Bake 8–10 minutes on an *ungreased* cookie sheet at 400 degrees. *Note:* Roll the dough on waxed paper.

CHOCOLATE GOODIES

- 1½ cups sifted flour
- ¼ teaspoon soda
- ¼ teaspoon salt
- ½ cup margarine
- ½ cup brown sugar, firmly packed
- 1 egg
- 1 egg yolk
- ¼ teaspoon vanilla
  Pecans, chopped
  Chocolate Frosting
  (recipe follows)

Sift together flour, soda and salt. Blend together margarine and brown sugar, creaming well. Add 1 egg, egg yolk and vanilla. Add dry ingredients gradually; mix thoroughly.

Mold dough into balls, using a rounded teaspoonful of dough for each cookie. Dip bottom in egg white and place on cookie sheet. Bake at 350 degrees for 10–12 minutes. Do not overbake. Cool and frost generously. Sprinkle Chocolate Goodies with chopped pecans.

Note: If dough is too soft to mold into little balls, place in freezer for just a few minutes.

Chocolate Frosting:
- 2 (1-ounce) squares unsweetened chocolate *or* ⅓ cup chocolate chips
- ¼ cup milk
- 1 tablespoon milk
- 1 cup confectioners' sugar

Combine chocolate with milk and butter in top of double boiler. Heat over boiling water until chocolate melts. Blend until smooth. Remove from heat. Add 1 cup sifted confectioners' sugar (more if needed). Beat until smooth and glossy.

STRAWBERRY CREAM COOKIES

- 1 cup butter
- 1 cup sugar
- 1 egg yolk
- 1 (3-ounce) package cream cheese
- 1 tablespoon vanilla
- 2½ cups all-purpose flour
  Strawberry jam, or flavor of your choice

Cream butter, sugar and cream cheese. Add vanilla and egg yolk; mix. Then blend in flour. Chill to make dough easier to handle. Using floured hands, shape into 1-inch balls. Using a floured thimble, press a hole in the center of each ball. Fill with ¼ teaspoon of jam. Bake on an ungreased sheet at 350 degrees for 10–12 minutes. Cookies should be lightly browned on the bottom. Cool on wire rack. These cookies are easy to make and taste very special.

BROWNIE RASPBERRY BARS

Makes 40 bars

¾ cup butter *or* margarine
3 ounces unsweetened chocolate
1½ cups sugar
3 eggs
1½ teaspoons vanilla
1⅓ cups flour
12 ounces raspberry *or* apricot preserves
6 ounces semisweet chocolate chips

Preheat oven to 325 degrees. In medium saucepan, melt butter and unsweetened chocolate over low heat. Remove from heat and stir in sugar. Blend in eggs, 1 at a time. Add vanilla; stir in flour. Spread in a greased 15 x 10-inch jelly roll pan. Bake for 20–25 minutes, or until set (do not underbake). Cool. Spread preserves on top of brownies. Cut brownies in half lengthwise, then crosswise to form 4 rectangles. Stack 2 rectangles, preserve side up. Turn edges if necessary. Cut into 2 x 2-inch bars and place on rack over waxed paper. Repeat with remaining rectangles. Heat chocolate chips over low heat until melted. Drizzle over each bar; chill to harden chocolate.

JUMBO PEANUT BUTTER APPLE COOKIES

Makes 1½ dozen

1 cup sifted flour
1 cup sifted whole-wheat flour
2 teaspoons baking soda
1 teaspoon cinnamon
¾ teaspoon salt
⅓ cup butter, softened
⅔ cup chunk-style peanut butter
¼ cup sugar
1¾ cups brown sugar
2 eggs
1 teaspoon vanilla
1 cup rolled oats

1 cup peeled, diced apples
½ cup raisins

Mix and sift first 5 ingredients. Cream butter, peanut butter and sugars. Add eggs and vanilla; mix. Add sifted dry ingredients to creamed mixture and mix well. Stir in oats, apples and raisins. Using about ¼ cup of dough for each, shape into balls. Place on ungreased cookie sheet and flatten slightly. Bake in a 350-degree oven for about 12–15 minutes. Let stand on cookie sheet 1 minute before removing to wire cooling rack.

CHOCOLATE MACAROONS

Makes 6 dozen

1 (18.5-ounce) package devil's food cake mix with pudding
1 cup flaked coconut, toasted
½ cup regular oats, uncooked and toasted
¾ cup butter *or* margarine, melted
2 teaspoons vanilla
2 eggs, slightly beaten
6 (1.45-ounce) milk chocolate candy bars
¾ cup flaked coconut

Combine first 6 ingredients; chill 30 minutes. Drop by heaping teaspoonfuls 2 inches apart on ungreased cookie sheets. Bake at 350 degrees for 10 minutes. Immediately top each cookie with 1 chocolate square; spread to front; sprinkle cookies with coconut.

PISTACHIO PUDDING COOKIES

Makes 7 dozen

2¼ cups unsifted all-purpose flour
1 teaspoon baking soda
1 cup margarine, well-softened
¼ cup granulated white sugar
¾ cup brownulated light brown sugar
½ teaspoon vanilla

½ teaspoon almond extract
1 (4-ounce) package pistachio instant pudding (used dry)
2 eggs
1 (12-ounce) package butterscotch morsels
1 cup chopped walnuts
Few drops green food coloring, if desired

Mix flour and baking soda in medium bowl. Combine margarine, both sugars, both extracts and instant pudding powder in large mixing bowl. Beat until smooth. Beat in eggs, 1 at a time. Gradually stir in flour mixture. Stir in morsels and nuts. Batter will be very stiff; mix well with floured hands. Cover bowl; chill several hours or overnight for easier shaping. Form into smooth balls by teaspoonfuls. Place 2 inches apart on ungreased cookie sheets. Bake at 375 degrees for 8–10 minutes. Do not overbake. If desired, drizzle with confectioners' sugar icing mixed with a few drops of green food coloring.

SHORTBREAD COOKIES

Makes 4 dozen

1 cup butter *or* margarine, softened
½ cup sugar
1 teaspoon vanilla
2¼ cups flour

Preheat oven to 325 degrees. Cream together the butter and sugar, then add vanilla and blend until light and fluffy. Stir in flour until well-mixed. Place dough on a floured surface and knead until smooth (do not overwork). Place dough in refrigerator until chilled.

Remove a small portion of dough at a time so the rest will remain chilled. Roll the dough to ¼-inch thickness and cut with cookie cutters. Place cookies on an ungreased cookie sheet and bake for 12–15 minutes, or until the cookies are light brown. Remove cookies to a flat surface to cool. Sprinkle cinnamon/sugar or colored sugars on top of cookies before baking, if desired.

GRANDMA'S SUGAR-RAISIN COOKIES
Makes 6 dozen

1½ cups seedless raisins
1½ cups sugar
1 cup shortening
2 eggs
1 teaspoon vanilla
3 cups flour
1 teaspoon baking powder
1 teaspoon baking soda
½ teaspoon salt
½ teaspoon nutmeg
Sugar

Simmer raisins in water to barely cover, until water is all absorbed. Set aside to cool. Cream sugar and shortening; add eggs and vanilla; beat thoroughly. Sift together the dry ingredients, except last sugar, and add to creamed mixture. Stir in raisins. Roll dough into 1-inch balls; roll in sugar. Place balls 2 inches apart on greased cookie sheets; flatten with bottom of sugar-dipped glass. Bake at 400 degrees for 10 minutes until lightly browned.

HOLIDAY MERINGUE SQUARES
Makes 24

¼ cup butter
1 cup blanched almonds, halved
2 egg whites
¼ teaspoon cream of tartar
½ teaspoon salt
1 teaspoon vanilla
1 cup sugar
½ cup crushed soda crackers
1 cup chocolate chips
1 cup candied cherries, halved

Heat butter and almonds in small saucepan; cool to room temperature. Beat egg whites, cream of tartar, salt and vanilla until foamy. Gradually add sugar, beating until mixture is stiff.

Fold in cracker crumbs, chocolate chips and cherries. Carefully fold in nuts. Spread in well-buttered 13 x 9 x 2-inch baking pan.

Bake in a 350-degree oven for 30–35 minutes, or until golden brown. While warm cut into 2-inch bars.

HOLIDAY MERINGUE COOKIES
Makes 3 dozen

2 egg whites
Dash salt
⅛ teaspoon cream of tartar
¾ cup sugar
½ teaspoon vanilla
1 cup miniature chocolate chips
1 cup chopped walnuts
Crushed peppermint candy (3–4 tablespoons)

Beat egg whites in small mixer bo at high speed until foamy. Add crea of tartar and salt; beat to form so peaks. Add sugar, 1 tablespoon at time, beating after each addition. M ringue should be stiff and shiny. Fold vanilla, chocolate chips and nuts. Dr by teaspoonfuls onto lightly greas cookie sheets, leaving about 1½-inc space between cookies. Sprinkle wi candy. Bake 40 minutes at 250 degree Cool on wire racks. Store in airtig container.

SOFT SUGAR COOKIES

½ cup butter *or* margarine
1½ cups white sugar
2 eggs
1 teaspoon vanilla
3 cups unsifted enriched flour
1 teaspoon salt
½ teaspoon baking powder
½ teaspoon baking soda
1 cup dairy sour cream

Cream butter or margarine with sugar; add vanilla. Add eggs and beat well. Mix flour, salt, baking powder and baking soda. Add to creamed mixture alternately with sour cream. You may add chocolate chips or raisins, or sprinkle with colored sugar, or sugar and cinnamon before baking. Drop on greased and floured cookie sheets. Bake at 400 degrees for 10–12 minutes.

PEANUT BUTTER COOKIES

½ cup (1 stick) margarine
½ cup sugar
½ cup brown sugar
1 egg
½ cup peanut butter
¼ teaspoon vanilla extract
1½ cups sifted flour
1 teaspoon baking soda
¼ teaspoon salt

Cream margarine until fluffy. Add sugars and egg; beat well. Beat in peanut butter and vanilla. Sift flour, soda and salt together; add to creamed mixture. Roll dough by hand into 1-inch balls and place on a greased cookie sheet. Flatten with a fork and bake in a 350-degree oven for 10–12 minutes.

MRS. MARTIN'S COOKIES

2 cups butter
2 cups granulated sugar
2 cups brown sugar
4 eggs
2 tablespoons vanilla
4 cups flour
5 cups oatmeal
1 teaspoon salt
2 teaspoons baking powder
2 teaspoons baking soda
1 (24-ounce) package chocolate chips *plus* 8-ounce Hershey bar
3 cups chopped nuts

Cream butter and sugars; add eggs and vanilla. Combine dry ingredients and add to creamed mixture. Add chips and grated Hershey bar. Add chopped nuts. Put on cookie sheet about 2 inches apart. Bake at 375 degrees for about 6 minutes.

CITRUS SUGAR COOKIES

Makes 5 dozen

- ½ cup butter *or* margarine
- 1 cup sugar, divided
- 2 eggs
- 1 tablespoon frozen orange juice concentrate, thawed and undiluted
- 3 tablespoons grated orange rind, divided
- 2 cups flour
- 2 teaspoons baking powder

Cream butter and ½ cup sugar until light and fluffy. Add eggs, 1 at a time, beating well after each addition. Blend in orange juice and 1 tablespoon grated orange rind. Combine flour and baking powder; blend into creamed mixture. Wrap dough in waxed paper and refrigerate for 3 hours. Roll out on lightly floured surface to ¼-inch thickness. Cut with a 2-inch cookie cutter. Place on greased cookie sheet. Combine ½ cup sugar and 2 tablespoons grated orange rind; sprinkle mixture over cookies. Bake at 375 degrees for 8–10 minutes.

ALMOND HOLLY LEAVES

Makes 12 dozen

- 1 pound butter, softened
- 1 cup sifted confectioners' sugar
- 2 eggs, beaten
- 4 cups all-purpose flour
- 1 cup almonds, toasted and finely chopped

Cream butter; gradually add confectioners' sugar, beating well. Add eggs; beat well. Stir in flour and almonds. Roll dough to ¼-inch thickness on a floured surface with a floured rolling pin. Cut into holly-leaf shapes with 1½-inch cookie cutter. Place cookies on ungreased cookie sheets, and bake in 350-degree oven for 10 minutes, or until edges are golden. Cool on wire racks.

WALNUT BALLS

Makes 3 dozen

- 1½ cups walnuts
- ½ cup butter *or* margarine (1 stick)
- 1 egg, separated
- ½ cup sugar
- ¾ teaspoon grated lemon peel
- 1 cup sifted all-purpose flour
- ¼ teaspoon cinnamon
- ¼ teaspoon salt
- ⅛ teaspoon cloves
- ½ cup apricot *or* seedless raspberry jam

Grate 1 cup walnuts, or very finely chop. Chop remaining ½ cup walnuts. These may be put in blender, ¼ cup at a time, and blended. Cream butter, egg yolk, sugar and lemon peel together. Resift flour with spices and salt. Blend into creamed mixture; add grated walnuts (1 cup) and mix well. Chill dough ½ hour or longer for easier handling. Shape into small balls. Beat egg white lightly. Dip balls in egg white, then roll in chopped walnuts (½ cup). Place on greased baking sheet, and make an indentation in top of each. Fill with jam. Bake at 350 degrees for about 18 minutes. Remove to wire racks to cool.

CINNAMON-PEANUT BUTTER COOKIES

Makes 4 dozen

- 1 cup all-purpose flour
- ½ teaspoon salt
- 1 teaspoon ground cinnamon
- ½ cup butter *or* margarine, at room temperature
- ½ cup light brown sugar, packed
- ½ cup granulated sugar
- ½ cup creamy peanut butter
- 1 large egg
- 1 teaspoon vanilla extract

Preheat oven to 350 degrees. Combine flour, salt and cinnamon. Combine remaining ingredients in large bowl. Beat with electric mixer until blended. *Drop heaping teaspoons, 1½ inches apart, onto ungreased cookie sheet. Bake 10–12 minutes, just until lightly golden. Do not overbake. Remove to wire rack to cool.

*My own secret (not in original recipe)—Place the bowl of batter, covered, in refrigerator to chill overnight before baking. The batter will be firmer and easier to handle. Instead of dropping the batter by teaspoonfuls, wet your hands slightly, and pick up a teaspoonful of batter and roll it around in your hands. Place the balls on cookie sheet and flatten slightly. It makes a beautiful, perfectly rounded cookie.

UP ON THE ROOFTOP SUNDAE BARS

Makes 36 bars

- 1 (22½-ounce) package fudge brownie mix
- ½ cup very hot water
- ½ cup oil
- 1 egg

Topping:

- 1 (7-ounce) jar marshmallow creme
- 1½ cups peanuts
- 6 (1.45-ounce) package chocolate candy bars, broken into sections

Heat oven to 350 degrees. Grease bottom only of 13 x 9-inch pan. In large bowl, combine brownie mix, hot water, oil and egg; beat 50 strokes with spoon. Spread in prepared pan. Bake at 350 degrees for 30–35 minutes. *Do not overbake.* Remove from oven; immediately spread marshmallow creme over baked brownies. Sprinkle evenly with peanuts; top with candy bar sections. Return to oven for 2 minutes, or until chocolate is melted. Spread evenly to cover. Refrigerate until chocolate is firm; cut into bars.

RED APPLE DROP COOKIES
Makes 4 dozen

- 2 cups all-purpose flour
- 1 teaspoon baking soda
- ½ teaspoon allspice
- ½ teaspoon cloves
- 1 cup walnuts, finely chopped
- 1¼ cups unpared red apples, finely chopped
- 1 cup dark raisins
- ½ cup butter *or* margarine, softened
- 1½ cups brown sugar
- 1 egg, unbeaten
- ⅓ cup apple juice

Sift flour, baking soda and spices; stir in walnuts, apple and raisins; set aside. Cream butter and sugar; add egg and apple juice. Stir in flour mixture; combine thoroughly. Drop by tablespoonfuls, 2 inches apart, onto lightly greased cookie sheet. Bake at 400 degrees for 8 minutes, or until golden brown.

CHOCOLATE FUDGE COOKIES

- 1¼ cups brown sugar
- ½ cup butter
- 1 egg
- ½ cup milk
- 2 teaspoons baking powder
- 2 cups flour
- 1 teaspoon vanilla
- ¼ teaspoon salt
- 2½ squares chocolate, melted

Cream butter and add sugar gradually. Add egg and beat. Mix baking powder with salt and flour, then add vanilla to milk. Add liquid and dry ingredients alternately to egg mixture. Add dry ingredients first and last. Add melted chocolate. Drop from teaspoon onto greased baking sheets and bake 10 minutes in a moderately hot 375-degree oven.

These cookies are delicious plain or iced with chocolate frosting!

IRISH SNAPS

- 1 cup butter
- 2 cups sugar
- 1 egg
- 1 lemon *or* orange, grated rind
- 2 teaspoons nutmeg
- 1 cup water
- ¼ cup brandy *or* wine
- 5 cups flour

Cream the butter and sugar together well. Add the rest of the ingredients in the order given above. Mix well and chill 30 minutes. Roll very thin. Cut in shapes. Bake on a greased cookie sheet in a 375-degree oven for about 10 minutes. Sprinkle the cookies with green sugar before baking.

"SOFT AS A PUSSY CAT" COOKIES

- 2 cups sugar
- 1 cup butter, softened
- 3 eggs
- 1 cup sour cream
- 2 teaspoons vanilla
- 4 cups flour
- 1 teaspoon baking powder
- 1 teaspoon baking soda
  Dash salt

Preheat oven to 350 degrees. Cream sugar and butter; add eggs, sour cream and vanilla. Then add dry ingredients. Use electric mixer to mix thoroughly. Drop by tablespoons on greased sheets; bake 8 minutes. Watch closely. These cookies should be a light color. Do not brown. Remove from oven and cool. Frost with a thin icing made from confectioners' sugar and a little milk to moisten. Decorate, if desired, with ground nuts, coconut or candy sprinkles.

ZUCCHINI COOKIES

- 1 cup grated zucchini
- 1 cup sugar
- ½ cup shortening *or* margarine
- 1 egg
- 2 cups flour
- 1 teaspoon ground cinnamon
- ½ teaspoon ground nutmeg
- ¾ teaspoon baking powder
- ½ teaspoon baking soda
- ¾ cup crushed pineapple, drained
- 1 cup chopped nuts
- 1 cup raisins

Cream sugar, shortening and egg. Add grated zucchini and crushed pineapple. Stir in dry ingredients; stir in nuts and raisins. On greased cookie sheet, drop by rounded teaspoonfuls. Bake at 375 degrees for 15 minutes, or until no imprint is left when you press top of cookie lightly. These do not brown on top. While still warm, glaze with a thin confectioners' sugar, canned milk and vanilla frosting.

Note: Dough will keep well for a week if covered and refrigerated.

SPECIAL SUGAR COOKIES

- ½ cup confectioners' sugar
- ½ cup white sugar
- 1 stick butter, softened
- ½ cup vegetable oil
- ½ teaspoon vanilla
- 2 cups all-purpose flour, plus 2 tablespoons
- 1 egg, beaten
- ½ teaspoon soda
- ½ teaspoon salt
- ½ teaspoon cream of tartar

Cream two sugars, butter and oil; add beaten egg and vanilla; beat until fluffy. Sift dry ingredients; add to first mixture. Drop by teaspoonfuls onto cookie sheet. Dip a glass bottom into sugar and press cookies down lightly. Bake at 375 degrees for 10 minutes.

CREAM CHEESE CHOCOLATE CHIP COOKIES

Makes 4 dozen

- 1 cup margarine
- 1 cup sugar
- 1 (3-ounce) package cream cheese
- 2 eggs
- 1 teaspoon vanilla
- ½ teaspoon lemon extract
- ½ cups flour
- 1 teaspoon baking powder
- ½ teaspoon baking soda
- 1 cup coarsely chopped pecans *or* walnuts
- 1 cup semisweet chocolate pieces

Cream margarine, then add sugar, [bea]ting until smooth and fluffy. Add [cre]am cheese; blend in eggs, vanilla, [and] lemon extract. Mix flour, baking [pow]der and baking soda together; stir [in]to cream cheese mixture. Add nuts [and] chocolate pieces. Drop by teaspoon [on] lightly greased cookie sheet. Bake at [35]0 degrees for 12–15 minutes.

ALMOND MACAROONS

Makes 1½ dozen

- 1 egg white
- ¼ teaspoon salt
- ¾ cup confectioners' sugar
- 1 cup finely minced almonds *or*
- 1 cup finely grated coconut
- ½ teaspoon almond extract

Lightly grease a cookie sheet. Pre[he]at oven to 250 degrees. Beat egg [wh]ite with salt until stiff. Gradually [ad]d ⅔ cup sugar, beating well. Fold in [re]maining sugar, nuts or coconut. Add [fla]voring, folding in. Beat well. Drop [by] teaspoonfuls on prepared sheet and [ba]ke for 25 minutes in 250-degree oven. [St]ore in a covered container for 1 week [to] develop best flavor.

CHERRY CHIP COOKIES

- 1 cup sugar
- ¾ cup butter, softened
- ¼ cup milk
- 1 teaspoon almond extract
- 1 cup cherry chips
- 1 egg
- 2 cups flour
- 1 teaspoon baking powder
- ¾ teaspoon salt
- ½ cup chopped nuts

Heat oven to 350 degrees. In large bowl cream butter and sugar. Add egg and extract; mix well. In small bowl combine flour, salt and baking powder. Add milk to creamed mixture; mix well. Add flour mixture to creamed mixture; mix well. Stir in chips and nuts. Drop by teaspoonfuls onto cookie sheets. Bake 9–12 minutes, or until lightly browned.

ORANGE CHOCOLATE CRUNCH

- 2 cups fresh orange sections (6 oranges)
- ½ cup orange juice
- 2 eggs
- 1 teaspoon vanilla
- ¼ teaspoon almond extract
- 1⅔ cups flour
- 1 cup sugar
- 1 teaspoon baking powder
- ½ teaspoon baking soda
- ½ teaspoon salt
- ½ cup brown sugar
- 1 cup chopped nuts
- 6 ounces semisweet chocolate chips

Peel and section oranges; cut into small pieces. Combine oranges and juice; add to beaten eggs. Add extract and mix in dry ingredients. Put into a floured and greased 9 x 13-inch pan. Combine brown sugar, nuts and chips; sprinkle over top. Bake at 350 degrees for 40–50 minutes.

FRUITCAKE BARS

- 1 cup brown sugar, packed
- 1¼ cups water
- ⅓ cup shortening
- 2 cups raisins
- 2 cups flour
- 1 teaspoon salt
- 1 teaspoon soda
- 1 teaspoon baking powder
- ½ teaspoon nutmeg
- 1 teaspoon cloves
- 2 teaspoons cinnamon
- ½ cup chopped nuts

Heat oven to 350 degrees. Mix brown sugar, water, shortening and raisins in saucepan. Bring to a boil; remove from heat and cool. Sift flour; blend in dry ingredients; stir into cooled mixture. Mix in nuts. Spread dough evenly in greased pan, 13 x 9 x 2 inches. Bake at 350 degrees for 35–40 minutes, or until no imprint remains when touched. Cool and cut into 2 x 2½-inch bars. Many people like "fruitless" fruitcake; they should love these bars.

PEANUT BUTTER COOKIES

- 2 cups sifted all-purpose flour
- 2 teaspoons baking powder
- ½ teaspoon salt
- ⅔ cup peanut butter
- 1 egg, slightly beaten
- 1½ cups (1 can) sweetened condensed milk
- 1 teaspoon vanilla
- ½ cup finely chopped nut meats (optional)

Sift blended dry ingredients. In large mixing bowl, blend peanut butter and egg. Stir in half of the condensed milk; blend in half of the dry ingredients. Repeat; stir in vanilla and nuts. Drop by tablespoon about 2 inches apart onto well-greased cookie sheet. Bake at 350 degrees for 10–12 minutes, or until cookie edges are lightly browned. Remove at once from cookie sheet.

PUMPKIN-FILLED COOKIES

Filling:
- 1 cup pumpkin
- ½ cup sugar
- ½ teaspoon cinnamon
- ½ teaspoon ginger
- ¼ teaspoon nutmeg
- ¼ teaspoon salt

Blend ingredients together. Set aside.

Cookies:
- 3 cups flour
- 1 teaspoon salt
- ½ teaspoon baking soda
- ½ cup brown sugar
- ¾ cup soft shortening
- 1 egg
- ¼ cup molasses
- 1 cup rolled oats

Mix and sift together flour, salt and baking soda. Combine sugar, shortening, egg and molasses; mix well. Add dry ingredients to molasses mixture. Add oats. Chill 30 minutes. Roll out ⅛ inch thick; place 1 tablespoon filling on 1 cookie and cover with second cookie. Press together; slit top. Bake 375 degrees for 15 minutes.

COFFEE CHOCOLATE CHUNK COOKIES
Makes 3 dozen

- ½ cup shortening
- ¼ cup, plus 2 tablespoons sugar
- ¼ cup, plus 2 tablespoons brown sugar
- 1 tablespoon instant coffee granules
- 1 egg
- ½ teaspoon vanilla extract
- ½ teaspoon water
- 1⅛ cups flour
- ½ teaspoon baking soda
- ½ teaspoon salt
- 1 (4-ounce) package Baker's German Sweet Chocolate

Coarsely chop chocolate; set aside. Cream first 4 ingredients in large bowl at medium speed of electric mixer. Add egg, vanilla and water. Beat well. Combine dry ingredients (except chocolate); add to creamed mixture. Combine well. Stir in chocolate. Drop by teaspoon onto greased baking sheets. Flatten slightly with fork. Bake at 350 degrees for 8–10 minutes. Remove to wire racks to cool.

JAM SANDWICH COOKIES
Makes 24 filled cookies

- ½ cup butter
- ½ cup packed brown sugar
- ¼ cup honey
- 1 egg
- ½ teaspoon vanilla
- 1¾ cups all-purpose flour
- 1 teaspoon baking soda
- ¼ teaspoon salt
- Raspberry or other jam

Cream together butter, brown sug and honey. Beat in egg and vanil. Combine flour, baking soda and sa Blend flour mixture into creamed mi ture. Chill dough for 30 minutes. Sha dough into small balls (about 1 inch diameter). Place on lightly greas baking sheets. Flatten balls slightly wi bottom of glass dipped in flour. Bake 350 degrees for 8–10 minutes, or un golden. Cool on baking sheet for fe minutes; remove to wire racks to co completely. When cool, put together pairs filled with jam. If desired, squee: filled cookies slightly until jam is vi ible on edges. Roll edges in cocon Especially pretty with red jam a coconut.

PECAN SANDIES
Makes 4 dozen

- ¼ cup soft margarine
- 1 (8-ounce) package softened cream cheese
- 1 egg
- 1 teaspoon pecan nut flavoring
- 1 (2-layer size) package dry cake mix
- 1 cup chopped pecans

Cream softened margarine and cream cheese. Add egg and flavoring. Beat well. Add dry cake mix; then add chopped pecans. Drop by teaspoonfuls onto greased cookie sheet. Bake in preheated 350-degree oven for 12 minutes, or until browned and done.

COCONUT ALMOND FUDGE BARS
Makes 24 bars

- 2 cups (1 package) fudge cake mix
- 1 package coconut almond frosting mix
- 1 cup applesauce
- 1 egg

In large mixing bowl, combine cake mix, frosting mix, applesauce and egg. Mix well. Grease and flour bottom and sides of 13 x 9-inch pan. Bake at 350 degrees for 30 minutes. Cool 15 minutes and cut into bars.

POTATO CHIP COOKIES
Makes 2 dozen

- 1 cup margarine (2 sticks)
- ½ cup sugar
- 1 teaspoon vanilla
- 1 cup crushed potato chips
- 1 cup all-purpose flour

Preheat oven to 350 degrees. Mi margarine, sugar and vanilla together Blend well. Add potato chips and stir i flour. Form small balls from mixture and place on an ungreased cookie sheet Press balls flat with the bottom of a glass that has been dipped in sugar. Bake 16–18 minutes, or until lightly browned.

BLACK WALNUT CHOCOLATE DROP COOKIES

Makes 4 dozen

1¾ cups sifted flour
½ teaspoon baking soda
1 teaspoon baking powder
¼ teaspoon salt
1 cup chopped black walnuts
½ cup butter
1¼ cups brown sugar, sifted and packed
1 egg
2 ounces unsweetened chocolate, melted and cooled
1 teaspoon vanilla extract
½ cup milk

Mix and sift flour, soda, baking powder and salt; add nuts and mix. Cream butter; add sugar gradually and cream until fluffy. Add well-beaten egg and chocolate. Add extract to milk. Add dry mixture alternately with milk to creamed mixture, mixing just enough for each addition to combine ingredients. Drop by spoonfuls on ungreased baking sheets. Bake in preheated 375-degree oven for about 12 minutes. When cool, spread with Chocolate Frosting.

Chocolate Frosting:
1½ ounces unsweetened chocolate, melted
1 egg yolk
3 tablespoons light cream
1¼ cups sifted confectioners' sugar

Combine chocolate, slightly beaten egg yolk and cream; add sugar and mix well.

BUTTERSCOTCH COCONUT COOKIES

2 cups flour
½ teaspoon soda
½ teaspoon salt
½ cup margarine, softened
½ cup granulated sugar
½ cup packed brown sugar

2 eggs
1 teaspoon vanilla
1 cup butterscotch chips
½ cup chopped pecans
2½ cups coconut
Pecan halves (if desired)
Candied cherry halves (if desired)

Preheat oven to 375 degrees. Combine in a small bowl the flour, soda and salt; set aside. Using larger bowl, combine softened margarine and both sugars; beat until very light and fluffy. Beat in eggs (one at a time) and vanilla. Add flour mixture; mix well. Stir in butterscotch chips and nuts. Drop dough into coconut. With lightly floured or greased hand, roll to coat with coconut. Form into balls. Bake at 375 degrees on ungreased cookie sheet for 10–12 minutes. Garnish each cookie with pecan half before baking if desired or place half candied cherry on each cookie as you remove from oven. Remove to cooling rack and allow to cool.

REESE'S CUP TARTS

Makes 4–5 dozen

½ cup butter
½ cup peanut butter
½ cup granulated sugar
½ cup brown sugar
1 egg
1 teaspoon vanilla
1½ cups all-purpose flour
1 teaspoon soda
½ teaspoon salt
Reese's miniature peanut-butter cups—foil removed

Cream butters and sugars thoroughly. Add egg and vanilla. Beat well. Combine flour, soda and salt. Add to creamed mixture. Take rounded teaspoons of dough and place in greased miniature muffin pans. Bake at 350 degrees for 8–10 minutes, or until cookie puffs up and is barely done. Remove from oven and immediately push a peanut-butter cup into each cookie-filled muffin cup. The cookies will deflate and form a tart shell around the peanut butter cup. Let cool in pan, then refrigerate until shine leaves the chocolate. Gently lift each tart out with tip of sharp knife.

MOLASSES CRISPS

Makes 4 dozen

¾ cup margarine *or* butter
1 cup brown sugar, packed
1 egg
⅓ cup dark molasses
1 cup non-fat dry milk powder
2½ cups unsifted rye flour
2 teaspoons baking soda
1 teaspoon cinnamon
1 teaspoon nutmeg
1 teaspoon ginger
¼ teaspoon salt
1 cup finely chopped peanuts

In large mixing bowl, cream butter and sugar until light and fluffy; beat in egg and molasses.

Sift together powdered milk, flour, soda, spices and salt. Add to mixture in bowl; stir in nuts.

Shape dough into 1¼-inch balls. Roll in granulated sugar (or shake in bag of sugar). Place 2 inches apart on lightly greased baking sheets. Bake in a 375-degree oven for 10–12 minutes. Cool on wire rack.

SANTA'S CHRISTMAS COOKIES

Makes 48 cookies

2 eggs
1½ cups sugar
1 cup margarine
1 teaspoon cinnamon
1 teaspoon salt
1 teaspoon baking soda
2½ cups flour
½ pound candied red cherries, chopped
½ pound candied green cherries, chopped
2 pounds dates, chopped
1 pound pecans, chopped

Combine and mix eggs, sugar and margarine. Combine cinnamon, salt, soda and flour. Mix well. Stir in fruits and nuts. Drop on an *ungreased* cookie sheet. Bake in a 350-degree oven for 15 minutes.

CHOCO SURPRISE COOKIES

Makes 8 dozen

- 1 cup all-purpose flour
- 1 teaspoon baking powder
- 1 teaspoon cinnamon
- 1 cup peanut butter (creamy)
- ½ cup margarine, softened
- 1 cup firmly packed brown sugar
- 2 eggs, well-beaten
- 1 (16-ounce) package milk chocolate stars (or Hershey Kisses with tips cut off) Confectioners' sugar

Combine first 3 ingredients and set aside. Combine and cream until fluffy, the peanut butter, margarine, brown sugar and eggs. Add dry ingredients. Cover dough; chill 1 hour or overnight.

Shape 1 teaspoon dough around star; place on lightly greased cookie sheet or on Teflon cookie sheet. Bake at 350 degrees for 9–11 minutes, or until lightly browned. Cool slightly on wire racks; then roll in confectioners' sugar. Cool completely before storing.

ICED PEANUT BUTTER COOKIES

- ½ cup margarine
- ½ cup sugar
- ½ cup brown sugar
- 2 eggs
- ⅓ cup peanut butter
- ½ teaspoon baking soda
- ¼ teaspoon salt
- ½ teaspoon vanilla
- 1 cup flour
- 1 cup rolled oats
- 1 cup chocolate chips

Mix together margarine, sugar and brown sugar. Blend in eggs, peanut butter, baking soda, vanilla, flour, salt and rolled oats. Spread in a greased 13 x 9 x 2-inch pan and bake at 350 degrees for 20 minutes. As soon as the pan is removed from the oven, sprinkle chocolate bits on the top. Return to oven for a few minutes to melt the chocolate; remove again, spreading chocolate evenly; allow to cool.

Icing:
- ¼ cup peanut butter
- ½ cup confectioners' sugar
- Milk (2–4 teaspoons)

Combine peanut butter and confectioners' sugar. Moisten with milk until consistency to spread. Ice cooled cookies.

ALMOND SNOWBALL COOKIES

Makes 5 dozen

- ½ cup butter or margarine
- ¼ cup evaporated milk
- ½ teaspoon grated lemon rind
- 1¾ cups sifted flour
- ¾ cup sugar
- ½ teaspoon salt
- 1 cup finely chopped almonds
- 6 tablespoons confectioners' sugar
- ½ pound candied cherries

Cream butter; beat in milk, a little at a time, until all is blended with butter. Add lemon rind. Sift flour with sugar and salt; gradually add to butter mixture. Add nuts; mix well. Pinch off pieces of dough, about a teaspoon. Flatten dough in palm of hand. Place a cherry on dough; pinch dough up around cherry completely. Roll between palms. Place on lightly greased, floured cookie sheet. Bake at 375 degrees for 12 minutes. Roll in confectioners' sugar while still warm.

CANTON ALMOND COOKIES

Makes 5 dozen

- 3 cups all-purpose flour
- 1 cup sugar
- ¼ teaspoon salt
- ½ teaspoon baking soda
- 1 cup shortening, room temperature
- 1 egg, lightly beaten
- ¼ teaspoon vanilla extract
- ½ teaspoon almond extract
- 1 cup almonds, blanched and split

Mix flour, sugar, salt and baking soda. Add shortening; cut in until mixture resembles cornmeal. Add egg, vanilla extract and almond extract. Mix until egg is absorbed and mixture smooth. Shape into ¾-inch balls; place on ungreased baking sheet. Flatten each cookie with a flour-dipped fork; press an almond half into the center. Bake at 350 degrees for 20 minutes, or until pale golden brown. Remove from baking sheet; cool on rack.

OATMEAL-RAISIN COOKIES

- 3 eggs, well-beaten
- 1 cup raisins
- 1 teaspoon vanilla
- 1 cup shortening
- 1 cup brown sugar
- 1 cup granulated sugar
- 2½ cups flour
- 1 teaspoon salt
- 2 teaspoons soda
- 1 teaspoon cinnamon
- 2 cups oatmeal
- ½ cup chopped nuts

Combine eggs, raisins and vanilla. Let mixture stand for 1 hour or more. Thoroughly cream together shortening, brown and white sugars. Sift flour, salt, soda and cinnamon. Mix well; blend in egg/raisin mixture, oats and nuts. (Dough will be very stiff.) Roll the dough into balls, the size of a large walnut; roll the balls in a cinnamon-sugar mixture (1 teaspoon cinnamon mixed with 1 cup sugar). Place on cookie sheet about 3 inches apart. Bake at 350 degrees for 10–12 minutes, or until lightly browned. Remove from oven and let cool a few minutes before removing from cookie sheet. These will keep several weeks, stored in a tightly covered container. Put waxed paper between layers of cookies.

PECAN BARS

1 stick margarine
1¼ cups white flour
2 eggs, beaten
1 cup light brown sugar
½ cup chopped pecans
½ cup shredded coconut
½ cup chopped and drained maraschino cherries
1 tablespoon Grape Nuts cereal
2 tablespoons white flour
½ teaspoon baking powder
1 teaspoon almond extract

In large mixer bowl, make a crumb mixture of margarine and flour. Pat down firmly into non-stick 9 x 13-inch pan. Bake for 10 minutes in 350-degree oven. Remove from oven.

Mix together all other ingredients and spread over prepared base. Return to oven and bake at 350 degrees for 20 minutes. Cool in pan, then cut into bars with sharp knife.

JINGLE-JAM MERINGUES
Makes 3 dozen

⅔ cup margarine
2 egg yolks, unbeaten
1 teaspoon vanilla
2 teaspoons baking powder
½ cup thick raspberry jam
1 cup sugar
2 tablespoons milk
2½ cups flour, sifted
⅛ teaspoon salt

Meringue Frosting:
2 egg whites
½ cup plus 2 tablespoons sugar
⅔ cup chopped pecans or walnuts

Cream together margarine and sugar until light and fluffy. Beat in egg yolks, milk and vanilla. Sift flour, baking powder and salt together and stir into creamed mixture; mix thoroughly. Make balls of heaping teaspoonfuls of mixture. Place on greased baking sheet. Flatten balls to ¼-inch thickness; top

each with ½ teaspoon jam. Beat egg whites until stiff, adding sugar gradually; fold in nuts. Spread meringue on cookies, completely covering the jam. Bake at 350 degrees for 15 minutes.

These cookies are a little different and very delicious. Any flavor jam can be used. Instead of the jam, you might like to use peanut butter and jam or jelly mixed for Goobers.

TOFFEE COOKIES
Makes 3 dozen

1½ cups flour
1 teaspoon baking powder
½ teaspoon salt
½ cup margarine
¾ cup packed brown sugar
1 egg
1 teaspoon vanilla
1 cup finely chopped Heath bars
⅓ cup coarsely chopped pecans

Mix egg, sugar, margarine and vanilla until smooth and creamy. Stir in dry ingredients. Blend in chopped candy bars and nuts. Drop by spoonfuls, 2 inches apart, on greased cookie sheet. Bake at 350 degrees for 12–15 minutes. Remove from cookie sheet. A great crunchy cookie!!

WALNUT MACAROONS

1 egg white
⅔ cup white sugar
⅛ teaspoon salt
¼ teaspoon almond extract
⅓ cup very finely chopped walnuts

Beat egg white very stiff, adding sugar slowly. Add salt very gradually while beating; still beating, add extract and chopped nuts. Drop by teaspoonfuls onto cookie sheet (Teflon or non-stick sheet if possible). Bake at 325 degrees for 15 minutes. Cool on rack.

HOLIDAY FRUITCAKE BARS
Makes 48

½ cup margarine or butter
1 package nut quick bread mix
1 cup coconut
1 (16-ounce) package (2 cups) mixed candied fruit, diced
1 cup chopped dates
1 cup coarsely chopped nuts
1 (14-ounce) can sweetened condensed milk (not evaporated)

Heat oven to 350 degrees. Melt margarine in a 15 x 10 x 1-inch jelly roll pan. Sprinkle evenly with dry quick bread mix. Sprinkle with coconut. Distribute candied fruit evenly over coconut. Distribute dates over candied fruit. Sprinkle with nuts. Press mixture lightly. Pour condensed milk over top, spreading evenly. Bake at 350 degrees for 20–30 minutes, or until set and lightly browned. Cool 30 minutes. While slightly warm, cut into bars and remove from pan. Cool completely.

BROWN SUGAR MACAROONS
Makes 2 dozen

1 fresh egg white, slightly beaten
1 cup brown sugar
1 cup chopped pecans, finely chopped
¼ teaspoon salt
1 teaspoon vanilla

Add sugar to beaten egg white. Then add remaining ingredients; mix. Drop in very small amounts onto a greased cookie sheet and bake in a 350-degree oven until a medium-brown color. Cool on the cookie sheet. ¼ cup grated coconut may be added for variety.

GINGERSNAPS

2 cups flour
1 tablespoon ground ginger
2 teaspoons baking soda
1 teaspoon cinnamon
½ teaspoon salt
¾ cup shortening
1 cup sugar
1 egg
¼ cup molasses

Measure flour, ginger, soda, cinnamon and salt; put aside. Cream shortening until soft. Gradually add sugar, creaming until light and fluffy. Beat in egg and molasses. Add dry ingredients over creamed mixture; blend well. Form teaspoonfuls of dough into small balls by rolling them lightly between palms of hands. Roll dough balls in granulated sugar to cover entire surface. Place 2 inches apart on ungreased cookie sheet. Bake at 350 degrees for 12–15 minutes until tops are crackly and cookies are brown.

PRIDE OF OHIO COOKIES

1 cup brown sugar
1 cup white sugar
1 cup shortening
1 cup flour
2 eggs
1 cup coconut
1 cup nut meats, chopped
1 teaspoon vanilla
1 teaspoon soda
1 teaspoon baking powder
½ teaspoon salt
3 cups quick rolled oats

Beat eggs in mixing bowl; add sugars and softened shortening. Blend well. Stir in coconut, nuts and vanilla. Sift flour and measure, then add soda, baking powder and salt, then sift again. Combine with other mixture. Stir in rolled oats; mix thoroughly by hand. Roll in small balls the size of a walnut and place on ungreased cookie sheet. Bake at 375 degrees for about 9 minutes, or until nicely browned.

CHERRY-NUT MACAROONS
Makes 4 dozen

1 (7-ounce) package flaked coconut (about 2⅔ cups)
2 cups fresh bread crumbs (about 4 slices)
1 (14-ounce) can sweetened condensed milk (*not* evaporated milk)
1 cup coarsely chopped nuts
48 maraschino cherries (about 2 cups), drained, reserving 2 tablespoons syrup

Preheat oven to 350 degrees. In large bowl, combine coconut and bread crumbs; stir in sweetened condensed milk, nuts and reserved syrup. Mix well. Drop by rounded teaspoonfuls onto generously greased baking sheets; gently press a cherry (can use halves) into center of each macaroon. Bake 10–12 minutes, or until lightly browned. Immediately remove from baking sheets. Cool on wire racks. Store loosely covered at room temperature.

OATS AND PEANUT COOKIES

1 cup shortening
¾ cup sugar
¾ cup dark brown sugar
2 eggs
2 teaspoons hot water
2 cups oats
1¼ cups flour
1 teaspoon baking soda
½ teaspoon salt
½ cup raisins
1 (8-ounce) package candy-coated chocolate pieces with peanuts

Cream shortening and sugars. Add eggs and water, beating well. Combine oats, flour, soda and salt. Add to creamed mixture, mixing well. Stir in raisins and candy. Drop by teaspoonfuls onto greased cookie sheets. Bake at 350 degrees for 9–10 minutes until lightly browned. Cool slightly before removing from sheets.

CANDY CANE COOKIES
Makes 30

¾ cup butter *or* margarine, softened
¾ cup sugar
1 egg
½ teaspoon vanilla
½ teaspoon peppermint extract
2 cups flour
½ teaspoon salt
¼ teaspoon baking powder
⅓ cup flaked coconut
1 teaspoon red food coloring

Cream butter and sugar; beat in egg, vanilla and extract. Sift flour with salt and baking powder; stir into creamed mixture. Divide dough in half. Stir coconut into 1 portion; blend food coloring into remaining dough. Cover; chill doughs for 10 minutes.

Divide each dough into 30 balls; keep half of each dough chilled until ready to use. With hands, roll each ball into 5-inch rope. For each cane, pinch together 1 end of red rope and 1 end of white rope; twist ropes together. Pinch together remaining ends. Place on ungreased cookie sheet; curve to form cane. Leave space between canes, as they expand during baking. Repeat with remaining balls. Bake at 375 degrees for 10 minutes.

CORNFLAKE MACAROONS
Makes 2½ dozen

3 egg whites
1 cup sugar
¼ teaspoon almond extract
¼ teaspoon vanilla extract
1½ cups flaked coconut
3 cups cornflakes

Beat egg whites until stiff but not dry; gradually add sugar. Add flavorings; fold in coconut and cornflakes. Drop by teaspoonfuls onto well-greased cookie sheets. Bake at 300 degrees for about 20 minutes. Remove from cookie sheet as soon as removed from oven.

BASIC BUTTER COOKIES
Makes 30 cookies

- 1 cup all-purpose flour
- ½ cup cornstarch
- ½ cup confectioners' sugar
- ¾ cup (1½ sticks) real butter, room temperature
- ½ cup coarsely chopped walnuts

Preheat oven to 300 degrees. Sift first 3 ingredients into large bowl. Add butter and mix well. Stir in walnuts. Drop by teaspoonfuls onto baking sheets. Bake until cookies are lightly golden, about 20–25 minutes.

Note: Real butter is the secret of these buttery-tasting cookies.

SUGAR COOKIES

- 1 cup confectioners' sugar
- 1 cup white sugar
- 1 cup butter (do not substitute margarine)
- 1 cup shortening
- 2 eggs
- 1½ teaspoons vanilla
- 1½ teaspoons salt
- 1½ teaspoons cream of tartar
- 1½ teaspoons soda
- 4¼ cups sifted flour

Blend first 4 ingredients until light and creamy. Add eggs and vanilla. Sift dry ingredients and add to creamed mixture; mix until well-blended. Form into balls. Put on greased cookie sheets. Flatten with glass dipped in sugar. Bake in 350-degree oven for 10 minutes.

PINEAPPLE-COCONUT COOKIES
Makes 3½ dozen

- ½ cup sugar
- ¼ cup brown sugar
- ¼ cup margarine
- ¼ cup shortening
- 1 egg
- 1 teaspoon vanilla
- 1¼ cups flour
- ¾ teaspoon salt
- ½ teaspoon soda
- ¼ teaspoon ginger
- 1 cup coconut
- ½ cup crushed pineapple, well-drained
- ½ cup chopped nuts

Cream first 6 ingredients together until light and fluffy. Stir dry ingredients together and beat into creamy mixture. Stir in coconut, pineapple and nuts. Drop teaspoonfuls 2 inches apart on a greased cookie sheet. Bake at 375 degrees for 8–10 minutes. Let stand 30 seconds on sheet after removing from oven, then cool on wire racks.

CARROT CHEDDAR COOKIES

- 1½ cups oats (quick *or* old-fashioned), uncooked
- 1 cup mild cheddar cheese (4 ounces), shredded
- 1 cup shredded carrots (or canned, no juice)
- ¾ cup all-purpose flour
- ⅔ cup soft butter *or* margarine
- ⅓ cup firmly packed brown sugar
- 1 egg, beaten
- ½ cup small raisins *or* chopped dates
- 1 teaspoon cinnamon
- 1 teaspoon vanilla
- ½ teaspoon salt
- ¼ teaspoon soda
- ⅛ teaspoon cloves

Combine all ingredients and mix well. Drop by rounded tablespoonfuls onto ungreased cookie sheet and flatten. Bake for 16–18 minutes at 350–375 degrees. Store tightly covered.

The small amount of sugar is more nutritious and permits those on low-calorie diets to enjoy.

GIANT OATMEAL PEANUT BUTTER CHIP COOKIES
Makes 2 dozen

- 1 cup butter *or* margarine
- 1 cup white sugar
- 1 cup brown sugar
- 2 eggs
- 1 teaspoon vanilla
- ½ teaspoon orange extract
- 1½ cups all-purpose flour
- ½ teaspoon salt
- ½ teaspoon baking soda
- 2 teaspoons cinnamon
- 2 teaspoons allspice
- 2 teaspoons cloves
- 1 teaspoon ginger
- 1 cup peanut butter chips
- ½ cup chopped dry-roasted peanuts
- 3 cups quick-cooking oats

In large bowl, cream butter and both sugars until light and fluffy. Beat in eggs, vanilla and orange extract. Sift together flour, salt, soda and spices. Stir into butter mixture. Stir in peanut butter chips, chopped peanuts and oats. Let dough sit at room temperature for 2 hours. Drop about ¼ cup dough at a time onto greased cookie sheets. Flatten dough slightly with back of spoon. Bake at 375 degrees for 10 minutes. Do not overbake. Let cool on cookie sheets 5 minutes before removing with spatula.

FUN RUM COOKIES
Makes 5 dozen

- 2 cups graham cracker crumbs
- 2 cups chopped walnuts *or* pecans
- 1½ to 2 teaspoons rum extract
- 1 can ready-to-spread vanilla *or* chocolate fudge frosting
  Confectioners' sugar

Combine all ingredients, except confectioners' sugar, in large bowl. Stir and blend well. Using 1 teaspoon at a time, form into a ball in palm of hands. Roll in confectioners' sugar. Store in tightly covered jar.

CRUNCHY OATMEAL COOKIES

Makes 4 dozen

- 1 cup flour
- 2 teaspoons baking soda
- 1 teaspoon baking powder
- ½ teaspoon salt
- 1 cup shortening
- 2 cups cornflakes
- 1 cup sugar
- 1 cup brown sugar, packed
- 2 eggs
- 1 teaspoon vanilla extract
- 2 cups uncooked, quick-cooking oats

Combine flour, soda, baking powder and salt. Set aside. In large bowl, cream shortening and sugars; beat in eggs and vanilla. Add flour mixture, mixing well. Stir in oats and cornflakes. Drop by heaping tablespoonfuls onto lightly greased cookie sheets. Bake at 325 degrees for 12–14 minutes.

Cool for 2 minutes on cookie sheet; remove to wire racks and cool completely.

FRUIT-N-HONEY COOKIES

- ¼ cup brown sugar
- ½ cup honey
- ½ cup butter *or* margarine
- 2 eggs
- 1½ cups flour
- ½ teaspoon salt
- ½ teaspoon baking soda
- 1 teaspoon cinnamon
- ½ cup milk
- ½ cup raisins
- ½ cup ground nuts
- ¼ cup coconut

Cream brown sugar, honey and butter together in a mixing bowl. Add eggs. Sift together dry ingredients. Add to creamed mixture alternately with milk. Mix well. Stir in raisins, nuts and coconut. Drop by teaspoonfuls onto greased cookie sheet. Bake at 400 degrees for 6–8 minutes.

BUTTER SHAMROCKS

- ½ cup butter
- 1 cup sugar
- 2 eggs, well-beaten
- 1 tablespoon milk
- ½ teaspoon salt
- 2 teaspoons baking powder
- 1 teaspoon vanilla
- 1½ cups flour
- 1 egg white
- Green sugar

Cream the butter; add the sugar, eggs, milk and 1 cup of the flour, sifted with the baking powder and salt. Add enough flour to make the dough easy to roll. Add the vanilla. Chill dough. Roll thin. Cut with a shamrock cutter. Brush with egg white and sprinkle with green sugar. Bake on a greased cookie sheet in a 350-degree oven for 10 minutes. Ovens vary, so watch closely so they do not get too brown. Green sugar may be purchased, or make it by mixing granulated sugar with green coloring. Let dry before using.

CANDLESTICK BARS

- 1 (14-ounce) package gingerbread mix
- 1 (8-ounce) can applesauce
- ½ cup raisins
- 1 (4-ounce) jar chopped mixed candied fruits and peels
- 1 (14-ounce) package white creamy frosting mix
- 2 tablespoons lemon juice

Combine gingerbread mix and applesauce; beat 2 minutes at medium speed or 2 minutes with spoon. Stir in raisins, fruits and peels. Spread in 15½ x 10½ x 1-inch jelly roll pan. Bake at 375 degrees for 15 minutes. Prepare frosting and add lemon juice, substituting lemon juice for half the liquid. Spread on cooled bars. Decorate with red and yellow gumdrops to look like a candle. Use red candy for candle and yellow candy for flame.

OLD-FASHIONED SOFT MOLASSES COOKIES

Makes 2 dozen

- 2½ cups sifted all-purpose flour
- 2 teaspoons soda
- 1 teaspoon cinnamon
- 1 teaspoon ginger
- 1 egg, unbeaten
- ½ cup water
- ¼ teaspoon salt
- ½ cup shortening
- ½ cup sugar
- ½ cup molasses

Sift together flour, soda, cinnamon, ginger and salt. Cream shortening and sugar until light and fluffy. Add egg and molasses; mix well.

Add dry ingredients to the mixture alternately with water, beginning and ending with dry ingredients.

Drop heaping teaspoonfuls on ungreased baking sheet. Bake in moderate 350-degree oven for about 8 minutes.

SOUR CREAM NUTMEG COOKIES

Makes 3 dozen

- 2 cups sifted flour
- 1 teaspoon nutmeg
- ½ teaspoon baking soda
- 2 teaspoons baking powder
- ¼ teaspoon salt
- ½ cup shortening
- 1 cup sugar
- 1 egg
- ½ cup sour cream
- ½ cup chopped nuts

Sift flour, nutmeg, baking soda, baking powder and salt together. Cream shortening and sugar until light and fluffy. Add egg; beat well. Add sour cream and sifted dry ingredients alternately, beating well after each addition. Add nuts. Drop by teaspoonfuls 2 inches apart onto well-greased baking sheets.

Bake in moderate oven 375 degrees for 10–12 minutes.

SOUR CREAM DATE DREAMS

¼ cup shortening
¾ cup brown sugar
½ teaspoon vanilla
1 egg, beaten
1¼ cups flour
½ teaspoon soda
¼ teaspoon baking powder
⅔ cup dates, chopped
   Walnut halves
¼ teaspoon salt
¼ teaspoon cinnamon
⅛ teaspoon nutmeg
½ cup sour cream

Cream together shortening, sugar and vanilla. Add egg; mix well. Sift together dry ingredients and add to shortening mixture alternately with sour cream. Stir in dates.

Drop by teaspoonfuls onto greased cookie sheet. Top each with a walnut half and bake at 400 degrees for about 8–10 minutes.

HAWAIIAN OATMEAL COOKIES

Makes 3 dozen

1 cup flour
1 teaspoon baking powder
1 teaspoon baking soda
¾ teaspoon salt
½ cup shortening
½ cup granulated sugar
½ cup brown sugar, packed
1 egg
½ teaspoon vanilla
1 cup rolled oats
1 cup shredded coconut

Sift together flour, baking powder, baking soda and salt; set aside. Cream shortening and sugars until light and fluffy; add egg; mix well. Add vanilla, then flour mixture. Add oats and coconut; mix until well-blended. Shape into small walnut-size balls; place on ungreased cookie sheets. Bake at 350 degrees about 12–15 minutes, or until golden.

CLOUD 9 COOKIES

Makes 3 dozen

2 egg whites, stiffly beaten
⅔ cup sugar
⅛ teaspoon salt
1 cup chopped almonds
1 cup miniature chocolate chips

Preheat oven to 350 degrees for 15 minutes; turn off when putting cookies in oven. Fold sugar, salt, nuts and chips into stiffly beaten egg whites. Drop by teaspoonfuls onto a well-greased cookie sheet. Leave in oven 2½ hours or overnight, but do not open oven door until time to remove cookies. A good lunchbox or after-school snack.

WRAP-AROUND CHERRY COOKIES

2 tablespoons white sugar
5 tablespoons confectioners' sugar
½ cup butter
1 cup all-purpose flour
   Maraschino cherries

Mix together all ingredients, except cherries; wrap small amount of dough around well-drained maraschino cherries. Bake at 350 degrees for 12–15 minutes. Remove from pan; cool on rack. Use cherry juice to make confectioners' sugar icing or glaze.

FIG SQUARES

3 eggs
¾ cup sugar
1 teaspoon vanilla
1 cup flour
⅛ teaspoon salt
2 teaspoons baking powder
1 (8-ounce) package (1½ cups) figs, chopped
1 cup walnuts, chopped

Beat eggs until light. Add sugar and vanilla; mix well. Add sifted dry ingredients and mix well. Fold in figs and walnuts. Bake in greased 9-inch square pan at 350 degrees for 30 minutes. Cool; cut in squares; sprinkle with sifted confectioners' sugar. Serve these with hot spiced tea!

STARLIGHT MINT SURPRISE COOKIES

Makes 4½ dozen

3 cups flour
1 teaspoon soda
½ teaspoon salt
1 cup butter
1 cup sugar
½ cup brown sugar
2 eggs
1 teaspoon vanilla
1 package chocolate mint wafers

Mix first 3 ingredients; set aside. Cream butter, sugars, eggs and vanilla. Add flour mixture. Cover and chill 2 hours. Enclose each chocolate mint wafer in 1 tablespoon dough. Place on greased cookie sheet, 2 inches apart. Top with pecan half. Bake for 10 minutes in a 375-degree oven.

PECAN BALLS

Makes 5 dozen

1 cup soft butter
½ cup granulated sugar *or* ½ cup confectioners' sugar
¼ teaspoon salt
1 teaspoon vanilla
2¼ cups flour
1 cup chopped pecans

Mix butter, sugar, salt and vanilla. Work in flour. The last bit of flour may be worked in with hands. Add nuts. Chill dough. Roll into 1-inch balls. Place on ungreased baking sheet and bake at 350 degrees for 10–12 minutes, until set, but not browned. Roll in sifted confectioners' sugar while warm. Cool; roll again.

DATE WALNUT CHEWS

2 eggs, beaten
1 cup sugar
2 teaspoons baking powder
1 cup chopped walnuts
3/4 cup flour
1 1/4 teaspoons vanilla
1 cup chopped dates

Mix in order given. Place batter in 8 x 8-inch pan; bake in a moderate 350-degree oven for 25–30 minutes. Cool and cut into squares. Top will be crusty.

CHOCOLATE CHERRY DROP COOKIES

1 package cherry cake mix
1/2 cup flour
1/2 cup oil
1/4 cup water
1 egg
1 cup chocolate chips

Blend all ingredients, except chocolate chips, using a mixer. Stir in chips by hand. Drop by teaspoonfuls onto an *ungreased* cookie sheet. Bake in a 350-degree oven for 10–12 minutes, or just until edges begin to brown. Cool on cookie sheet about 1 minute before removing.

MARVELOUS MACAROONS
Makes 2½ dozen

2 2/3 cups flake coconut
2/3 cup sugar
1/4 cup all-purpose flour
1/4 teaspoon salt
4 egg whites, beaten to stiff

peaks
1 teaspoon almond extract
1 cup chopped almonds

Combine coconut, sugar, flour and salt in mixing bowl. Stir in egg whites and almond extract. Stir in almonds; mix well. Drop from teaspoon onto lightly greased baking sheets. Garnish with candied cherry half, if desired. Bake at 325 degrees for 20–25 minutes, or until edges of cookies are golden brown. Remove immediately.

CANDIED ORANGE PEEL COOKIES
Makes 3 dozen

2 eggs
2/3 cup shortening
1 cup sugar
2/3 cup sour cream
1/2 cup candied orange peel
2 1/3 cups all-purpose flour
2 teaspoons baking powder
1/4 teaspoon salt
1/2 teaspoon baking soda

Beat together first 5 ingredients. Sift together dry ingredients; add to liquid ingredients. Drop by teaspoonfuls onto greased cookie sheet; press small piece of candied peel into top of each cookie. Bake at 375 degrees for 12 minutes, or until lightly browned.

ANGEL COOKIES

1½ cups bread crumbs
1/2 cup chopped nuts
1/2 teaspoon vanilla or almond extract
2/3 cup sweetened condensed milk
3 drops red food coloring
30 nut halves (walnut or pecan)

Soak bread crumbs in condensed milk to which the extract and coloring have been added. Add chopped nuts. Drop by spoonfuls onto greased cookie sheets. Top each with a nut half; bake at 350 degrees for 12 minutes.

WALNUT CLUSTERS
Makes 50

1/4 cup butter
1/2 cup sugar
1 egg, unbeaten
1 1/4 teaspoons vanilla
1 1/2 squares unsweetened chocolate, melted
1/2 cup flour
1/4 teaspoon baking powder
1/2 teaspoon salt
2 cups unbroken walnuts

Cream butter and sugar until fluffy. Add egg and vanilla; blend well. Stir in chocolate, then flour sifted with baking powder and salt. Add walnuts. Drop by teaspoonfuls onto greased baking sheet. Bake at 350 degrees for 10 minutes. Cookies should be soft, almost like candy.

MINCEMEAT SQUARES
Makes 24 bars

2½ cups flour
1½ teaspoons baking soda
1/2 teaspoon salt
1½ cups quick-cooking rolled oats
1 cup firmly packed dark brown sugar
3/4 cup (1½ sticks) butter *or* margarine
1 (16-ounce) jar prepared mincemeat

Sift flour, baking soda and salt into large bowl. Stir in rolled oats and brown sugar until blended. Cut in butter or margarine with pastry blender until mixture is crumbly. Pat half the mixture into greased 11 x 7 x 1-inch baking pan. Spread mincemeat on top. Sprinkle remaining oat mixture over and press into mincemeat. Bake in moderate oven at 375 degrees for 25 minutes, or until topping is golden. Cool in pan on wire rack for 15 minutes.

With sharp knife, cut 3 times lengthwise and 5 times crosswise to make 24 bars. Remove from pan with spatula and store, layered between waxed paper, in metal tin with tight-fitting lid.

MEXICAN YULETIDE COOKIES

Makes 6½ dozen

- 1 cup butter
- ¾ cup confectioners' sugar
- 1 egg
- 1½ teaspoons vanilla
- ⅛ teaspoon salt
- 2 cups flour
- 1 cup uncooked oatmeal
- 1 cup chopped pecans
  Confectioners' sugar for rolling

Cream butter; add sugar gradually; beat in egg and vanilla. Blend in salt, flour, oatmeal and pecans. Shape rounded teaspoonfuls of dough into balls. Place on ungreased cookie sheets. Bake at 325 degrees for 20 minutes. Roll in confectioners' sugar while warm.

RICH DROP COOKIES

- 2 cups sifted flour
- ½ teaspoon baking soda
- 1½ teaspoons cream of tartar
- 1 cup white sugar
- ½ teaspoon salt
- 1 cup shortening
- 1 teaspoon vanilla
- 1 egg

Cream sugar and shortening. Add egg, vanilla and salt. Beat until smooth and fluffy. Sift flour, baking soda and cream of tartar. Add to creamed mixture. Roll into little balls; place on cookie sheet. Decorate with cherry half or colored sprinkles. Bake at 325 degrees for 10–15 minutes.

LEMON-PINEAPPLE DROPS

Makes 4 dozen

- ½ cup shortening
- 2 eggs
- 1 (3-ounce) package lemon-flavored gelatin
- 1 (1-pound) package cake mix
- 1 (8¼-ounce) can crushed pineapple, well-drained

In mixing bowl, combine shortening and eggs. Blend in dry gelatin. Add half of dry cake mix. Beat at medium speed of mixer until fluffy. Add remaining cake mix. Blend on low speed, scraping sides of bowl constantly. Stir in pineapple. Drop rounded teaspoonfuls 2 inches apart on ungreased cookie sheet. Bake at 375 degrees for 10–12 minutes.

CRISPY CORN-FLAKES COOKIES

- 3 cups cornflakes cereal
- 1 cup sugar
- 1 cup walnuts, coarsely chopped
- ¼ teaspoon almond extract
- 2 egg yolks, beaten
- 2 egg whites

Combine first 5 ingredients. Beat egg whites until stiff; fold into cornflakes mixture. Drop by tablespoonfuls onto a well-greased baking sheet. Bake at 350 degrees until pale amber. Allow to cool before removing from cookie sheet.

LITTLE ANGEL CLOUDS

Makes 2 dozen

- 3 cups cake flour, sifted
- 4 tablespoons confectioners' sugar
- ½ cup pecans or walnuts, finely ground
- ½ cup soft butter or margarine
- ½ tablespoon vanilla extract

Mix cake flour, confectioners' sugar, pecans (or walnuts), butter and vanilla. Shape mixture by hand into balls about the size of a walnut. Place on a greased cookie sheet. Bake at 350 degrees for 20 minutes; roll in confectioners' sugar.

HEAVENLY CRUNCH

- 1 package from a box of graham crackers
- 2 sticks margarine
- ½ cup sugar
- ⅔ cup chopped pecans

Spread crackers in large jelly roll pan. Chop pecans and sprinkle over crackers. Melt margarine in saucepan. Add sugar; boil 3 minutes. Pour over crackers. Bake in 350-degree oven for 10–15 minutes. Remove from pan before they cool completely. Break into sections. These are delicious!

PECAN PIE SURPRISE BARS

- 1 package Pillsbury yellow cake mix
- ½ cup butter or margarine, melted
- 1 egg
- 1 cup chopped pecans

Grease bottom and sides of 13 x 9-inch baking pan. Reserve ⅔ cup dry cake mix for filling. In large mixing bowl, combine remaining dry cake mix, butter and 1 egg; mix until crumbly. Press into prepared pan. Bake at 350 degrees for 15–20 minutes until light golden brown. Meanwhile, prepare filling (recipe follows). Pour filling over partially baked crust; sprinkle with pecans. Return to oven, bake for 30–35 minutes until filling is set. Cool; cut into 36 bars.

Filling:

- ⅔ cup reserved cake mix
- ½ cup firmly packed brown sugar
- 1½ cups dark brown syrup
- 1 teaspoon vanilla
- 3 eggs

In large mixer bowl, combine all ingredients; beat at medium speed 1–2 minutes.

OLD FAMILY FAVORITE TOFFEE SQUARES

1 cup margarine *or* half margarine and half butter
1 cup brown sugar
1 egg yolk
1 teaspoon vanilla
2 cups flour
1 cup chocolate chips
¼ teaspoon Crisco
Ground walnuts

Cream shortening and sugar. Add egg yolk and vanilla; blend together. Add flour, mix together again. Spread this mixture onto a cookie sheet by pinching pieces of dough and pressing dough to cover the cookie sheet, working with your fingers. Bake 15 minutes at 325 degrees.

Melt chocolate chips. Add ¼ teaspoon Crisco to chocolate to keep it soft.

After dough is baked, spread with chocolate, while warm. Thinly spread chocolate with your fingers instead of a knife. While chocolate is still warm, sprinkle with ground walnuts. After chocolate is set, cut cookies into 1½-inch squares.

Luscious!!

BROWN SUGAR CHEWS

1 egg
1 cup brown sugar, packed
1 teaspoon vanilla
½ cup flour
¼ teaspoon salt
¼ teaspoon soda
1 cup coarsely chopped walnuts

Stir together egg, brown sugar and vanilla. Add ½ cup flour sifted with salt and soda. Stir in nuts. Turn into a greased 8 x 8 x 2-inch baking pan and bake at 350 degrees for 18–20 minutes. Cool in pan and cut into squares.

WALNUT MERINGUE BARS

Makes 4 dozen

2½ cups all-purpose flour
5 eggs, separated
6 tablespoons sugar
1 cup sweet butter
2 teaspoons vanilla
2 cups apricot jam
1 cup sugar
3 cups ground walnuts
Confectioners' sugar

In a bowl, combine flour, egg yolks, sugar, butter and vanilla. Blend with fork until dough comes away from sides of bowl. Press dough into an 11 x 16-inch pan. Spread with jam. Beat egg whites until stiff, gradually beating in 1 cup sugar. Fold in nuts. Spread over dough. Bake at 350 degrees for 40 minutes. Sprinkle with confectioners' sugar. Cool and cut into bars.

Any kind of jam can be substituted for the apricot. The cookie is very rich, so make the bars small.

BUTTER PECAN TURTLE BARS

Makes 2 dozen

Crust:
2 cups flour
2 cups firmly packed brown sugar
½ cup soft butter

Combine all ingredients. Mix at medium speed with mixer, 2–3 minutes, or until particles are fine. Pat into ungreased 9 x 12-inch pan.

Filling:
1 cup pecan halves or hickory nuts
⅔ cup butter
½ cup firmly packed brown sugar
1 cup milk chocolate chips

Spread nuts over crust. Cook, stirring constantly, the butter and brown sugar over medium heat until entire surface of mixture begins to boil, a[bout] 1 minute. Pour over pecans. Bake 20 minutes at 350 degrees. Rem[ove] from oven; sprinkle with choco[late] chips. Marble chips after they [are] melted.

JEWELED COOKIE BARS

2 eggs
1 cup sugar
1 teaspoon vanilla
1 cup sifted flour
½ teaspoon salt
½ cup chopped, toasted blanched almonds
½ cup cut-up gumdrops
½ cup gumdrops for topping, cu[t] up

Beat eggs until foamy; beat in sug[ar] and vanilla. Sift together flour and sa[lt] stir into creamed mixture. Fold in [al-]monds and gumdrops. Spread in we[ll] greased and floured 9-inch square pa[n]. Sprinkle extra gumdrops over top [of] batter. Bake in 350-degree oven f[or] 30–35 minutes until top has a dull cru[st.] Cut into squares while still warm, the[n] cool before removing from pan.

OLD-FASHIONED RAISIN BARS

1 cup raisins
1 cup water
½ cup shortening
½ teaspoon soda
Pinch of salt
2 cups flour
1 cup sugar
1 teaspoon cinnamon
½ teaspoon cloves
½ cup nuts (optional)

Boil raisins and water; remove from heat; add shortening and soda to melt. Add dry ingredients and nuts. Sprea[d] on cookie sheet and bake 20 minutes a[t] 375 degrees. Top with a thin confec[-]tioners' sugar icing. Cut into bars.

MISSISSIPPI MUD BARS

2 cups sugar
1 cup margarine
3 tablespoons cocoa
4 eggs
1½ cups flour
1¼ cups coconut
1½ cups chopped nuts
1 (7-ounce) jar marshmallow creme

Cream together sugar, margarine and cocoa. Add eggs and mix well. Add flour, coconut and nuts. Blend thoroughly.

Bake in greased 12 x 15-inch cookie sheet at 350 degrees for 25–30 minutes. Remove from oven and spread with marshmallow creme.

Frosting:

1 pound confectioners' sugar
½ cup evaporated milk
½ cup cocoa
½ cup soft margarine
1 teaspoon vanilla

Cream together frosting ingredients, blending well. When bars are cool, frost.

DATE BARS

1 pound dates
1 cup walnut meats
½ cup flour
¼ teaspoon baking powder
¼ teaspoon salt
1 cup sugar
2 eggs
¼ cup melted butter
Confectioners' sugar

Pit dates and cut into quarters. Mix together flour, baking powder, salt and sugar. Add dates and nuts to flour mixture. Beat eggs. Add melted butter and combine mixtures. Bake in 8 x 12-inch pan for 30 minutes in moderate oven of 350 degrees. When slightly cool, cut into bars. Roll each bar in confectioners' sugar.

ALMOND BARS

2 cups brown sugar
1 cup white sugar
¾ cup melted butter
¾ cup melted lard
4½ cups sifted flour
1 cup almonds, sliced
3 eggs, well-beaten
1 teaspoon soda
1 scant teaspoon salt

Cream butter and lard; add sugars and well-beaten eggs. Sift flour with soda and salt. Combine with creamed mixture; add almonds. Pack into bread pan. (I roll in waxed paper.) Chill in refrigerator 24 hours. Slice and bake until brown at 350 degrees. (I substitute margarine for both butter and lard.) This recipe has been passed down through the family for years.

GRANOLA BARS

6 eggs
3 cups granola cereal
1 cup raisins, chopped
½ cup almonds, finely chopped
½ cup sesame seeds
¼ cup sunflower seeds

Beat eggs in medium-size bowl. Add remaining ingredients; mix well with spoon. Batter will be thick. Let mixture stand 15 minutes. Pour mixture into well-greased 9-inch square pan. Press mixture into pan and smooth top. Bake at 350 degrees for 25–30 minutes, until done (lightly browned and firm). Remove from oven and cut into 1 x 2-inch bars while still hot. Remove from pan by loosening edges gently with a spatula. Cool. Store in an airtight container.

CHEESECAKE BARS

1 box Duncan Hines Golden Butter Recipe cake mix
1 egg

1 stick margarine
1 (8-ounce) package cream cheese
2 eggs
1 (1-pound) box confectioners' sugar

Blend together the first 3 ingredients. Crumble and press into greased oblong pan. Then mix next 3 ingredients together and spread on top of bottom layer. Bake at 350 degrees for 35–40 minutes, or until golden brown. Cool completely and cut into bars.

LEMON DROPS
Makes 4 dozen

3 eggs, separated
1 teaspoon grated lemon rind
½ teaspoon lemon extract
½ cup confectioners' sugar
⅓ cup sifted flour

Beat egg yolks until thick and lemon-colored. Stir in rind and extract. Beat egg whites until stiff but not dry. Gradually add confectioners' sugar and beat until stiff. Fold in egg yolk mixture. Gently fold in flour. Drop by teaspoon onto paper-lined baking sheets. Bake in moderate 350-degree oven about 12 minutes, or until golden brown.

ROCKY ROAD S'MORES BARS

½ cup margarine
½ cup packed brown sugar
1 cup flour
½ cup graham cracker crumbs
2 cups miniature marshmallows
1 (6-ounce) package semisweet chocolate pieces
½ cup chopped walnuts (optional)

Beat margarine and brown sugar until light and fluffy. Add combined flour and crumbs; mix well. Press onto bottom of greased 9-inch square pan. Sprinkle with remaining ingredients. Bake at 375 degrees for 15–20 minutes, or until golden brown. Cool; cut into bars.

Desserts
DELICIOUS

LINCOLN LOG
Serves 5

Cake:
- 5   eggs, separated
- 6   tablespoons sugar
- ½   cup all-purpose flour
- ½   teaspoon vanilla extract

Mocha Cream Filling and Frosting:
- 1   cup butter *or* margarine, softened
- 4½   tablespoons confectioners' sugar
- 2   tablespoons unsweetened cocoa
- 2   tablespoons strong, cooled coffee
- 2   cups whipping cream, whipped

Beat egg yolks with sugar; mix in flour and vanilla. Fold in stiffly beaten egg whites; spread mixture on a buttered waxed-paper–lined jelly roll pan. Bake at 350 degrees for 15 minutes; transfer to a dampened cloth dusted with confectioners' sugar. Roll cake in cloth; cool. Beat butter and confectioners' sugar; stir in cocoa and coffee. Unroll pastry; cover with a thin layer of mocha cream and whipped cream. Reroll cake (without cloth); cut off 2 ends diagonally; reserve. Cover cake and 2 slices with remaining mocha cream; place 1 slice on top of cake, the other slice on the side of cake (to resemble branches). With a fork, trace lines into the cream to simulate the bark.

ICE-CREAM DESSERT
Serves 12-15

- 1/2 cup butter, melted
- 1 (10-ounce) package shortbread cookies, crushed
- 2 (3-ounce) packages instant vanilla pudding
- 2 cups milk
- 1 teaspoon vanilla
- 4 cups vanilla ice cream
- 1 (4-1/2-ounce) container frozen whipped topping
- 3 Heath candy bars, crushed

Combine butter and cookie crumbs. Pat into a 9x13-inch pan. Bake at 350 degrees for 15 minutes. Cool. With electric mixer blend pudding, milk, and vanilla. Add ice cream and mix well. Spread over cooled crust. Let set until firm. Cover with whipped topping and sprinkle with crushed candy bars. Refrigerate until serving.

CRANBERRY FLUFF
Serves 6

- 1 can whole cranberry sauce
- 1-1/2 cups finely crushed vanilla-wafer crumbs (about 20 wafers)
- 1 cup heavy cream, whipped

With fork, break up cranberry sauce. Blend in crumbs. Fold in whipped cream. Pile lightly in sherbet glasses; refrigerate 30 to 60 minutes.

RASPBERRY BANANA ROYAL
Serves 6

- 1 cup water
- ¾ cup cold water
- 1 (3-ounce) package raspberry gelatin
- 1 tablespoon lemon juice
- 1 medium banana, sliced
- ½ cup pineapple tidbits (optional)

In saucepan, heat 1 cup of water to boiling. Remove from heat; add gelatin and stir until dissolved. Add cold water and lemon juice. Chill in refrigerator until thickened, about 2 hours. Fold in banana and pineapple tidbits. Pour into mold; chill until firm. To serve, unmold on lettuce.

CHOCOLATE-BANANA ROLL-UPS

- 2 ripe bananas
- 4 large prepared pancakes
- 2 (8-ounce) cans chocolate pudding

Preheat oven to 350 degrees. Cut bananas in half lengthwise. Place a banana slice on each pancake. Roll pancake and bananas and secure with toothpicks. Grease cookie sheet. Place banana roll-ups on sheet. Bake in a 350-degree oven for 10 minutes. When done, use tongs to remove to serving plate. Spoon chocolate pudding on top.

ANGEL FOOD CAKE WITH FLUFFY FROSTING

1 (already prepared) angel food cake
1 envelope Dream Whip
1 (4-serving) package any flavor instant pudding
1½ cups cold milk

Combine Dream Whip, pudding mix and cold milk. Beat at high speed to soft peaks (4–6 minutes). Frost angel food cake. Store in refrigerator.

LEMON REFRIGERATOR PUDDING
Serves 10

1 (21-ounce) can lemon pie filling
2 (11-ounce) cans mandarin oranges, drained
½ cup flaked coconut
2 cups miniature marshmallows
1 cup dairy sour cream
Cocktail cherries

Combine all ingredients, except cocktail cherries. Chill in refrigerator until needed; then serve decorated with cherries.

SHERBET DESSERT

1 teaspoon vanilla
1 pint whipping cream *or* Dream Whip
18 soft coconut macaroons, crumbled
½ cup nuts
1 quart lime sherbet
1 quart raspberry sherbet

Combine vanilla and whipping cream or Dream Whip. Beat on high speed with electric mixer until creamy and fluffy. Mix macaroons and nuts in whipping cream. Take half the mixture and spread in pan. Spoon lime sherbet and raspberry sherbet over this, then top with remaining cream mixture. Place in freezer. Makes enough for one 9 x 13-inch pan or two 8 x 8-inch pans.

WAFFLE SUNDAES

2 frozen blueberry waffles (jumbo size), toasted
2 scoops strawberry *or* vanilla ice cream
  Banana slices
  Strawberry preserves
  Whipped topping

For each serving, top 1 waffle with 1 scoop ice cream. Arrange banana slices around ice cream. Spoon preserves over ice cream. Garnish with whipped topping. Serve immediately.

Quick and easy to fix.

RICE AND CHERRY SUPREME

1 cup whipping cream
½ cup sugar
3 cups cold cooked rice
½ teaspoon vanilla
1 can cherry pie filling

Beat cream and sugar together. Gently fold in rice, vanilla and cherry pie filling.

CINNAMON PINK APPLES

4 apples
1 cup water
¼ cup brown sugar
  Red cinnamon candies

Core apples and fill the insides with cinnamon candies. Mix water and brown sugar. Pour sugar mixture into a pan and arrange apples. Bake at 375 degrees for 45 minutes.

CHERRY WHIP

1 stick margarine
2 cups graham cracker crumbs
1 cup cold milk
2 envelopes whipped topping mix
1 teaspoon vanilla
1 cup sugar
1 (8-ounce) package cream cheese
1 large can cherry pie filling

Melt margarine over low heat. Mix with 2 cups graham cracker crumbs. Put into 9 x 13 x 2-inch pan. In a large bowl, whip until stiff, 1 cup cold milk with 2 envelopes whipped topping mix. Add 1 teaspoon vanilla, cup sugar and cream cheese (softened). Spread over crumb mixture. Spoon 1 large can cherry pie filling over whipped mixture. Set in refrigerator overnight. Slice and serve.

BANANA SPLIT
Serves 4

1 (3⅝-ounce) package chocolate pudding and pie filling
2 cups milk
4 bananas, sliced lengthwise
½ gallon vanilla ice cream
1 (8½-ounce) can pineapple tidbits, drained
½ cup chopped pecans
1 cup whipped cream
4 maraschino cherries, drained

Prepare pudding with 2 cups milk according to package directions. Cover surface of pudding with waxed paper or plastic wrap; refrigerate until cool.

Put 1 sliced banana in each of 4 serving dishes. Top with 3 scoops of ice cream; cover with ¼ of pudding; sprinkle with pineapple tidbits and pecans. Garnish with whipped cream and a cherry.

LIME CHEESECAKE
Serves 10–12

- 1 cup shredded coconut
- 2 tablespoons flour
- 2 tablespoons margarine, melted
- 1 envelope unflavored gelatin
- 2 (8-ounce) packages cream cheese
- 3 eggs, separated
- ¾ cup sugar
- ¼ cup lime juice
  Grated lime rind
  Green food coloring (optional)
- 1 cup whipping cream, whipped

Combine coconut, flour and margarine; press into a 9-inch springform pan. Bake at 350 degrees for 12–15 minutes. Soften gelatin in ¼ cup cold water. Soften cream cheese. Combine egg yolks, ¾ cup water and sugar in saucepan; cook, stirring constantly, over medium heat for 5 minutes. Stir in gelatin until dissolved. Add gelatin mixture gradually to cream cheese; mix until blended. Stir in lime juice, 1 teaspoon lime rind and several drops of green food coloring, if desired. Fold in whipped cream and stiffly beaten egg whites; pour over crust. Chill until firm. Garnish with lime rind. A dreamy, delightful dessert!

FRUIT PARFAITS

- 2 tablespoons frozen orange juice concentrate
- 1 tablespoon sugar
- ½ cup whipped topping
- 1 orange, peeled, sectioned and cut up
- 1 banana, sliced
- ½ cup pineapple chunks
- ⅓ cup marshmallows

Combine orange juice and sugar; mix well. Fold in whipped topping. In another bowl, combine fruit pieces. In 2 parfait glasses, alternately layer fruit, marshmallows and then whipped topping; repeat. Chill. May be topped with a maraschino cherry.

CHOCOLATE WAFER PUDDING
Serves 6–8

- 1 (3¼-ounce) package vanilla pudding and pie filling
- 2 cups milk
- 8 chocolate wafers
- 1 cup whipped cream
- 2 tablespoons chocolate syrup (optional)

Prepare pudding with 2 cups milk according to package directions. Cover surface of pudding with waxed paper or plastic wrap; refrigerate until cool.

Alternate layers of chocolate wafers and pudding in a 1-quart casserole, ending with vanilla pudding. Garnish with whipped cream and drizzle with chocolate syrup, if desired.

PEACH BLUEBERRY COBBLER
Serves 8

- ½ cup sugar
- 1 tablespoon cornstarch
- ¾ cup orange juice
- 1½ cups fresh *or* frozen peach slices
- 1½ cups blueberries
- ½ cup all-purpose flour
- ½ cup whole-wheat flour
- 1½ teaspoon baking powder
- ⅓ cup milk
- 1 tablespoon vegetable oil
- 1 teaspoon sugar

In small saucepan, stir together ½ cup sugar, cornstarch and orange juice. Cook until bubbly; add peaches and blueberries; cook until hot. Keep warm. Stir together flours and baking powder; add milk and oil and stir until mixture forms a ball. On floured surface, pat into an 8-inch circle. Cut into wedges. Spoon hot berry mixture into 9-inch pie plate and top immediately with pastry wedges. Sprinkle with sugar. Bake in 425-degree oven for 20–30 minutes, or until pastry is browned.

ICE CREAM GELATIN DESSERT
Serves 5

- 1 (3-ounce) package gelatin, any flavor
- 1 cup boiling water
- ½ cup cold water
- 1 cup vanilla ice cream (or your favorite flavor)
- 1 cup canned fruit, drained (fruit cocktail, sliced peaches or mandarin oranges)

Dissolve gelatin with boiling water in an 8-inch or 9-inch metal pan. (The pan helps the gelatin cool faster.) Then remove ½ cup and pour into a bowl. Add ½ cup cold water to the gelatin in the pan and place in the freezer until it thickens (10–15 minutes).

Meanwhile, add 1 cup ice cream to the gelatin in the bowl; stir until smooth. Remove thickened gelatin from the freezer and, if desired, stir in fruit, reserving a few pieces for garnish.

Spoon thickened gelatin and fruit into individual dessert glasses.

Top with ice cream/gelatin mixture. Chill 30 minutes. Garnish and serve.

HOLIDAY MINCEMEAT-STUFFED APPLES
Serves 8

- 8 medium-size Granny Smith apples
- 4 tablespoons butter *or* margarine
- 1 tablespoon rum extract
- 8 tablespoons mincemeat

Wash and core apples; do not peel. Place apples in an ovenproof dish. Fill cavities with butter, rum extract and mincemeat. Bake at 350 degrees for 25 minutes, or until apples are tender. Serve with baked pork loin, lamb or baked ham.

MILK DUD DESSERT

6   egg yolks
1   cup sugar
1   cup rusk crumbs
½   cup chopped walnuts
1   teaspoon vanilla
1   teaspoon baking
    powder
6   egg whites
4   small packages Milk
    Duds
¹/₂ cup milk
1   cup confectioners'
    sugar
2   tablespoons butter
½   pint whipping cream

Beat egg yolks; add sugar and beat again.

Mix together rusk crumbs, nuts, vanilla and baking powder. Add to egg mixture. Fold in stiffly beaten egg whites. Bake in 9 x 13-inch greased pan at 350 degrees for 30 minutes. Cool. Melt Milk Duds, milk, confectioners' sugar and butter until smooth, stirring constantly. Let stand until cool and creamy. Whip the cream; spread over baked portion. Pour sauce on top and refrigerate overnight.

PEANUT BUTTER PARFAIT
Serves 4

1   cup brown sugar
⅓   cup milk
¼   cup white corn syrup
1   tablespoon butter
¼   cup peanut butter
    Vanilla ice cream
    Peanuts

Combine first 4 ingredients in medium saucepan. Cook over medium heat until sugar dissolves and butter melts, stirring constantly. Remove from heat; add peanut butter. Beat with rotary beater or mixer until smooth; cool. Alternate layers of peanut sauce and ice cream in parfait glasses, beginning and ending with ice cream. Top with peanuts.

WHIPPED DESSERT TOPPING
Makes 1-2/3 cups

1/2 cup instant non-fat dry milk
1/2 cup ice water
2 tablespoons lemon juice
1/4 cup sugar
1/2 teaspoon vanilla

In a bowl combine nonfat dry milk, ice water, and lemon juice. Use an electric mixer and beat until mixture is very stiff. Beat in sugar and vanilla; beat until sugar is dissolved and mixture is smooth and creamy. Serve at once. Use as topping for desserts.

Variations: Make as directed, then blend in 2 tablespoons cocoa; or make as above and fold in 1/4 cup flaked coconut.

CREAM CHEESE AND CHERRY DESSERT
Serves 18–20

Crust:
2   cups crushed pretzels
1   cup melted butter *or*
    margarine
¾   cup sugar

Filling:
1   (8-ounce) package
    cream cheese, softened
1   cup confectioners'
    sugar
1   (8-ounce) container
    whipped topping

Topping:
1   (30-ounce) can cherry
    pie filling

For crust: Combine ingredients and press into a 9 x 13-inch pan, reserving some for garnish.
For filling: Combine and beat cream cheese with confectioners' sugar. Add whipped topping to the cheese mixture, ½ cup at a time, mixing gently. Spread over crust.

Spread pie filling over top and sprinkle with reserved pretzel mixture. Refrigerate 2–3 hours.

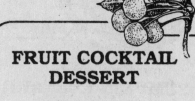

FRUIT COCKTAIL DESSERT

The topping melts as it cooks and makes a tasty dessert.

1   (16-ounce) can fruit cocktail,
    drained
1   egg, beaten
1   cup sugar
1   teaspoon soda
1   cup flour
⅛   teaspoon salt
½   cup chopped nuts
½   cup brown sugar

Add egg to fruit and then fold in dry ingredients. Pour the batter into a 9-inch round or square microwave-safe baking dish.

Combine nuts and brown sugar and pour over batter.

Place small glass or custard cup, open end up, in center of baking dish before placing batter in dish. Microwave, uncovered, 7–8 minutes. For varying power, use 5 minutes on 50 percent power and 4–5 minutes on HIGH.

Helpful hint: The glass inserted in the center gives a "doughnut" shape which works more effectively in getting baked goods done.

BAKED BANANAS

2   bananas
    Lemon juice
    Brown sugar *or* granulated
    sugar with cinnamon
    Butter

Peel bananas and slice in half lengthwise. Place in a buttered pie plate or casserole. Sprinkle with lemon juice and sugar. Dot with butter. Bake at 350 degrees for 15 minutes. This is also a delicious way to make a dessert using pears or apples.

PRETTY PUMPKIN CUSTARD

- 2 cups canned pumpkin
- 1 cup soft bread crumbs
- 2 eggs, separated
- 1½ cups sweet milk
- 1 cup sugar
- 3 tablespoons butter, melted
- ¼ teaspoon salt
- 1¼ teaspoons orange extract

Combine all ingredients 1 at a time, except egg whites; mix well after each addition. Pour into oven-proof dish or individual custard cups. Bake at 325 degrees until mixture thickens and browns. Beat egg whites until stiff; add 2 tablespoons sugar. Spread on top of custard; place under broiler until golden brown.

IRISH COFFEE PUDDING

Use this for your centerpiece.

- 6 eggs
- ⅓ cup Irish whiskey
- ¾ cup sugar
- 1¼ cups heavy cream
- 1 cup strong, black espresso
- 2 tablespoons finely crushed walnuts
- 3 tablespoons gelatin
- 1 cup whipped cream
- 2 tablespoons chopped walnuts

Separate eggs and beat yolks with sugar. Heat coffee and dissolve gelatin in it. Add to egg-sugar mixture. Heat over double boiler until thickened; add whiskey or extract; beat until creamy. Place bowl over cracked ice and stir until it begins to set. Whip cream and fold in; then whip egg whites and fold in.
Pour into mold or waxed-paper–lined bowl; press an oiled jar into center to form a well. Chill to set. Fold nuts into whipped cream; fill center.

HAPPY DAY CAKE
Serves 8–10

- 1 (3¾-ounce) package chocolate fudge pudding and pie filling
- 2 cups milk
- 1 (11¼-ounce) frozen pound cake
- ⅓ cup coconut
- ½ gallon vanilla ice cream (optional)

Prepare pudding with 2 cups milk according to package directions. Cover surface of pudding with waxed paper or plastic wrap; refrigerate until cool.
Slice pound cake lengthwise into 3 layers. Spread pudding between each layer and frost top with pudding. Sprinkle with coconut. Serve with a scoop of vanilla ice cream, if desired.

SCALLOPED APPLES

- 4 medium (1–1¼ pounds) tart apples, peeled, cored and sliced
- ½ cup sugar
- ¼ teaspoon cinnamon
- ¼ teaspoon cloves
- ½ cup butter *or* margarine
- 2 cups fresh bread crumbs (4 slices bread)

Toss apples with sugar and spices. In skillet, melt butter; add crumbs and toss lightly, stirring. In greased 8-inch square baking pan, layer half the apples, then half the crumbs. Top with layers of remaining apples and crumbs. Bake in preheated 350-degree oven for 45 minutes, or until tender. Serve warm as a side dish with pork or ham, or as a dessert topped with vanilla ice cream.

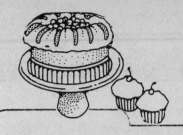

HEAVENLY HASH CAKE
Serves 12–16

- 1 (12-ounce) package semisweet chocolate chips
- 4 eggs, separated
- 2 tablespoons sugar
- 1 teaspoon vanilla extract
- ½ teaspoon salt
- 1 pint whipping cream
- 1 cup pecans, broken
- 1 large angel food cake

Melt chocolate chips over low heat. Beat egg yolks and add to chocolate. Beat egg whites and add 2 tablespoons sugar. Add egg whites to chocolate mixture. Stir and add pecans, vanilla and salt. Whip cream and fold in last.
Break angel food cake into chunks and cover bottom of tube pan or deep bowl. Cover with layer of chocolate mixture; add another layer of cake pieces and cover with chocolate mixture. Then add another layer of cake pieces and cover with remaining chocolate mixture.
Chill in refrigerator overnight. Turn onto cake plate and slice to serve.

CRANBERRY FLUFF
Serves 6

- 1 pound cranberries, chopped
- 1 cup sugar
- ½ cup seeded grapes, halved
- ½ cup small marshmallows
- ½ cup chopped pecans
- ½ cup maraschino cherries, halved
- ½ pint whipping cream, whipped

Combine fruits, marshmallows and nuts; fold in whipping cream. Transfer mixture to a serving bowl. Chill in refrigerator 1–2 hours.

CRANBERRY PUDDING

1 cup flour
½ cup sugar
1½ teaspoons baking powder
Salt
1 cup halved cranberries
1½ tablespoons melted butter
½ cup milk

Mix the dry ingredients. Blend in butter and milk. Add cranberries. Bake in greased 9 x 9-inch pan at 375 degrees for 30 minutes.

Sauce:
½ cup butter
1 cup brown sugar
¾ cup cream (evaporated milk is fine)

Place ingredients in saucepan on medium heat until well-blended. Serve pudding in squares with warm sauce.

BLUEBERRY SALAD
Serves 12

1 (3-ounce) package blackberry gelatin
2 cups boiling water
1 (15-ounce) can blueberries with juice (*or* 1 pound of your own, frozen)
1 (8-ounce) can crushed pineapple, drained

Topping:
1 (8-ounce) package cream cheese, softened
¼ cup sugar
¼ pint sour cream
½ teaspoon vanilla
½ cup nuts

Dissolve gelatin in boiling water. Add blueberries and pineapple; pour into 9 x 12-inch glass baking dish. Refrigerate until set.

Blend cream cheese and sugar. Add sour cream slowly and then vanilla. Spread over gelatin salad and sprinkle with nuts. Refrigerate until serving time.

This salad may be varied with the use of black raspberry gelatin.

MOCHA FLUFF
Serves 4

1 envelope gelatin
¼ cup water
¼ cup sugar
¼ teaspoon salt
1½ cups hot, strong coffee
2 tablespoons lemon juice
2 egg whites, stiffly beaten

Soften gelatin in cold water. Add sugar, salt and hot coffee, stirring thoroughly to dissolve. Add lemon juice and cool. When nearly set, beat until stiff. Add egg whites and continue beating until mixture holds its shape. Turn into molds and chill.

CHERRY EMPANADAS
Makes 12-14

1-1/2 cups flour
1 teaspoon baking powder
1/2 teaspoon salt
8 tablespoons shortening
4-6 teaspoons water
1 small can cherry pie filling (or filling of your choice)
Confectioners' sugar
Cinnamon

Mix flour, baking powder, and salt; cut in shortening. Add water and mix. Roll out 1/8 inch thick and cut into 3-inch circular pieces. Fill each half round piece with fruit filling. Moisten edges; fold over and seal. Bake in 400-degree oven for 15 minutes. Cool slightly; roll each cooked empanada in confectioners' sugar mixed with cinnamon.

QUICK BAKED ALASKA
Serves 4

4 packaged dessert shells
Jam *or* jelly
4 scoops of favorite ice cream
Whipped cream

Turn oven temperature to 475 degrees. Spread dessert shells with jam or jelly. Place on baking sheet. Bake dessert shells with jam or jelly for 5 minutes. Place a scoop of ice cream in center; top with whipped cream; serve.

PEANUT BUTTER INSTANT PUDDING
Serves 4

⅓ cup creamy peanut butter
2 cups cold milk
1 (3¾-ounce) package vanilla, 1 (4-ounce) package butterscotch or 1 (4½-ounce) package chocolate *instant* pudding

Stir peanut butter and milk together. Add pudding mix and beat slowly with rotary beater for 1–2 minutes, or until well-blended. Pudding will be soft. Let stand for 5 minutes and serve.

GINGER PEACH CAKE
Serves 6–8

2 tablespoons margarine
1 package ginger bread mix
½ cup water
2 cups sliced peaches
Whipped cream for topping

Preheat oven to 375 degrees. Grease bottom and sides of baking pan. In bowl, combine gingerbread mix and water. Blend at low speed; then beat 2 minutes at medium speed. Stir in peaches. Pour into baking pan. Bake in oven for 35 minutes. Serve warm topped with whipped cream.

HOT FUDGE TURTLE SUNDAES
Serves 2

⅓ cup semisweet chocolate
   pieces
1 tablespoon milk
⅓ cup miniature marshmallows
   Vanilla ice cream
   Toasted pecan halves

Combine chocolate pieces and milk in top of double boiler; heat over simmering water until chocolate is melted. Remove from heat and stir in marshmallows until partially melted. Scoop ice cream into 2 dessert dishes and top with chocolate mixture. Top with pecan halves.

AMBROSIA PARFAITS

1 (8-ounce) can mandarin orange segments, drained
¼ cup chopped, toasted
   blanched almonds
2 cups prepared whipped topping
1 package *instant* toasted coconut pudding
2 cups cold milk
   Mint sprigs

Reserve 5 orange segments for garnish. Fold oranges and almonds into topping. Combine pudding with milk, beating slowly for 2 minutes. Alternate topping and pudding in parfait glasses. Garnish with oranges and mint.

CREAMY CHOCOMINT TORTE
Serves 12

2 envelopes unflavored gelatin
½ cup sugar

4 eggs, separated
1½ cups milk
½ cup creme de menthe
2½ cups chocolate sandwich
   cookie crumbs
¼ cup butter *or* margarine, melted
2 cups (1 pint) whipping *or*
   heavy cream, whipped

In medium saucepan, mix unflavored gelatin with ¼ cup sugar; blend in egg yolks beaten with milk. Let stand 1 minute. Stir over low heat until gelatin is completely dissolved, about 5 minutes; add liqueur. Pour into large bowl and chill, stirring occasionally, until mixture mounds slightly when dropped from spoon. Meanwhile, in small bowl, combine cookie crumbs and butter. Reserve 1½ cups mixture. Press remaining onto bottom of 9-inch springform pan; chill.

In medium bowl, beat egg whites until soft peaks form; gradually add remaining sugar and beat until stiff. Fold egg whites, then whipped cream into gelatin mixture. Turn ⅓ mixture into prepared pan and top with ¾ cup reserved cookie crumbs; repeat, ending with gelatin mixture. Chill until set. Garnish, if desired, with additional whipped cream and miniature chocolate-mint candy bars.

CANDY CANE DESSERT
Serves 9

1 graham cracker crust (your favorite recipe)
1 (8-ounce) container frozen whipped topping, thawed
1 small package miniature marshmallows
4 large candy canes, crushed
   (about ½ cup)

Place graham cracker crust in bottom of 11 x 7-inch pan. Combine whipped topping, marshmallows and ¾ of the candy. Spoon on crust. Spread remaining crushed candy cane over mixture. Chill thoroughly.

EASY CHERRY COBBLER

2 cans tart cherries,
   undrained
1 package white cake mix
1 stick margarine, melted
1 cup nuts

Pour cherries in bottom of 9 x 13-inch pan, then sprinkle dry cake mix over cherries and *do not stir*. Pour melted margarine over cake mix; sprinkle nuts on top. *Do not mix.* Bake at 400 degrees for 30 minutes, or until set. Delicious topped with ice cream.

CHOCOLATE FLUFF AND STUFF

¾ cup water
2 envelopes unflavored gelatin
⅔ cup sugar
¼ cup cocoa
½ cup milk
½ teaspoon vanilla
2 cups frozen whipped dessert topping, thawed

Place water in 1-cup measure; cover Microwave on HIGH, 2–2½ minutes or until boiling. Add gelatin; stir to dissolve. Set aside.

In small bowl combine sugar and cocoa. Slowly blend in milk, stirring to dissolve sugar and cocoa. Stir in vanilla. Blend in dissolved gelatin. Skim off any foam. Pour ½ cup of chocolate gelatin mixture into small bowl. Blend in whipped topping. Pour remaining gelatin mixture into an 8 x 8-inch baking dish. Spoon chocolate-whipped topping mixture over and spread evenly with spatula.

Refrigerate until firm, about 1 hour. Cut into 16 squares.

APPLE DUMPLINGS

2 cups flour
2-1/2 teaspoons baking powder
1/2 teaspoon salt
1/2 cup shortening
1/4 cup milk
8 apples
8 tablespoons sugar
4 tablespoons butter
Cinnamon and sugar mixed

Sift flour, salt, and baking powder. Cut in shortening. Add milk and stir. Knead lightly on a floured board. Roll 1/8-inch thick. Divide dough into 8 parts. Peel and core apples. Place one apple on each section of dough. Fill hollow of apple with 1 tablespoon of sugar and 1 teaspoon of butter. Fold dough over apple, pressing edges together. Place in a shallow baking pan. Sprinkle with sugar-cinnamon mixture and dot with remaining butter. Bake at 400 degrees for 30-40 minutes. Serve with cream or half-and-half.

GOURMET ORANGE BAKED ALASKA
Serves 6

1 pint orange sherbet
3 large oranges
3 egg whites, stiffly beaten
1/4 teaspoon cream of tartar
1/4 cup plus 2 tablespoons sugar

Scoop sherbet into 6 balls; freeze at least 4 hours until very firm. Cut oranges crosswise in half; cut thin slice from bottom of each half. Cut around edges and membranes; remove fruit and membrane from orange shells. Line bottom of each shell with fruit; refrigerate. Beat egg whites

and cream of tartar. Beat in sugar, 1 tablespoon at a time; beat until stiff and glossy. Place orange shells on ungreased baking sheet; fill each with a frozen sherbet ball. Completely cover sherbet ball with meringue, sealing it to the edge of the shell. Bake at 400 degrees for 4-5 minutes, or until meringue is light golden brown. Serve immediately.

BLACK FOREST TRIFLE

1 (9-ounce) package chocolate cake mix
1/4 cup rum or brandy (optional)
1 can cherry pie filling
1 package instant chocolate pudding
1 medium Cool Whip

Bake cake as package directs. Cool and cut in cubes. Prepare pudding as package directs. Arrange one half cake cubes in glass bowl. Sprinkle 1 ounce rum or brandy. Layer one half of pudding, then one half of cherry pie filling; next, one half of Cool Whip. Repeat layering in order given.

Chill at least 3 hours before serving. Looks very pretty in a tall stemmed bowl.

PUMPKIN DESSERT

1-1/3 cups graham cracker crumbs
1/4 cup sugar
1/4 cup soft butter
60 marshmallows
2 cups pumpkin
1 teaspoon cinnamon
1/2 teaspoon ginger
1/2 teaspoon salt
2 packages whipped topping mix, prepared according to package directions
1 cup sweetened whipped cream
Toasted coconut

Mix graham cracker crumbs with sugar and soft butter. Press into a 9x13-inch pan. Bake at 375 degrees for 8 to 10 minutes. Let cool. Melt marshmallows, pumpkin, spices, and salt in a double boiler or other large pan. Fold in whipped topping and spread the mixture over graham cracker crust. Spread the whipped cream over top of pumpkin mixture. Top with toasted coconut. Chill in refrigerator before serving.

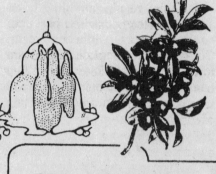

OLD-FASHIONED BLUEBERRY BUCKLE
Serves 6

2 cups flour
3 teaspoons baking powder
1/2 cup margarine
1/2 cup sugar
1 egg, beaten
1/2 cup milk
1/2 teaspoon almond flavoring

Topping:
2 cups fresh or frozen blueberries
2 teaspoons lemon juice
1/4 cup sugar
1/3 cup flour
1/2 teaspoon cinnamon
1/4 cup margarine

Sift flour with baking powder. Set aside. In mixing bowl cream margarine and sugar. Add egg; beat until creamy. Combine milk and almond flavoring; add to creamed mixture alternately with flour; beat until smooth. Pour into buttered 9-inch square pan. Sprinkle lemon juice over blueberries and spread over batter. Mix sugar, flour, cinnamon and margarine thoroughly with fingers until crumbly. Spread over blueberries. Bake at 350 degrees for 45-50 minutes, or until it tests done. Serve warm or cold, with cream, if desired.

PARADISE DESSERT
Serves 8

1 box regular-size lemon gelatin
1 pint boiling water
1/2 cup blanched almonds
12 large marshmallows, diced small
12 maraschino cherries, chopped
6 crushed macaroon cookies
4 tablespoons sugar
1/4 teaspoon salt
1-1/2 cups Cool Whip

Dissolve gelatin in boiling water and chill. When thickened beat until consistency of whipped cream. Combine next 6 ingredients and add to gelatin mixture. Fold in Cool Whip and turn into a 7x5-inch loaf pan and chill until firm. Unmold and slice into 3/4-inch slices to serve.

RASPBERRY REFRIGERATOR DESSERT
Serves 15-18

2 (10-ounce) packages frozen red raspberries
1 cup water
1/2 cup sugar
2 teaspoons lemon juice
4 tablespoons cornstarch
1/4 cup cold water
50 large marshmallows
1 cup milk
2 cups heavy cream or 2 packages Dream Whip
1-1/4 cups graham cracker crumbs
1/4 cup chopped nuts
1/4 cup melted butter or margarine

Heat raspberries with water, sugar, and lemon juice. Dissolve cornstarch in 1/4 cup water; stir into raspberries and cook until thickened and clear. Cool. Melt marshmallows in milk over boiling water in a double boiler. Cool thoroughly. Whip cream or Dream Whip and fold into marshmallow mixture. Mix graham cracker crumbs, nuts, and butter in a 13x9x2-1/2 inch pan. Press firmly into bottom of pan. Spread marshmallow cream mixture over crumbs. Spread raspberry mixture over top. Refrigerate until firm.

EASY PEACH BUTTERSCOTCH CRISP
Serves 6

2 (16-ounce) cans sliced peaches, well drained
1/4 cup raisins
1 (3-3/4 ounce) package *instant* butterscotch pudding mix
1/2 cup flour
1/3 cup chopped dry roasted peanuts
1/4 cup old fashioned rolled oats
1/2 cup butter or margarine

Heat oven to 400 degrees. In an 8-inch square baking pan place peaches and raisins; set aside. In small bowl combine remaining ingredients, cutting in the butter or margarine until mixture is crumbly. Sprinkle crumbly mixture over peaches and raisins. Bake 15-20 minutes or until bubbly around edges. Serve with ice cream.

STRAWBERRY CHEESE DELIGHT

2 (3-ounce) packages lady fingers
2 (10-ounce) packages frozen strawberries
1/4 cup cold water
1-1/2 tablespoons cornstarch
1 (8-ounce) package cream cheese, softened
1 cup confectioners' sugar
1 pint whipping cream, whipped
1 teaspoon vanilla

In 2 quart saucepan, bring berries to a gentle boil. Mix the cold water and cornstarch in a cup and slowly pour into the berries, stirring until thickened. Set aside to cool.

In mixing bowl beat softened cream cheese with confectioners' sugar until smooth. Fold in whipped cream and vanilla; set aside.

Line bottom of 13x9 inch pan with lady fingers. Top with cream cheese mixture. Finally top with the strawberry mixture. Refrigerate until ready to serve.

CRANBERRY APPLE CRISP
Serves 9

5 cups sliced tart apples (about 6 medium apples)
1-1/2 cups Ocean Spray fresh or frozen cranberries
1/3 cup granulated sugar
1/2 cup all-purpose flour
1/2 cup brown sugar
1 teaspoon cinnamon
1/4 cup butter or margarine

Preheat oven to 375 degrees. Lightly grease a 9-inch square baking pan. Layer apple slices and cranberries in pan, sprinkling with granulated sugar as you layer. In a bowl, cut and mix together flour, brown sugar, and cinnamon. Cut in butter until light and crumbly. Sprinkle topping evenly over apples and cranberries. Bake 45 minutes, until apples are tender.

RHUBARB CRISP
Serves 6-8

1 cup flour
3/4 cup oatmeal
1 cup brown sugar
1 teaspoon cinnamon
1/2 cup margarine, melted
4 cups diced rhubarb

Sauce:
1 cup white sugar
2 tablespoons cornstarch
1 cup water
1 teaspoon vanilla

Preheat oven to 350 degrees. Mix flour, oatmeal, brown sugar, cinnamon, and melted margarine until crumbly. Divide in half; press one half of mixture into bottom of 9x9-inch pan. Cover bottom layer with 4 cups diced rhubarb.

In medium saucepan, combine white sugar, cornstarch, water, and vanilla. Cook until thickened and clear. Pour over rhubarb. Pat remaining crumb mixture on top. Bake at 350 degrees for 1 hour.

RHUBARB BERRY DELIGHT

Filling:
1-1/2 cups fresh or frozen chopped rhubarb
1 cup fresh or frozen, sliced strawberries
1/2 cup granulated sugar
1 tablespoon corn starch

Mix all ingredients well in a large bowl. Fill a 10-inch glass pie plate with the fruit mixture. Set aside while preparing topping.

Topping:
1/2 cup brown sugar
1/2 cup dry oats
1/2 cup all-purpose flour
1/2 cup butter or margarine

Mix all ingredients until crumbly. Sprinkle over fruit mixture until covered. Bake at 350 degrees for 20 minutes until fruit is tender and topping is golden brown. Serve warm with fresh whipped cream for a decorative touch.

BLUEBERRY SWIRL ICE CREAM
Makes 1-1/2 quarts

1 recipe Cheesecake Ice Cream (see above)
1/2 cup water
1/4 cup sugar
1 teaspoon cornstarch
1 tablespoon lemon juice
1 cup fresh or frozen blueberries, unsweetened
1/8 teaspoon cinnamon

Combine water and sugar in a saucepan. Bring to a boil, stirring to dissolve sugar. Dissolve cornstarch in lemon juice. Add to ingredients in pan, stirring until thickened. Add blueberries and cinnamon. Boil for about 2 minutes, mashing the berries slightly with the back of a large spoon or potato masher. Remove from heat. Chill thoroughly. Swirl into soft Cheesecake Ice Cream after removing it from freezer. Refreeze until firm.

BUTTERFINGER ICE CREAM

1 can Eagle Brand milk
8 eggs (or Egg Beaters)
1/2 cup peanut butter
1 can evaporated milk
3 cups sugar
Milk to fill freezer
4 King-size Butterfinger candy bars or 8 (11-ounce) size

Mix first 6 ingredients, then add chopped or broken Butterfingers. Freeze in 1-1/2 gallon ice cream freezer.

BUTTERSCOTCH ICE CREAM
Makes 1 quart

1 quart vanilla ice cream, softened
1/2 cup butterscotch-flavored morsels
1/2 cup toasted walnuts
1/2 cup chopped toasted coconut

In large bowl, combine ice cream, butterscotch-flavored morsels, walnuts, and coconut. Stir until well blended. Pour into airtight container; freeze until firm.

CHOCOLATY CHOCOLATE ICE CREAM
Serves 4

3 tablespoons cocoa
3/4 cup whole milk
1/2 cup water
2 teaspoons sugar
1/2 teaspoon vanilla

In mixing bowl mix milk and cocoa thoroughly. Add sugar, water, and vanilla; beat well. Pour into refrigerator tray and freeze until firm.

STRAWBERRY ICE CREAM

1 (14-ounce) can sweetened condensed milk
1 (10-ounce) package frozen strawberries in syrup, thawed
2 cups whipping cream

Whirl thawed strawberries in blender until smooth. Combine strawberries with condensed milk, then fold in whipped cream, and freeze, according to the directions for Chocolate Ice Cream (recipe follows).

NO-FUSS CHOCOLATE ICE CREAM
Makes 1-1/2 quarts

1 (14-ounce) can sweetened condensed milk
2/3 cup chocolate syrup
2 cups whipping cream

In large bowl, stir together the condensed milk and chocolate syrup. Whip cream until stiff. Gently fold into chocolate/condensed milk mixture. Line a 9 x 5-inch loaf pan (or other 2-quart container) with aluminum foil. Pour ice cream mixture into lined pan and cover with foil. Freeze for 6 hours or until firm. To serve, scoop ice cream directly from pan or remove from pan in one piece; peel off foil, and slice.

"COOKIES AND CREAM" ICE CREAM
Makes 1-1/2 quarts

3 egg yolks
1 (14-ounce) can sweetened condensed milk
2 tablespoons water
4 teaspoons vanilla extract
1 cup coarsely-crushed chocolate sandwich cookies
2 cups whipping cream

In large bowl, beat egg yolks. Stir in milk, water, and vanilla. Fold in cookies and whipped cream. Pour into aluminum foil-lined 9 x 5-inch loaf pan or other 2-quart container. Cover. Freeze 6 hours or until firm.

CHOCOLATE ICE CREAM
Makes 4 servings

3/4 cup milk powder
3 tablespoons cocoa
1/2 cup water
8 teaspoons sugar
1/2 teaspoon vanilla

Mix milk powder and cocoa thoroughly. Add sugar, water, and vanilla. Beat until smooth and pour into refrigerator tray. Freeze until firm.

WHITE CHOCOLATE ICE CREAM
Makes 1 quart

1 cup water
3/4 cup sugar
6 egg yolks
1 tablespoon vanilla
10 ounces Swiss or French white chocolate, melted
2 cups whipping cream

In heavy medium-size saucepan, blend water and sugar. Cook over low heat until sugar dissolves, swirling pan occasionally. Bring to a boil. Let boil 5 minutes. Meanwhile, combine egg yolks and vanilla in large bowl of electric mixer and beat at high speed until light and fluffy, about 7 minutes. Slowly, add hot syrup to yolk mixture, beating constantly until thickened and completely cooked, about 10 minutes. Gradually add white chocolate and continue beating until cooked, about 7 minutes. Stir in cream. Cover and freeze until set, at least 5 or 6 hours, or overnight.

CHEESECAKE ICE CREAM
Makes about 2 quarts

2 egg yolks
1 cup sugar, divided
1 cup half-and-half
2 (8-ounce) packages cream cheese
1/2 teaspoon grated lemon rind
1/2 teaspoon grated orange rind
1 tablespoon lemon juice

1/2 teaspoon vanilla
1 pint plain yogurt

In heavy saucepan, beat egg yolks with 1/2 cup sugar. Beat in half-and-half. Cook over low heat, stirring constantly, until just thick enough to coat back of spoon. Do not boil. Remove from heat. Chill thoroughly. Beat cream cheese until light. Add remaining sugar, lemon, and orange rinds, lemon juice, and vanilla. Continue to beat until smooth. Freeze in flat trays, then beat with rotary beater or in food processor.

LEMON ICE CREAM
Serves 6

2 eggs
1/2 cup sugar
1/2 cup light corn syrup
1-1/4 cups milk
1 cup whipping cream or Dream Whip
1/4 cup lemon juice
2 teaspoons grated lemon peel (2 lemons)

Beat eggs until light and lemon-colored. Add sugar gradually, beating constantly. Add corn syrup, milk, whipping cream, lemon juice, and grated lemon peel. Mix well. Put in 9x5-inch loaf pan. Freeze until firm, about 9 hours (covering with aluminum foil). Turn out into chilled bowl; beat until light. Return to 9x5-inch loaf pan. Cover; freeze until firm, 9 hours.

FRESH PEACH ICE CREAM
Makes about 2 quarts

2 eggs
3/4 cup sugar
1/8 teaspoon salt
3/4 cup light corn syrup
1 cup heavy cream

1 cup milk
3 cups peeled and sliced fresh ripe peaches
1 tablespoon, plus 2 teaspoons lemon juice
1/8 teaspoon almond extract

In large bowl of mixer beat eggs, sugar, and salt until thick and light-colored. Beat in corn syrup and cream until well blended. In blender, whirl until smooth, milk, peaches, lemon juice, and almond extract. Beat into cream mixture until well-blended. Freeze until almost firm. Beat until smooth. Freeze again, then beat again. Turn into chilled 9 x 9-inch baking pan or 9 x 5 x 3-inch loaf pan. Freeze until firm, then cover airtight.

PEPPERMINT ICE CREAM
Serves 6

1 envelope unflavored gelatin
1/2 cup cold milk
1-1/4 cups crushed peppermint candy
2 cups whipped whipping cream
1-1/2 cups scalded milk

Soften gelatin in cold milk; dissolve in hot milk. Add 1 cup candy and dissolve. Freeze. Break up and beat until smooth. Fold in cream and 1/4 cup candy. Freeze.

RASPBERRY ICE CREAM
Makes 2 quarts

1 (10-ounce) package frozen raspberries, thawed
1/2 cup sugar
2-1/2 cups milk
1-1/2 cups whipping cream
1-1/2 teaspoons vanilla extract

Process undrained raspberries with food mill to remove seeds. Combine raspberries and remaining ingredients. Stir until sugar is dissolved. Pour mixture into 1 gallon freezer can. Freeze according to manufacturer's instructions. Let ripen at least 1 hour. Delicious!!

BUTTERSCOTCH TAPIOCA
Serves 4

3 tablespoons quick-cooking tapioca
1/8 teaspoon salt
2 cups milk
1 tablespoon butter
1/2 cup dark brown sugar
1/4 cup finely chopped pecans

Mix tapioca, salt, and milk in a pan and let stand for 5 minutes. Cook over moderate heat, stirring constantly, for about 6 minutes, until mixture comes to a full boil. Remove from heat. Melt butter in a small skillet and stir in brown sugar. Cook over moderate heat, stirring until sugar melts and bubbles for 1 minute. Stir into tapioca mixture and add pecans. Serve warm or chilled.

ELEGANT CHOCOLATE ANGEL TORTE
Serves 12

1/3 cup Hershey's cocoa
1 (14.5 ounce) package angel food cake mix
2.8-ounce package (2 envelopes) whipped topping mix
1 cup *cold* milk
1 teaspoon vanilla
1 cup strawberry purée*
Strawberries

Combine cocoa and contents of cake flour packet. Proceed with mixing cake as directed on package. Bake and cool as directed. Slice cooled cake crosswise into four 1-inch slices. Combine topping mix, cold milk, and vanilla in large mixer bowl; prepare according to package directions. Blend in strawberry purée. Place bottom cake slice on serving plate; spread with one-fourth of topping.

Stack next cake layer; spread with topping. Continue layering cake and topping. Garnish with strawberries. Refrigerate. To serve, use sharp serrated knife and cut with a gentle sawing motion.
*Mash or puree 2 cups sliced fresh strawberries (or frozen berries, thawed) in blender or food processor to measure 1 cup.

BUTTERSCOTCH TORTE
Serves 8

1 package fluffy white frosting mix (for 2-layer cake)
1 teaspoon vanilla
1 cup graham-cracker crumbs
1 (6-ounce) package butterscotch chips
1/2 cup coconut
1/2 cup chopped pecans

Prepare frosting mix according to package directions. Add vanilla. Fold in all other ingredients carefully, and spread in a greased 9-inch plate. Bake in a 350-degree oven for 30 minutes or until lightly browned. Serve with vanilla ice cream or a dab of whipped cream, if desired.

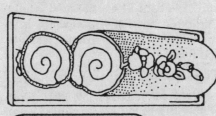

APPLE CHEESE TORTE

1/2 cup butter, softened
2/3 cup sugar, plus 1/4 cup sugar
3/4 teaspoon vanilla
1 cup flour
1 (8-ounce) package cream cheese, softened
1 egg
1/2 teaspoon cinnamon
4 cups peeled, sliced apples
1/4 cup sliced almonds

Preheat oven to 450 degrees. Cream butter, 1/3 cup sugar, and 1/4 tea-

spoon vanilla. Blend in flour. Spread dough onto bottom and 1-1/2 inches up the sides of a 9-inch spring-form pan.

Combine cream cheese and 1/4 cup sugar. Mix well. Add egg and remaining 1/2 teaspoon vanilla. Pour into pastry-lined pan. Combine 1/3 cup sugar and cinnamon. Add apples, spoon over cheese layer. Sprinkle with sliced almonds. Bake at 450 degrees for 10 minutes; reduce heat to 400 degrees and bake for 35 minutes. Cool before removing from pan.

CHOCOLATE ECLAIR TORTE
Serves 12-16

2 (6-ounce) packages instant vanilla pudding
3 cups milk
1 (10-ounce) container whipped topping
Graham crackers

Beat pudding and milk for two minutes. Add whipped topping. Line bottom of 9x13-inch pan with whole graham crackers. Pour half of pudding mixture over crackers. Put another layer of whole graham crackers and the rest of pudding mixture. Then top with last layer of whole graham crackers. Frost with Eclair Frosting (recipe follows).

Eclair Frosting:
4 (1-ounce) packages Nestle's Chocobake or 4 squares melted semisweet chocolate
1-1/2 cups confectioners' sugar
2 tablespoons butter or margarine
2 tablespoons white corn syrup
1 teaspoon vanilla
3 tablespoons milk

Mix thoroughly. Place on top of torte. Refrigerate overnight before serving.

OLD-FASHIONED RICE PUDDING
Serves 6

1 quart skim milk
1 teaspoon Sweet 'N Low sugar
   substitute
1/4 cup raw white rice
1 tablespoon butter
1/4 teaspoon salt
1/4 teaspoon nutmeg
1 teaspoon vanilla

Preheat oven at 325 degrees. In a lightly greased 1-1/2 quart casserole, combine all ingredients. Bake uncovered, stirring frequently, for the first hour. The complete cooking time is 2-1/2 hours. This may be served topped with low-calorie whipped cream or crushed fruit. (115 calories per serving)

FIGGY PUDDING
Serves 8-10

1-1/2 cups all-purpose flour
1 teaspoon baking powder
1/2 teaspoon baking soda
1/2 teaspoon cinnamon
1/2 teaspoon nutmeg
1/2 teaspoon ginger
1 cup chopped cranberries
1 cup shredded carrots
1 cup packed brown sugar
1/2 cup cooking oil
1/2 cup honey
2 beaten eggs

In a large bowl, combine dry ingredients. In a bowl, combine carrots, cranberries, brown sugar, oil, honey, and eggs. Add carrot mixture to dry ingredients. Pour into greased 7-cup mold. Bake in a 325-degree oven for 30 to 40 minutes or until it tests done. Serve with Orange Hard Sauce (recipe follows).

Orange Hard Sauce:
   Makes 1/2 cup
1/4 cup butter, softened
1 cup sifted confectioners' sugar
1/4 teaspoon shredded orange peel
1 tablespoon orange juice

Beat butter and sugar together in a small bowl. Beat in peel and juice until well-blended. Spoon into small serving bowl. Chill.

PARTY PUNCH BOWL DESSERT

1 box yellow cake mix
2 large boxes strawberry gelatin
2 large containers Cool Whip
2 large (10-ounce) packages frozen
   sliced strawberries
2 large packages regular vanilla
   pudding (*not* instant)
Fresh strawberries for garnish

Use 2 (8-inch) round layer cake pans and a clear glass punch bowl. Make cake according to box directions. Cool; cut layers horizontally by pulling string through so you have 4 layers. Make vanilla pudding according to package directions and let cool. Mix 2-1/2 cups boiling water with 2 packages strawberry gelatin to dissolve. Add the 2 packages of partially thawed berries. Put in refrigerator until mixture thickens—but do not let it get too firm.

To assemble:
   In the punch bowl add 1/4 of the gelatin mixture.
First layer of cake, 1/4 more gelatin, spread a layer of Cool Whip, then a layer of pudding.
Second layer of cake, gelatin, Cool Whip, pudding
Third layer of cake, gelatin, Cool Whip, pudding
Fourth layer of cake only, topped with thick layer of Cool Whip. Garnish with fresh, sliced berries. You can make this the night before but *do not* put last layer of Cool Whip on until an hour or so before serving. Use large serving spoon to scoop out servings. Prepare for raving reviews on appearance and taste!

CARAMEL TOPPED RICE CUSTARD
Serves 6

12 caramel candies
2-1/4 cups milk, divided
2 cups cooked rice, cooled
4 eggs
1/3 cup packed brown sugar
1 teaspoon vanilla extract
1/4 teaspoon salt

Combine caramels and 1/4 cup milk in small saucepan. Cook, stirring, over medium-low heat until caramels melt. Pour equal amounts into 6 buttered, 3/4-cup custard cups. Spoon 1/3 cup rice into each cup. Blend remaining ingredients; pour evenly into each cup. Place cups in shallow pan, containing 1 inch water. Bake at 350 degrees for 45 minutes, or until custard is set. Loosen custard with knife and invert onto dessert plates. Garnish with chopped nuts or coconut, if desired. Serve warm.

STRAWBERRIES WITH SOUR CREAM CUSTARD

1/2 cup sugar
2-1/2 tablespoons cornstarch
1-1/2 cups milk
4 eggs, beaten
1/2 cup sour cream
1-1/2 teaspoons vanilla
1-2 pints fresh strawberries
   (washed, hulled and halved)

Combine sugar and cornstarch in medium saucepan. Gradually, stir in milk and cook over medium heat, stirring constantly until it boils. Boil and stir 1 minute. Remove from heat. Blend milk mixture *into egg mixture* in saucepan. Add sour cream and vanilla; beat with whisk until well blended. Cool *immediately* by placing in a bowl of ice cold water for a few minutes. Cover and chill thoroughly. To serve, spoon custard sauce over strawberries. Will literally melt in your mouth.

Strawberry Almond Fritters are also completely different from the usual.

VANILLA ICE CREAM
Serves 6

2 eggs
1/2 cup sugar
1/8 teaspoon salt
1/2 cup light corn syrup
1-1/3 cups heavy cream
2/3 cup milk
1 teaspoon lemon juice
Seeds scraped from split 6-inch
    vanilla bean

In large bowl of electric mixer beat eggs, sugar, and salt until thick and light-colored. Beat in remaining ingredients until well blended. Freeze until almost firm. Beat until smooth. Freeze again, then beat again. Turn into chilled 9 x 9-inch baking pan or 9 x 5 x 3-inch loaf pan. Freeze until firm, then cover airtight. Makes about 1 quart.

PEACH SHERBET

1 (1-pound) can peaches
1 tablespoon Tang powder
Pinch of salt
1/4 cup ice water

Empty can of peaches into freezer tray to freeze. When frozen, break into small pieces. Combine ingredients in blender and blend until smooth. Pour into chilled sherbet glasses, or freeze until ready to serve.

RASPBERRY SHERBET
Makes 1-1/2 pints

3/4 cup sugar
1/4 cup water
1 cup raspberry juice
1/4 cup lemon juice
Pinch of salt
1 cup evaporated milk

Boil sugar and water to a thin syrup. Add fruit juices and salt. Chill milk in ice cream can. Pour cold fruit juice mixture slowly into the milk. Freeze with ratio 1:8 salt-ice mixture.

APPLE-CHEESE PUDDING
Serves 6

2 cups firmly packed dark brown
    sugar
1 quart water
1 stick cinnamon
1 clove
6 slices stale bread, toasted and
    cubed
3 apples, pared, cored, and sliced
1 cup raisins
1 cup chopped blanched almonds
1/2 pound Monterey Jack or similar
    cheese, cubed

Put brown sugar, water, cinnamon, and clove into a saucepan and bring to boiling; reduce heat and simmer until a light syrup is formed. Discard spices; set syrup aside. Meanwhile, arrange a layer of toast cubes in a buttered casserole. Cover with a layer of apples, raisins, almonds, and cheese. Repeat until all ingredients are used. Pour syrup over all. Bake at 350 degrees for 30 minutes. Serve hot.

SOUR-CREAM APPLE PUDDING

5 large apples
1 cup brown sugar
1/4 cup butter
1 cup graham-cracker crumbs
1/2 cup flour
1 teaspoon cinnamon
1 cup sour cream

Peel and cut apples. Mix flour, sugar, and cinnamon together; combine with apples. Cut butter over surface of apples. Top with sour cream. Sprinkle the top surface with graham-cracker crumbs. Bake at 375 degrees for 20-25 minutes.

BLACK BREAD PUDDING
Serves 6

6 eggs, separated
1/2 cup sugar
1/4 teaspoon salt
1 cup stale bread crumbs (made from
    rye, pumpernickel or whole wheat
    bread)
3/4 teaspoon cinnamon
1/4 teaspoon cloves
2 tablespoons melted butter
Stale dry bread crumbs, fine

Beat egg yolks at high speed in a small bowl until thick. Gradually beat in sugar. Continue beating at high speed until mixture is very thick and piles softly. Using clean beaters and a large bowl, beat egg whites with salt until stiff, not dry, peaks form. Fold bread crumbs, cinnamon, and cloves into beaten yolks. Then fold in 1 tablespoon melted butter. Fold in egg whites. Brush a 2-quart deep casserole with remaining 1 tablespoon melted butter. Coat dish with bread crumbs. Gently turn soufflé mixture into prepared dish. Bake at 350 degrees for 25-30 minutes, or until set in center.

BAKED RICE PUDDING
Serves 6-8

1 cup sugar
1-1/2 teaspoons cornstarch
1/8 teaspoon ground nutmeg
3 eggs, beaten
2 cups milk
1 cup raisins
2/3 cup cooked regular rice
1/2 teaspoon vanilla extract

Combine sugar, cornstarch, and nutmeg in a medium mixing bowl. Add eggs, beating until well-combined. Add milk, raisins, rice, and vanilla, stirring until well-blended. Pour mixture into a greased 8-inch square pan. Place prepared pan in a 13x9x2-inch baking pan; add boiling water to a depth of 1 inch. Bake at 325 degrees for 1 hour or until a knife inserted in center comes out clean. Spoon into individual serving bowls. Serve hot! This recipe is great for leftover rice.

STRAWBERRY MERINGUE TORTE

3 egg whites
1/2 teaspoon baking powder
1 cup sugar
10 squares or 10 soda crackers rolled fine
1/2 cup pecans, rolled fine
3 cups sliced strawberries
Cool Whip

Beat egg whites and baking powder until frothy. Gradually beat in sugar until whites are stiff. Fold in crackers and pecans. Spread in 9-inch pie pan, which has been greased thoroughly with butter. Bake 30 minutes in 300 degree oven.

Fill meringue tart with strawberries; top with Cool Whip when ready to serve.

STRAWBERRY ALMOND BUTTER

1/2 pound margarine
1 pound powdered sugar
1 pound strawberries
1/2 cup finely ground almonds

Cream butter with powdered sugar and work in the pound of hulled strawberries that have been forced through a colander. When well mixed, stir in almonds and pinch of salt, if desired.

For a change-of-pace dessert, strawberries with sour cream custard is a "conversation piece." This recipe will serve 6 and it looks delightful in a glass bowl that has been chilled.

FROZEN STRAWBERRY DESSERT

24 large marshmallows
1 (10-ounce) package frozen strawberries (thawed)
1 cup sifted flour
1/2 cup milk
1 envelope Dream Whip
1 stick margarine

Have margarine at room temperature. Cut margarine into flour to make crumbs. Press into bottom of 7x11-inch pan. Bake at 400 degrees until brown. Cool. Melt marshmallows in milk. Add strawberries and let cool. When cool, add prepared Dream Whip. Pour into crust and freeze. Best when eaten partially frozen.

I keep this dessert in the freezer for unexpected guests.

STRAWBERRY ALMOND FRITTERS

Strawberries
1 cup apricot jam
1 cup toasted almonds
1 cup cracker crumbs
2 eggs

Wash, hull, and dry strawberries on paper towel. Force apricot jam through coarse strainer. Finely chop toasted almonds and crush salted crackers until you have a cupful. Beat eggs slightly. Dip each berry in jam and roll in almonds. When all are coated, dip, two at a time, in egg and then crumbs. Chill. Before serving time, heat deep fat to 360 degrees and cook berries until they are golden brown. Serve at once, passing powdered sugar, if desired. These may be fried in skillet also.

Strawberries are not only for royalty, nor do we have to "sew a fine seam" to enjoy them. We are fortunate enough to have these delectable goodies available to us all year long. Whichever recipe you choose, it will add a noble note to your table.

STRAWBERRY GERMAN CREAM
Serves 6-8

1 (10-ounce) box frozen sliced strawberries, thawed
1 cup boiling water
1 (3-ounce) package strawberry gelatin
1 envelope dessert topping mix

Drain strawberries, reserving syrup. Pour boiling water over gelatin in bowl, stirring until gelatin is dissolve. Add enough cold water to reserv syrup to measure 1 cup; stir into di solved gelatin. Chill until almost s Prepare dessert topping mix as pac age directs. Beat gelatin until foam Fold gelatin and strawberries in topping mix. Pour into 1-quart mol Chill until firm; unmold. Serve wi sweetened whipped cream and ga nish with strawberries.

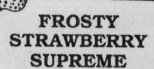

FROSTY STRAWBERRY SUPREME
Serves 9-12

1 cup all-purpose flour
1/4 cup finely chopped pecans
1/4 cup brown sugar, packed
1/2 cup melted margarine
2 cups egg whites
1 (10-ounce) package frozen strawberries, partially thawed
2/3 cup white granulated sugar
2 tablespoons lemon juice
1 cup whipped cream or non-dairy whipped topping.

Combine flour, nuts, brown suga and melted margarine. Mix well an spread into 13x9-inch pan. Bake a 350 degrees for about 20 to 25 min utes, stirring to crumble. Combin egg whites, sugar, strawberries, an lemon juice in a large deep mixin bowl. Beat with electric mixer at hig speed for 15 minutes. Fold in whippe cream or whipped topping. Place one half the crumbs in bottom of the par Pour in strawberry mixture, then to with remaining crumbs. Freeze unti firm. Cut into squares to serve. To each serving with whipped topping, i desired. This is really a "Supreme dessert.

Note: Use blueberries for a change o pace, adjusting to suit your own tast in regard to sugar.

Foreign & EXOTIC

SMOKED PORK PLATTER (AUSTRIA)
Serves 6–8

1 boneless smoked pork shoulder roll (approximately 2½ pounds)
  Water
4 medium potatoes, pared and halved
3 small onions, quartered
1 (27-ounce) can sauerkraut
1 teaspoon caraway seeds
¼ teaspoon pepper (optional)

Place pork shoulder roll in a Dutch oven and add enough water to cover meat. Cover and cook over low heat for 1½ hours. Remove meat from pan and pour off all but 2 cups of liquid. Add potatoes and onions to liquid in pan. Place meat on top. Cover and continue cooking for 30 minutes, or until meat and vegetables are done. During last 10 minutes of cooking time, add sauerkraut, caraway seeds and pepper. Remove meat and vegetables to hot platter.

STEAK ROLL (BRACIOLA)
Serves 8–10

3 eggs
1 center-cut round steak, ½ inch thick
6 slices salami

3 tablespoons Romano cheese
  Salt and pepper to taste

Beat eggs; cook in form of an omelet. Remove bone from steak and season meat. Place omelet on top of steak; then make a layer of salami slices on top of omelet. Sprinkle Romano cheese, salt and pepper over all and begin to roll steak, jelly roll fashion. The meat roll can be secured with heavy cord or rolled in aluminum foil. Bake at 350 degrees for 1 hour, depending on weight of meat. Slice and serve with a vegetable.

EGG FOO YONG (CHINESE)

6 eggs, beaten well
⅔ cup finely sliced onion
¼ cup finely chopped celery
1 cup bean sprouts, drained
1 to 1½ cups cooked chicken, turkey *or* pork roast*
  Salad oil

Combine eggs, onion, celery, bean sprouts and meat. Use a large griddle or skillet greased well with salad oil. For each patty, use about ¼ cup of egg mixture poured on hot griddle. Use a broad spatula to keep egg mixture from spreading too much. When the patties are set and brown, turn over to brown other side. Serve hot.

Hot Soy Sauce:
5 teaspoons soy sauce
2 teaspoons cornstarch
2 teaspoons sugar
2 teaspoons vinegar
¾ teaspoon salt
1 cup cold water

Serve with Egg Foo Yong.
*1–2 (6½-ounce) cans tuna may be substituted for chicken.

POTATOES ITALIANO
Serves 4 to 6

4 large baking potatoes
1 tablespoon olive or vegetable oil
1/4 cup grated Parmesan cheese
1 cup shredded Mozzarella cheese
3 medium tomatoes, sliced ,
1 large onion, peeled and thinly sliced
1/2 teaspoon oregano
1/2 teaspoon salt
1/8 teaspoon pepper
2 tablespoons butter

Peel and slice potatoes in 1/4-inch slices. Oil 9 x 13-inch casserole dish. Combine two cheeses, reserving some for topping. Arrange potatoes, tomatoes and onion slices in layers; sprinkle each layer with cheese and seasonings. Dot with butter and bake uncovered at 400 degrees for 30 minutes. Remove from oven and sprinkle with remaining cheese; bake for an additional 20 minutes.

INDONESIAN VEGETABLE SALAD (GADO-GADO)
Serves 6–8

- 4 cups shredded cabbage
- ½ cup flaked coconut
- 2 tablespoons peanut oil *or* vegetable oil
- ¼ cup thinly sliced green onions
- 2 cloves garlic, minced
- ½ cup peanut butter (smooth)
- 1 teaspoon light brown sugar
- 1 teaspoon salt
- ¼ teaspoon dried, ground chili peppers
- 2 teaspoons grated lemon rind
- ¾ cup light cream
- ¾ cup water
- 2 medium-size tomatoes, diced (Use ripe, but firm tomatoes; drain if overly juicy)
- 2 cucumbers, seeded and diced (small to medium size)
- 2 hard-cooked eggs, coarsely chopped

Cover cabbage with water; bring to a boil and cook only 2 minutes. Drain. Rinse coconut under cold water; drain and pat dry with paper towels. Heat oil in a skillet; sauté onions and garlic for 3 minutes. Stir in coconut, peanut butter, sugar, salt, chili peppers and lemon rind, and very gradually the cream mixed with water. Cook over low heat for 5 minutes, stirring frequently. Cool. In a bowl, toss together cabbage, tomatoes and cucumbers. Pour dressing over and mix lightly. Chill 1 hour before serving. Sprinkle with chopped egg just before serving.

SCANDINAVIAN PORK PATTIES (FRIKADELLER)
Serves 4

- 1 pound ground pork
- 1⅔ cups tart apples, peeled and coarsely shredded
- ⅓ cup bread crumbs, Italian style
- ½ teaspoon salt
  Freshly ground black pepper (to taste)
- 2 large eggs, beaten
- 2 tablespoons vegetable oil
- ½ cup currant jelly
- ½ cup port wine
- ½ cup heavy cream
  Chopped parsley

In medium bowl, combine pork, apples, bread crumbs, salt, pepper and beaten eggs. Mix well with hands and form into 8 (3-inch) patties. In large skillet, heat vegetable oil; add patties and cook over medium heat until browned on both sides and no longer pink in center, about 7 minutes a side. Remove patties to warm serving platter and keep warm. Drain off drippings in skillet and discard. Add jelly, wine and cream; cook and stir over medium heat until bubbly and reduced to the consistency of heavy cream, about 3–5 minutes. Pour sauce over patties and serve at once. Garnish with sprigs of chopped parsley.

CARROT SALAD (OMOK-HOURIA)
Serves 6 to 8

- 5 large carrots, scraped and washed, cut into 1/4" pieces
- 2 cloves garlic crushed
- 4 tablespoons very finely chopped fresh coriander leaves
- 4 tablespoons lemon juice
- 4 tablespoons olive oil
- 1-1/2 teaspoons salt
- 1/2 teaspoon pepper
- 1/8 teaspoon cayenne
- 2 hard-boiled eggs, sliced
- 12 black olives, pitted and cut in half
- 1 small tomato, thinly sliced

Place carrots in saucepan; cover with water; bring to boil; cook for 5 minutes over medium heat. Drain and allow to cool; place in food processor; process for a moment, until carrots are coarsely ground.

Transfer to mixing bowl; add garlic, coriander leaves, lemon juice, oil, salt, pepper and cayenne; mix. Place on flat serving plate. Decorate with eggs, olives and tomato.

GERMAN-STYLE BEANS
Serves 6

- 4 slices bacon
- ½ cup onion, chopped
- 1½ tablespoons sugar
- 1½ tablespoons flour
- ¼ teaspoon celery seed
- ½ teaspoon salt
- 2 (15½-ounce) cans green and shelled beans
- ⅓ cup vinegar

Cook bacon until crisp; remove and drain bacon. Add onion to bacon drippings. Cook until tender. Add sugar, flour, celery seed and salt. Cook until bubbly. Drain beans; reserve ⅓ cup liquid. Add bean liquid and vinegar to flour mixture. Stir; add beans. Simmer about 10–15 minutes, or until slightly thickened and thoroughly heated. Crumble bacon and add to beans.

BOEUF BOURGUIGNON

- 1 tablespoon oil
- 1 pound lean beef cubes
- 1 onion, thinly sliced
- 1 cup beef bouillon
- 1 cup dry red wine
- 12 small onions
- ½ pound whole mushrooms
  Salt and pepper to taste
- 1 tablespoon cornstarch
- 1 tablespoon cold water

Heat oil in heavy saucepan and brown beef cubes until deeply colored. Remove from pan and brown sliced onions until golden brown. Return beef cubes to pan; add bouillon and dry red wine. Simmer until beef cubes are almost tender. Add onions and cook until tender. Add mushrooms and heat through; adjust seasoning. Mix cornstarch and water. Add to beef stock and boil for 1 minute, or until sauce is thickened and clear. Serve with noodles or rice.

EGG NOODLES WITH PORK SAUCE (CHINA)

Serves 4

- 1 large onion, finely chopped
- 4 garlic cloves, finely chopped
- 2 tablespoons peanut oil
- 1 pound ground pork
- ¼ teaspoon hamburger seasoning
- 2 tablespoons Worcestershire sauce
- 1 tablespoon soy sauce
- 1 teaspoon brown sugar
- 1 teaspoon hoisin sauce
- ½ cup chicken broth
- 4 cups cooked, buttered egg noodles
  Chives *or* parsley chow mein noodles *or* rice noodles

Brown onion and garlic in oil. Add pork. Cook; drain grease. Add remaining seasonings and broth. Cook 15–20 minutes. Spoon sauce over egg noodles. Garnish with chives or parsley; top with chow mein noodles or rice noodles.

This recipe originated from China. I love the flavors of their cooking and I also have developed new flavors by combining some of their choice ingredients with my favorites.

SEZCHUAN BEEF

- 1 pound round, flank *or* sirloin steak
- 1–2 tablespoons vegetable oil
- ¼ cup slivered orange peel (optional)
- 1 clove garlic, minced
- ½ teaspoon ginger*
- ¼ to ½ teaspoon crushed red pepper flakes
  Steamed broccoli
- 2 tablespoons cornstarch
- 1 cup beef broth

- 2 tablespoons soy sauce
- 2 tablespoons sherry
- ¼ cup orange marmalade**
  Hot cooked rice
- ⅛ teaspoon Kitchen Bouquet sauce

Can partially freeze meat to make it easier to thinly slice diagonally. Heat oil in large skillet or wok over medium heat. Add half the beef; stir-fry 3 minutes until browned. Remove browned meat and add rest of beef; brown. Return all beef to the wok; add orange peel, ginger, garlic and red pepper flakes; stir-fry 1 minute. Stir together cornstarch, beef broth, soy sauce, sherry and Kitchen Bouquet in a bowl; then mix in orange marmalade. Add to beef in wok. Stirring constantly, bring to a boil over medium heat and boil 1–2 minutes. Serve over hot, cooked rice with steamed broccoli on the side.

For Sezchuan Chicken:

- 1 pound boneless chicken breasts, thinly sliced
- 1 cup cool chicken broth—prepared as above

*Can use (I do) fresh minced gingerroot to taste, about 1 teaspoon.
**Can substitute ¼ cup honey for orange peel and marmalade for a different, delicious sauce.

PAKISTANI CURRIED PEAS (CURRY MATAR PAKISTANI—INDIA)

Serves 4

- 1 teaspoon butter
- 1 teaspoon vegetable oil
- ½ cup sliced green onions
- ¼ teaspoon turmeric
- ½ teaspoon ground coriander
- ⅛ teaspoon ground red pepper
- 1½ teaspoons curry powder
- ¼ teaspoon salt
- 1 tablespoon Garam Masala (recipe follows)
- 1 (10-ounce) package frozen peas

Garam Masala:

- 1 tablespoon cardamom seeds
- 1 (2-inch) stick cinnamon
- 1 teaspoon cumin seeds
- 1 teaspoon whole cloves
- 1 teaspoon black peppercorns
- ¼ teaspoon nutmeg

Put all ingredients of Garam Masala in grinder for 30–40 seconds.

In saucepan heat butter and oil; add green onions; cook, stirring, 2 minutes. Stir in turmeric, coriander, red pepper, curry powder, salt and Garam Masala. Cook, stirring occasionally, about 10 minutes. Add peas. Reduce heat; cook about 10 minutes. Serve with plain hot rice and Indian bread (chapati or poori).

PAPRIKAS POTATOES (HUNGARY)

Serves 6–8

- 3 pounds potatoes, peeled and sliced to ¼-inch thickness
- 2 tablespoons shortening *or* bacon drippings
- 1 small onion, minced
- 3 cloves garlic, pressed
- 1 tablespoon salt
- 2 tablespoons Hungarian paprika
- 2 cups chicken broth
- 2 cups water
- 1 cup sour cream

In medium-size Dutch oven, melt shortening and sauté onion and garlic until limp. Add paprika and salt. Stir and cook for about 1 minute. Add chicken broth and water. Bring to boil. Add potatoes; bring back to boil and reduce heat to simmer. Continue cooking until potatoes are tender. Stir with care occasionally. Stir in sour cream and bring back just to boil. Ready to serve.

The Hungarian love of sour cream, paprika and garlic is used to enhance the lowly potato into a tasty side dish. Brought from Hungary by grandparents.

MIDDLE EAST TABOULEH SALAD
Serves 6–8

- 1 cup fine burghul (wheal pilaf)
- 2 cups chopped parsley
- ½ cup finely chopped green onions
- ¼ cup finely chopped mint
- ¼ cup olive oil
- ¼ cup lemon juice
- ½ teaspoon salt
- ½ teaspoon pepper, black
- 2 firm, ripe tomatoes, chopped
- 1 cucumber, sliced
- 1 green pepper, chopped

Wash burghul with cold water and drain at once, squeezing all water out, then add lemon juice, oil, salt and black pepper. Stir well. Let stand for a few minutes, or until burghul has absorbed the lemon and oil. Sliced and chopped vegetables must be pretty dry so that when you add the burghul, which has been mixed with oil and lemon juice, it will not be soggy but just hold together very nicely. Add your mint last. If you wish, you can also chop lettuce and add to your salad.

MEATBALLS WITH SAUERKRAUT (HUNGARY)
Serves 6

- ¾ pound ground beef chuck
- ¾ cup ground pork
- ¾ cup minced onion
- 3 cloves garlic, pressed
- 2 eggs, slightly beaten
- 1 tablespoon salt
- ½ teaspoon freshly ground pepper
- ¾ cup long-grain rice, partially cooked and cooled
- 2 tablespoons shortening (lard is best; next best, bacon drippings)
- 2 tablespoons flour
- 2 pounds sauerkraut
  Water

Additional salt to flavor, to personal taste
Pepper to taste

In large bowl mix thoroughly the first 8 ingredients. Set aside. In large Dutch oven, melt shortening and add flour. Under low heat cook flour until lightly browned. Add 1 cup water. Place sauerkraut in sieve and slightly wash under cold water. Remove pan from heat and place a layer of sauerkraut on bottom. With your hands, form the meat mixture into about 2½-inch balls. Place on top of sauerkraut. Cover with remaining kraut. Add water to cover by about 1 inch. Bring to boil, then reduce heat to simmer and cover. Cook for about 1½ hours, until meat is tender. Season the liquid with salt and pepper to taste. Serve in soup bowls with good rye bread.

POTICA (YUGOSLAVIAN CHRISTMAS BREAD)

- 3½ cups flour
- 1 package yeast
- 1 cup milk
- 2 tablespoons sugar
- 2 tablespoons butter
- 1 teaspoon salt
- 1 egg

Filling:

- 2 cups finely ground walnuts
- 1 egg, beaten
- ¼ cup brown sugar
- 2 tablespoons honey
- 2 tablespoons milk
- 1 tablespoon melted butter
- 1 teaspoon cinnamon
- ½ teaspoon vanilla

Stir together 1½ cups flour and yeast. Heat milk, sugar, butter and salt until warm. Add to flour/yeast mixture. Add egg and beat with el□ tric mixer at low speed. Scra□ bowl. Beat for 3 minutes at hi□ speed. Stir in remaining flour □ make a moderately stiff dough. T□ out and knead until smooth and el□ tic. Place in greased bowl and □ rise until doubled—about 1½ hou□ Combine filling ingredients and □ aside. Punch down dough and let □ for 10 minutes. Roll out until ve□ thin and approximately 20 x 30 inc□ es. Spread out nut filling and roll □ along longer side. Pinch edge □ seal. Place in U-shape on greas□ baking sheet. Let rise until double□ Bake at 350 degrees for 30–35 mi□ utes.

JAPANESE RICE A LA LUISE
Makes 8 cups

- 1 cup long-grain rice (toasted)
- ½ cup onions, sliced
- 2 tablespoons butter
- 1 cup sliced celery
- 2 cans small whole mushrooms
- 1 large bell pepper, sliced
- ½ cup blanched almonds, shredded
- 1 can water chestnuts, drained
- 1 can bamboo shoots, drained
- 3 cups chicken broth, fresh *or* canned
- 3 tablespoons soy sauce
- 1½ teaspoons salt
- ½ teaspoon pepper

Place rice in shallow pan; toast in □ preheated 350-degree oven unt□ lightly browned, stirring occasionally□ Melt butter in large saucepan an□ sauté onions until translucent. Add al□ other ingredients and stir over me□ dium heat until hot, but not boiling□ Add salt to taste, if necessary. Plac□ browned dry rice in a 3-quart casse□ role and pour contents of saucepa□ over it; stir. Cover and bake in 350□ degree oven until liquid is absorbed□ about 45 minutes.

BISCOUTI (ITALIAN BISCUIT COOKIES)

Makes 5–6 dozen

6 tablespoons Crisco shortening
1 cup sugar
3 eggs
1 teaspoon anise extract
5 teaspoons baking powder
¾ cup milk
6 cups flour, sifted

Cream together shortening and sugar. Add 1 egg at a time. Add anise extract. Add flour and baking powder alternately with milk. Grease pan. Bake at 400 degrees for 10–12 minutes. Cookies can be iced with confectioners' sugar and milk combination. (Add food coloring to icing for holiday flair, if desired.)

RED SNAPPER A LA VERACRUZANA (HUACHINANGO A LA VERACRUZANA)

Serves 4–6

1 (2½ pound) red snapper
2½ cups chopped tomatoes
2 onions, chopped
3 green peppers, chopped
3 cloves garlic, minced
1 bunch parsley, finely chopped
2 chili peppers, finely chopped (small elongated green chilies)
⅓ cup finely chopped green olives
⅓ cup capers
4 tablespoons vinegar
8 jalapeño peppers (cut in half, fried and cut in strips)
1 pint oil

1 teaspoon oregano
Salt and pepper
¼ pint dry sherry

Cut red snapper into 6-ounce fillets. Sauté tomatoes in a skillet; add onions, then green peppers, garlic, parsley and chili peppers. Add chopped olives, capers, vinegar and jalapeño strips. Blend in oil. Season with oregano, salt and pepper. Simmer slowly until all is tender and thickened. Add sherry during last part of cooking. In a separate skillet, heat a little oil and add rinsed red snapper fillets. Cover fish with sauce. Cover and cook over low heat 20 minutes. Keep fish from sticking with wide spatula. Serve with rice.

SOUPE AUX LEGUMES DU QUEBEC (VEGETABLE SOUP, "QUEBEC STYLE")

Serves 8

1½ to 2 pounds brisket of beef *or* beef shoulder
1 meatless beef bone
2 cups diced carrots
½ cup diced parsnips
3 large onions, cut in very thin slices
1 cup of finely chopped celery
1 teaspoon savory
½ teaspoon marjoram
¼ teaspoon aniseed
1 teaspoon peppercorns
2 tablespoons coarse salt
1 tablespoon sugar
1 (20-ounce) can tomatoes
3 quarts water

Place all ingredients in a large heavy pan. Bring to a boil; cover and simmer for approximately 4 hours. Mix a few times during the first hour. The dish may be served at the table as a "pot au feu," or the meat may be carved before presenting at the table.

This recipe is from my mother's collection of Canadian recipes.

GOLDEN-CRUST BREAD, POLISH STYLE

Makes 2 loaves

1 cup sour cream
¼ teaspoon soda
1¼ cups hot water
1 cake yeast
¼ cup sugar
½ teaspoon salt
2 tablespoons shortening, melted
6½ cups flour

Combine sour cream and soda; add water, yeast, sugar, salt and melted shortening. Gradually add flour. Mix until well-blended. Knead 5–8 minutes. Put in greased bowl and allow to rise in a warm place until double. Shape into 2 loaves. Allow to rise again until double. Bake in a 375-degree oven for 45 minutes. Let stand 45 minutes before cutting.

IRISH STEW

Serves 6

⅓ cup flour
1½ teaspoons salt
Dash of pepper
1½ pounds lean lamb, cut in 1-inch cubes
2 tablespoons fat
3 cups water
3 medium onions, sliced
4 medium potatoes, cubed
1 turnip, diced
5 medium carrots, quartered
1½ cups frozen peas
¼ cup water

Combine flour, salt and pepper. Coat meat. Save remaining flour. Brown meat in hot fat in a 4-quart saucepan. Add water and cover. Simmer until meat is tender, about 1½ hours. Add onions, potatoes, turnip and carrots. Cover. Simmer 15 minutes. Add peas. Cover and simmer until vegetables are tender. Blend water with remaining flour. Add to stew. Stir. Cook until thick.

HUNGARIAN SHORT RIBS
Serves 6

      4 pounds beef short ribs
      2 tablespoons oil
      2 large onions, sliced
    1/4 cup brown sugar
      1 small can tomato sauce
  2 1/2 cups water
    1/4 cup white vinegar
      1 teaspoon salt
      1 teaspoon dry mustard
      1 teaspoon
         Worcestershire sauce
      6 ounces medium-size noodles

In Dutch oven brown meat in the oil. Add onions. Blend tomato sauce with 1½ cups water, ¼ cup brown sugar, vinegar, salt, mustard and Worcestershire sauce. Pour over meat. Cover and simmer for 2–2½ hours, until meat is tender. Stir in noodles and remaining 1 cup water. Cover again and simmer for 15–20 minutes, or until noodles are tender.

REUBEN CROQUETTES (GERMAN)

    1/2 cup raw rice, cooked
      1 (1-pound) can kraut,
         well-drained
      1 can corned beef
    1/4 cup chopped onion
      3 eggs
      1 cup shredded Swiss cheese
      1 teaspoon salt
    1/4 teaspoon pepper
      2 tablespoons water
  1 1/2 cups fine bread crumbs

Chop the kraut and beef together very fine. Add onion, 2 eggs, cooked rice, cheese, salt and pepper. Mix well. Shape into 18 balls or patties. Use ¼ cup for each ball.

Mix the other egg and 2 tablespoons water together. Roll each croquette in bread crumbs, then in egg mixture and then in bread crumbs again. Let dry for 10 minutes.

If frying the croquettes, fry in shallow oil for 5–7 minutes; turn over once to brown on both sides.

If baking, bake at 400 degrees for 10 minutes in a pan; then turn and bake for another 10 minutes.

Serve with sauce (recipe follows).

Sauce for Croquettes:
      1 cup mayonnaise
    1/3 cup milk
    1/4 cup prepared mustard
      4 teaspoons lemon juice

Mix all together and serve over croquettes.

BEET BORSCHT (RUSSIAN SOUP)
Serves 6

      4 cups beef broth
      2 teaspoons salt
    1/2 teaspoon pepper
      4 cups raw beets, peeled and
         shredded
      3 cups shredded cabbage
      1 cup chopped onion
    1/2 cup sour cream
      2 tablespoons brown sugar
      1 can beer (optional)

In Dutch oven or large pan bring beef broth to a boil; add prepared beets, cabbage, onions, salt and pepper (unless broth is already seasoned). Simmer for about 35–40 minutes. Add brown sugar and beer. Reheat; serve in bowls; top with teaspoonful of sour cream.

Great served with thick slices of dark rye bread and butter.

HAWAIIAN SWEET-SOUR PORK
Serves 7

  1 1/2 pounds lean pork, cut in 2 x
         2½-inch strips
  2 1/2 cups pineapple chunks
    1/4 cup brown sugar
      2 tablespoons cornstarch
    1/4 cup vinegar
    2/3 tablespoon soy sauce
    1/4 teaspoon salt
      1 small green pepper, cut in
         strips
    1/4 cup thinly sliced onion

Brown pork in small amount vegetable oil. Add ½ cup wat cover and simmer (do not boil) u tender, about 1 hour or less. Dr pineapple and reserve syr Combine sugar and cornstarch. A pineapple syrup, vinegar, soy sa and salt. Add to pork. Cook and until mixture thickens. Add pine ple, green peppers and onion. Cc 2–3 minutes. Serve on hot steam rice.

EUROPEAN TORTE SQUARES

    1/2 pound butter (2 sticks)
      1 cup sugar
      6 egg yolks
      2 cups flour
      1 teaspoon salt
      1 teaspoon baking
         powder
         Grape jelly

Cream butter and sugar. Add the egg yolks and cream well. Sift flou salt and baking powder; add creamed mixture. Pat this mixture o a cookie sheet and spread top surfac with grape jelly. Top this with icin (recipe follows).

Icing:
      6 egg whites
      1 cup ground nuts
      1 cup sugar

Beat egg whites until they hol peaks. Add nuts and sugar; blend well Use this on top of torte. Cut in square and bake for 30 minutes at 375 de grees.

GREEK ZUCCHINI SCRAMBLE
Serves 2

2 small zucchini squash
3 tablespoons butter
2 large eggs
  Salt and pepper

Wash and scrape zucchini. Slice across into thin slices and drop into melted butter in large 12-inch skillet. Cover; let cook over low heat until tender and browned lightly, stirring occasionally to prevent sticking. Beat eggs; pour over zucchini in pan. Add salt and pepper. Stir gently until eggs are cooked.

FRENCH BREAKFAST PUFFS (PETIS FEUILLETES)
Serves 12

⅓ cup shortening
1 cup granulated sugar
1 egg
1½ cups sifted flour
1½ teaspoons baking powder
½ teaspoon salt
¼ teaspoon nutmeg
½ cup milk
⅓ cup melted butter
1 teaspoon cinnamon

Heat oven to 350 degrees; grease muffin tins. Mix shortening, ½ cup sugar and egg thoroughly. Sift together flour, baking powder, salt and nutmeg; stir in alternately with milk. Fill muffin tins two-thirds full. Bake for 20–25 minutes. Immediately remove from tins and roll in melted butter; roll in mixture of ½ cup sugar and cinnamon. Serve hot.

HOT SALAD DRESSING (HEIS SALAT SAUCE)
Serves 6

3 slices bacon
3 tablespoons vinegar
1 tablespoon sugar
½ teaspoon salt
1 tablespoon flour
½ teaspoon pepper
1 tablespoon sour cream
1 egg, well-beaten
  Lettuce, spinach *or* endive

Dice bacon and fry crisp; pour off some of the fat. Add vinegar, sugar, salt, flour and pepper; brown well. Stir in sour cream and egg; stir until thick and smooth. Pour over chopped lettuce, spinach greens or endive.

BRAMBORY NA KYSELO (SOUR POTATOES)
Serves 6

2½ pounds potatoes, peeled and sliced
½ teaspoon caraway seeds
¼ cup flour
¼ cup shortening
1 cup sour cream
1 tablespoon vinegar
½ teaspoon sugar
1 tablespoon chopped dill *or* chives
2 egg yolks

Boil potatoes in salted water with caraway seeds. Drain, and reserve liquid. Brown flour in shortening, stirring constantly; stir in 1–1½ cups of potato water. Simmer for 10–15 minutes. Add the remaining ingredients and potatoes. Serve as is, or add diced, boiled meat.

GREEK-STYLE BEEF STEW

2 pounds stew meat, cut in cubes
3 tablespoons oil
2 teaspoons parsley flakes
1 teaspoon salt
1 teaspoon pepper
4 whole cloves, broken up
¼ teaspoon each nutmeg and allspice
1 clove garlic, crushed
1 can whole tomatoes *or* stewed tomatoes
½ cup red wine
1 cup chopped onions
10 black olives

Brown meat in a Dutch oven. Combine flakes, salt, pepper, cloves, nutmeg and allspice. Add garlic. Add oil to meat mixture. Add remaining ingredients. Bring to a boil; cover. Bake at 350 degrees for 2 hours.

HUNGARIAN CHERRY EVEN-WEIGHT CAKE (EGYENSULY)

¾ pound (1½ cups) unsalted butter
¾ pound (1½ cups) sugar
6 large eggs
¾ pound (3 cups) sifted flour
  Pinch of salt
  Grated rind of 1 lemon
1 pound sweet *or* sour pitted cherries *or* sliced peaches

Preheat oven to 350 degrees. Grease and flour a 9-inch springform or loaf pan. Cream butter and sugar extremely well. Add each egg separately, beating after each addition. Sift flour with salt 4 times through a fine sifter held high in the air. Combine flour and lemon rind, then add gradually to batter. Mix well, scraping sides often. Fold in cherries or peaches. Bake for 1 hour, or until cake springs back when touched and pulls from sides of pan. Cool on a rack and turn out.

CARAWAY MEATBALLS (KUMMEL UND FLEISCH GERMAN)

Serves 4–6

1 tablespoon caraway seed
1 tablespoon diced onion
3 tablespoons red wine vinegar
1 pound ground beef
½ ground ground pork
1½ cups soft bread crumbs
¾ cup milk
1 egg
1½ teaspoons salt
   Pinch of pepper

Soak caraway seed, onion and vinegar for 10 minutes. Add remaining ingredients and mix well. Shape into meatballs; roll in flour. Brown in melted fat. Add 1 cup water. Cover. Simmer for 30 minutes.

BEEF MORTOUN (BOEUF MORTOUN-FRENCH)

Serves 6

2½ pounds cooked round roast
2 onions, finely chopped
2 tablespoons butter
2 tablespoons flour
1 cup beef stock
   Salt and pepper
   Bread crumbs

Slice beef thinly; trim away gristle and fat. Lay slices in a greased baking dish. Brown onions in butter. Add flour and cook to form paste. Add stock to make a thin gravy. Add salt and pepper; pour over beef. Sprinkle with bread crumbs. Heat in oven at 350 degrees for 30 minutes.

SWEET-AND-SOUR ITALIAN SALAD (INSALATA AGRO-DOLCE)

Serves 20

1 pint carrots, cooked, diced and drained
1 pint green peas, cooked, diced and drained
1 pint green beans, cooked, diced and drained
1 pint red beans, cooked, diced and drained
1 cup diced onion
1 cup chopped green pepper
¼ cup chopped pimiento
½ cup salad oil
1 teaspoon celery seed
1 cup sugar
1 cup white vinegar

Combine all ingredients in a large bowl; stir lightly. Marinate overnight in refrigerator.

BULKOKI

Serves 4–6

2 pounds sirloin, frozen and thinly sliced
¼ cup brown sugar
4–6 small cloves garlic, chopped *or* minced
2 tablespoons chopped onion
½ cup salad oil
¼ cup soy sauce
½ teaspoon pepper
   Fluffy cooked rice

Mix sugar, garlic, onion, salad oil, soy sauce and pepper for marinade. Marinate meat for 2–4 hours. Prepare rice. Remove meat from marinade and stir-fry in an ordinary skillet or wok for about 8 minutes, or until meat is done.

NORWEGIAN WAFERS

Makes 4 dozen

⅔ cup butter

---

4 hard-cooked egg yolks, sieved
½ cup honey
2 teaspoons vanilla
2¼ cups flour, sifted
1 cup miniature chocolate c

Preheat oven to 400 degr Combine butter, egg yolks, h and vanilla; blend well. Add f and chocolate chips. Divide do in half and roll between 2 shee waxed paper to ¼-inch thickn Cut in 2-inch circles. Bake 8 utes.

TAHINI DRESSING

Makes ¾ cup

3 tablespoons tahini (sesame seed paste)
6 tablespoons cold water
1 garlic clove
   Fresh lemon juice
2 teaspoons minced fresh parsley
   Paprika

Combine tahini and cold wat stir well until blended. Peel ga and put through a press into the ta ni mixture. Add lemon juice to ta and the minced parsley. Add a li sprinkling of paprika and mix aga

ITALIAN BEEF— MANZO AL ITALIANO

Serves 6

3 pounds beef roast, thinly slice
½ pound suet
1 teaspoon oregano
½ teaspoon red pepper
1 teaspoon onion salt
½ teaspoon garlic salt
1 teaspoon black pepper
1 teaspoon salt

Place beef in Dutch oven; cov with water. Add suet and seasoning cover. Simmer 2–3 hours until be is tender. Serve on French bread.

KOREAN VEGETABLE DISH

2 cloves garlic
1/4 cup vegetable oil
1 quart stewed tomatoes
1 package frozen spinach
1 cup uncooked rice

Brown garlic in oil. Add tomatoes and simmer for 1/2 hour. Add spinach and rice. Cover tightly, cook until rice is tender, adding more water or tomato juice if needed. Add salt and pepper to taste.

This is unusual and very tasty.

ALMOND AND SESAME SEED PIES (MAQRUD)

Makes about 24 pies

2-1/2 cups semolina flour
3 eggs
1 cup butter
1 teaspoon baking powder
1 teaspoon vanilla
1/4 cup pulverized almonds
1/4 cup pulverized sesame seeds
1/4 cup sugar
1 cup honey
1/2 cup water
2 teaspoons rose water
Oil for frying
Icing sugar

Make dough by thoroughly mixing semolina, eggs, butter, baking powder and vanilla (add a few tablespoons of water if the dough is thick); form into 2" long rolls, about 3/4" in diameter; set aside.

Make filling by mixing almonds, sesame seeds and sugar. In your palm, flatten each roll to about 1/4" thicknesses; place 1 heaping teaspoon of filling in middle; pinch to close, in the process turning the ends in to form a rectangular pie. Allow *maqruds* to rest a few moments while preparing syrup.

Make a syrup by placing honey and water in pot, stirring constantly bring to a boil; reduce heat to low and stir in rose water. Keep on low heat.

In frying pan, pour oil 3/4" thick; heat. Then fry pies over medium heat until light brown, turning over once.

Place pies in syrup for at least 2 minutes, remove; allow to cool. Sprinkle heavily with icing sugar and serve.

NOTE: If fresh coriander is not available, a mixture of half chives-half parsley can be substituted. Also, vegetable oil may be used instead of olive oil.

SPAGHETTI WITH RICOTTA AND WALNUT SAUCE

2 cloves garlic
1 cup walnuts
1 tablespoon snipped parsley
1 tablespoon chopped fresh basil or mint
1 pound ricotta cheese
1 cup grated Parmesan cheese
1 teaspoon seasoned salt
1/4 teaspoon pepper
(optional) pinch or two of red pepper

Put garlic, walnuts and herbs in blender, whirl until creamy. Turn out into bowl with remaining ingredients, mix thoroughly. Set aside. Cook and drain 3/4 pound spaghetti, add while hot to bowl mixture. Toss until pasta is well coated with sauce. Garnish with snipped parsley and a few chopped walnuts.

CHICKEN CHOW MEIN (CHINESE DISH)

Serves 4

1 whole chicken
1 stalk celery, chopped
2 onions, chopped
1 tablespoon butter
1 tablespoon soya sauce
Salt and Pepper
1 tablespoon Worcestershire sauce
3 tablespoons cornstarch

Cook chicken until tender. Remove bones. Stir-fry chopped celery and onion in butter. Add to chicken and broth; cook celery until tender. Add soya sauce, Worcestershire sauce, salt, and pepper. Make thickening with cornstarch. Add to chow mein. Serve over chow mein noodles.

AUSTRIAN SALZBURG DUMPLINGS

Serves 3 to 6

6 eggs, separated
1/2 cup granulated sugar
1/4 teaspoon vanilla extract
1/3 cup all-purpose flour
3 tablespoons unsalted butter
Powdered sugar

Preheat oven to 425 degrees. In medium bowl, beat egg whites until soft peaks form. Gradually beat in granulated sugar until stiff, but not dry. In small bowl, beat egg yolks; stir in vanilla and 2 tablespoons beaten egg whites; do not stir. Sift flour over egg mixture. Fold egg yolk mixture and flour into egg whites, quickly but carefully. Place butter in shallow baking dish; place in oven until butter melts. Spoon egg mixture into hot dish. Using 2 tablespoons, shape egg mixture into 3 to 6 equal rolls or mounds.

Place dish in center of oven. Bake 8 to 10 minutes or until golden brown. Sprinkle top with powdered sugar while hot. Serve immediately.

NOTE: This is a Soufflé type of dessert. deep out of drafts to keep from collapsing.

HUNGARIAN NOODLES OR KLUSE

Serves 5

2 cups flour
2 eggs
1 cup water
1 teaspoon salt

Beat all the above ingredients with a wooden spoon until the dough is soft, and bubbles form. Make dough somewhat stiff. Cut with a spoon into boiling salted water. Let noodles boil until they rise to the top and boil for 5 minutes. Drain and serve with chicken.

This recipe was made by my mother-in-law. She used to cool the mixture and then fry them with a pound of side pork and onion, like fried potatoes. She did this to serve a family of 15 at one time. This recipe is about 50 years old. It takes about 20 minutes to prepare.

HONEY-HAM CHOW MEIN

1 medium green pepper
1 medium onion
2 ribs celery
1 small can mushrooms
2 tablespoons vegetable oil
2 cups cooked ham strips
1 cup chicken bouillon
2 tablespoons honey
1 tablespoon corn starch
1 tablespoon soy sauce
1/4 cup water

Cut green pepper in strips, onion in slices, celery in pieces (for Chinese effect, cut on the bias) and mushrooms in slices. Heat oil; add onions and ham; cook until ham is slightly browned. Add bouillon, pepper, celery and mushrooms; cover tightly; cook slowly for 6 minutes. Mix remaining ingredients; add and cook for 2 minutes, stirring constantly. Serve with crisp noodles, or over a bed of rice.

ITALIAN VEGETABLE SALAD

1 head cauliflower, cut into pieces
1 bunch broccoli, cut into pieces
3 zucchini, sliced
5 tomatoes, cut into chunks or 1 basket of cherry tomatoes
1 can black pitted olives, sliced
1 (16 ounce) bottle of Seven Seas Italian Dressing
1 teaspoon salt
1/2 teaspoon pepper

Mix all ingredients together and let stand overnight in refrigerator. This is a great recipe for picnics or potlucks.

ENCHILADA CASSEROLE

12 corn tortillas
2 pounds hamburger
2 tablespoons chili powder
1/2 teaspoon garlic powder
1 medium onion, chopped
15 ounce can tomato sauce
Salt and pepper
1 cups grated Colby or Cheddar cheese
1 can cream of chicken soup
3/4 cup milk

Brown meat, garlic and onion. Add tomato sauce, chili powder, salt and pepper. Heat 9 x 13 inch pan. Line bottom with 6 tortillas. Add meat on top. Cover with 6 more tortillas. Spread chicken soup over these and then milk. Cover with cheese. Bake 25 minutes at 350 degrees. A very easy and tasty dish!

QUICK MEXICAN DISH

Serves 6-8

1 can cream of cheese soup
1 can cream of onion soup
16 ounce can tomatoes, chopped and drained
1 pound ground beef
1 package taco seasoning
8 ounce package Cheddar cheese -grated
11 ounce package Doritos, crushed
Onion, chopped
16 ounce can corn, drained
1 can green chilies, chopped

Brown meat and onion; drain. Add seasonings and corn. Mix together. Add soups and tomatoes. Grease an oblong baking dish. In bottom of dish crush Doritos to completely cover the bottom. Add meat mixture, then pour soup mixture over the meat. Top with cheese. Bake 350 degrees for 2 minutes.

Add sour cream on top of baked casserole, and sliced ripe olives. This is quick and easy!

ENCHILADA SQUARES

1 pound ground beef
1 cup chopped onion
4-ounce can diced green chilies, drained
4 eggs
8-ounce can tomato sauce
5-1/3-ounce can (2/3 cup) evaporated milk
1 (12-ounce) envelope enchilada sauce mix and 1 teaspoon chili powder
1 cup shredded Cheddar cheese
1/2 cup sliced black olives

Brown beef and onion, drain. Spread meat mixture in lightly buttered 10 x 6 x 2-inch baking dish. Sprinkle diced green chilies over meat mixtures. Beat eggs, tomato sauce, evaporated milk, enchilada sauce. Sprinkle sliced black olives over top.

If desired, sprinkle 2 cups corn chips over top.

Bake in a 350 degree oven for 25 minutes or until set. Sprinkle with cheese and bake 5 more minutes. Let set 10 minutes before cutting.

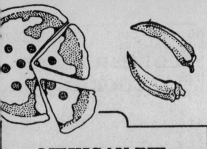

MEXICAN PIE

Crust:
2 cups beef broth
1 cup long-grain rice
1 tablespoon margarine
1 teaspoon salt
2 eggs, slightly beaten
2 tablespoons chopped pimiento

Filling:
1 pound ground beef
1 garlic clove, crushed
1 teaspoon cumin
1/2 teaspoon salt
1/2 cup mild taco sauce
1 egg, beaten

Guacamole:
1 large avocado, peeled and quartered
1 tablespoon chopped onion
1 tablespoon mild taco sauce
1/2 teaspoon salt
1/2 teaspoon lemon juice

1 cup sour cream

Crust: Grease a 10-inch pie pan. In medium saucepan, heat broth to boiling. Stir in rice, margarine and salt. Return to a boil. Cover reduce heat; simmer until rice is tender. Remove from heat; let cool slightly; stir in eggs and pimiento. Press against bottom and sides of pie plate.

Filling: Preheat oven to 350 degrees. In skillet, brown beef. Drain. Stir in garlic, cumin and salt; cook 2 more minutes. Remove from heat; stir in taco sauce and egg. Spoon filling into crust. Bake 25 minutes.

Guacamole: In small bowl, mash 3 avocado quarters (reserve 1 quarter for garnish). Stir in remaining ingredients. Cover and set aside.

Remove pie from oven. Spread guacamole over meat. Top with sour cream. Return to oven and bake 5 more minutes. Slice remaining avocado; sprinkle on pie.

CRAB MEAT PIES (BRIKS)
Makes 10 pies

4 tablespoons butter
2 medium sized onions, finely chopped
3 cloves garlic, crushed
1/4 cup finely chopped fresh coriander leaves
1 hot pepper, finely chopped
1 teaspoon salt
1/2 teaspoon pepper
4.5-ounce can crab meat, drained
1/2 cup Parmesan cheese
11 small eggs
10 sheets filo dough
Oil for frying

In frying pan, melt butter. Over medium heat, stir-fry onions, garlic, coriander leaves, hot pepper, salt and pepper for 10 minutes. Remove from heat. Make a filling by stirring in crab meat and cheese; set aside. Beat one of the eggs; set aside. Fold a sheet of filo dough over twice to make a square. Place 1/10 of the filling in center; form into a well. Keep dough soft by placing wet towel over sheets while making pies. Brush edges of square with beaten egg; break an egg into the well; fold over to form a triangle. Press edges together. Turn them in about 1/2"; brush again with egg to make sure they are well sealed. In frying pan, pour oil to 3/4" thickness; heat; gently slide in pies; fry over slightly higher than medium heat for about 2 minutes on each side, or until sides are golden brown. Remove and place on paper towels; drain. When all the pies are finished, serve immediately.

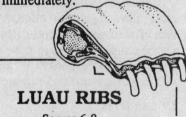

LUAU RIBS
Serves 6-8

1/2 cup brown sugar, firmly packed
2 teaspoons ginger
1/3 cup catsup
1/3 cup vinegar
2 cloves garlic, minced
2 (4-1/2-ounces each) cans apple and apricot baby food

2 tablespoons soy sauce or Worcestershire sauce
6 to 8 pounds meaty spareribs
1 teaspoon salt
Dash of pepper

Mix brown sugar and ginger. Combine with baby food, catsup, vinegar, soy sauce and garlic. Rub ribs with salt and pepper. Place ribs, meat side up, on rack in a shallow pan. Bake at 450 degrees for 15 minutes; pour off fat. Reduce oven temperature to 350 degrees. Baste ribs with sauce and continue baking for 1-1/2 hours (depending on your oven.) While baking, baste with sauce several times.

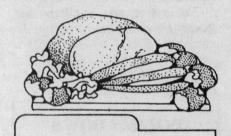

ITALIAN TURKEY LOAF

1-1/4 pounds ground turkey
1 cup egg plant, diced
1 onion, chopped
6-8 mushrooms, chopped
1 egg white, beaten
1/3 teaspoon sage
1/3 teaspoon tarragon
2 tablespoons low sodium tomato sauce
2 cups bran flakes cereal
1 medium pepper, chopped
2 medium tomatoes, peeled and chopped
1 whole egg, beaten
1/3 teaspoon oregano
1 clove garlic
1/4 teaspoon pepper

Place all ingredients, except tomato sauce, in large mixing bowl. Mix until well blended. Press mixture in loaf pan 8x5x3-inches. Spread tomato sauce evenly over top of loaf; bake at 350 degrees for 30 minutes. Remove from oven and drain off excess liquid. Return to oven for additional 45 minutes or until loaf is done. Allow to sit a few minutes before removing from pan and slicing.

FRENCH ONION SOUP
Serves 4

2 large onions, sliced thin and
    sautéed in butter until light brown
2 cups beef stock or beef bouillon
1/2 cup cream
1 teaspoon Worcestershire sauce
Salt and pepper to taste
Toast
Parmesan Cheese

Boil the sautéed onions in stock for 10 minutes. Add cream, salt and pepper to taste. Just before serving, add the Worcestershire sauce. Put a thin slice of toast covered with Parmesan cheese into each bowl.

SCOTTISH BANNOCKS

1 cup whole wheat flour
1 cup rolled oats
1 scant teaspoon baking soda
1-1/4 cups buttermilk
2 tablespoons vegetable oil
2 teaspoons honey

Mix flour, oats, and baking soda. In another bowl, mix remaining ingredients; then stir into dry ingredients until the combination is creamy smooth. Spoon batter into muffin tins and bake in preheated oven at 300-325 degrees for 20-25 minutes. The oatcakes will be golden brown with a top nicely textured from the rolled oats.

SCOTTISH BANANA COOKIES
Makes 5 dozen

2/3 cup butter
1 cup sugar
2 eggs
1 teaspoon almond flavoring
2-1/4 cups flour
2 tablespoons cornstarch
1 teaspoon baking powder
1/2 teaspoon baking soda
1/2 teaspoon salt
1-1/2 cups mashed bananas

Cream together butter and sugar until light and fluffy. Add eggs, one a a time, and beat well after each addition. Add almond flavoring. Sift together flour, cornstarch, baking powder, baking soda, and salt. Add alternately with mashed bananas.

Drop by teaspoonfuls onto greased cookie sheets. Bake in a 400 degree oven for 15 minutes.

POLISH BOWS

8 egg yolks
1 tablespoon vanilla
1 ounce whiskey
Sour cream (same amount as yolks)
1 teaspoon salt (level)
1 teaspoon baking powder
All the flour it will take

Put yolks into bowl; beat until yolks turn light yellow (about 5 minutes). Add sour cream; mix until well blended. Add vanilla; mix a little; add whiskey, salt and baking powder. Mix for short time until everything looks mixed. Start to add sifted flour until you can scoop it out of bowl. Scoop out onto more sifted flour on table. Knead until dough starts to make a popping noise; form loaf; wrap in plastic wrap; place in refrigerator overnight.

Next day, cut piece about 1-1/2-inches; roll out very thin. Cut into strips 2-inches wide and 6-inches long. Cut slit in center; put 1 end through slit.

When all dough is rolled out, slit and turned, you are ready to fry in shortening (about 4 at a time), until they look done.

ITALIAN BOW KNOT COOKES
Makes 6 dozen medium cookies

This recipe has made many a kaffe klatch more enjoyable. Keeps well, if they last that long.

4 cups flour
4 teaspoons baking powder
2 teaspoons salt
6 beaten eggs
1 cup sugar
1/2 cup oil
1-1/2 teaspoons lemon extract

Blend beaten eggs into dry ingredients, following with all other ingredients. Knead until smooth. Roll into pencil lengths and tie in bow knots. Bake on greased cookie sheets in a 400 degree oven for 15 minutes.

Lemon Icing:
1/4 cup butter
1 pound confectioners' sugar
Juice of 2 lemons

Cream butter; add remaining ingredients. Stir until well blended. If too thin, add more sugar. Too thick, add more lemon juice.

FUNNEL CAKES (DRECHTER KUCHE)

3 eggs
2 cups milk
1/4 cup sugar
3-4 cups flour
1/2 teaspoon salt
2 teaspoons baking powder

Beat eggs; add sugar and milk. Sift half the flour, salt, and baking powder together and add to milk and egg mixture. Beat the batter smooth and add only as much more flour as needed. Batter should be thin enough to run through a funnel. Drop from funnel into deep, hot fat (375 degrees). Spirals and endless intricate shapes can be made by swirling and criss-crossing while controlling the funnel spout with a finger. Serve hot with molasses, tart jelly, jam, or sprinkle with powdered sugar.

CHICKEN COUSCOUS
Serves 8 to 10

To prepare *couscous*, a coussoussiére which is a double boiler with the top part perforated is required.

NOTE: Cost is approximately $25 for a 6-quart pot.

2 cups couscous
5 tablespoons butter
4 tablespoons olive oil
1 pound chicken, cut into small serving pieces
2 medium sized onions, chopped
4 cloves garlic, crushed
1/4 cup finely chopped fresh coriander leaves
1 hot pepper, finely chopped
1 large carrot, scraped and sliced into 4 pieces lengthwise and cut into 1" pieces
4 small potatoes, quartered
2 zucchini about 6" long, sliced lengthwise and cut into 2" pieces
1 cup 1" cubes of turnips
2 cups choppéd cabbage
4 medium sized tomatoes, chopped
19-ounce can chick peas, with water
2 teaspoons salt
1 teaspoon ground caraway
1 teaspoon cumin
1/2 teaspoon pepper
Pinch of saffron
1/2 cup slivered almonds, toasted

In mixing bowl, place *couscous* and butter; knead with fingers until *couscous* kernels are coated; set aside.

In bottom half of coussoussiére, heat oil; sauté chicken pieces over medium heat until they begin to brown. Stir in onions, garlic, fresh coriander and hot pepper; stir-fry for 8 more minutes. Add 4 cups of water and all remaining ingredients except almonds and *couscous;* bring to a boil. Fit top of coussoussiére with the *couscous* on the bottom part. Seal two parts together with piece of cloth impregnated with flour (the cloth should be about 4" wide and long enough to fit around the coussoussiére, then folded 4 times lengthwise and dipped in 1 cup of water in which 1/4 cup of flour has been dissolved); then cook over medium heat for 20 minutes. Sprinkle 1 cup water over *couscous,* stirring constantly to make sure lumps do not form; cook for 40 minutes, stirring *couscous* occasionally.

Mound *couscous* on large serving plate; make a well on top; decorate *couscous* with almonds. With slotted spoon, remove meat and vegetables; arrange in well on top of *couscous*. Place remaining juice in gravy boat, to be added as desired

MOSTACCIOLI

1 pound ground beef
1/2 cup chopped green pepper
2 cups tomatoes
6-ounce can tomato paste
1/2 cup water
1/2 pound Cheddar cheese
Shredded Parmesan cheese
1 onion, chopped
1 bay leaf
1/2 teaspoon salt
1/4 teaspoon pepper
8-ounce Mostaccioli noodles (4 cups)

Brown meat slowly, along with green pepper and onion. Cook until tender. Stir in water, tomatoes, tomato paste and seasonings. In a 2-quart casserole, mix together cooked noodles, meat sauce and Cheddar cheese. Sprinkle with Parmesan cheese. Bake at 350 degrees for 30 minutes. Delicious family favorite.

MEXICAN OVEN FRIED CHICKEN
Serves 6
178 calories per serving

3 pound broiler-fryer, skinned and cut into serving-size pieces
1-1/2 cups Bloody Mary mix
1/2 cup crushed corn flakes
1/2 teaspoon dried oregano leaves
1/2 teaspoon ground cumin
1/2 teaspoon chili powder
1/2 teaspoon paprika
1/4 teaspoon onion salt
1/8 teaspoon garlic powder
Vegetable cooking spray

Combine chicken and Bloody Mary mix in a large bowl; cover and refrigerate 6 hours or overnight.

Combine next 7 ingredients. Drain chicken and dredge in mixture. Arrange chicken in jellyroll pan coated with cooking spray. Bake at 350 degrees for 50 - 60 minutes.

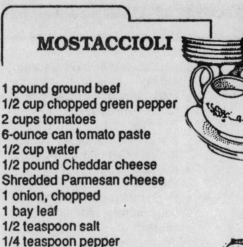

GERMAN SAUERKRAUT ROLLS

1-1/2 large cans sauerkraut
4 eggs
3/4 cup shortening or oil
1/2 teaspoon salt
3 cups flour
1/4 cup water

Drain juice from kraut. In skillet, heat oil or shortening; stir in kraut; add salt and pepper to taste. Fry about 20 minutes, or until browned; cool. Mix flour and salt; add eggs and water. Knead until dough is smooth and elastic, like noodle dough. On floured board, roll to 1/4 inch thick. Spread cooled kraut on top; roll up like jelly roll. Slice cross-wise; place cut pieces in frying pan. Cover with small amount of water; add salt. Cook over medium heat for one hour. OPTIONAL: For added flavor, place hot dogs or Polish sausage around dough.

Meat
DISHES

PATRICIA NIXON'S HOT CHICKEN SALAD
Serves 8

4 cups cold chicken, cut up into chunks (cooked)
2 tablespoons lemon juice
⅔ cup finely chopped toasted almonds
¾ cup mayonnaise
1 teaspoon salt
½ teaspoon monosodium glutamate
1 cup grated cheese
2 cups chopped celery
4 hard-cooked eggs, sliced
¾ cup cream of chicken soup
1 teaspoon onion, finely minced
2 pimientos, finely cut
1½ cups crushed potato chips

Combine all ingredients, except cheese, potato chips and almonds. Place in a large rectangular dish. Top with cheese, potato chips and almonds. Let stand overnight in refrigerator. Bake in a 400-degree oven for 20–25 minutes.

CHICKEN NOODLE MEDLEY
Serves 6

10 ounces green noodles
1 medium-size onion
1 bay leaf
2 tablespoons butter
1 teaspoon onion salt
⅛ teaspoon pepper

3 pounds broiler-fryer chicken, cut up
1 (10¾-ounce) can cream of mushroom soup
¾ cup milk
⅔ cup grated Parmesan cheese
2 tablespoons chopped chives
½ teaspoon sage
Paprika
1 (1-pound) package frozen baby carrots, drained and cooked

Preheat oven to 350 degrees. Cook noodles according to package directions, adding onion and bay leaf to cooking water. Drain noodles; discard onion and bay leaf. Toss together noodles, butter, onion salt and pepper. Spoon into buttered 13 x 9-inch baking dish. Sprinkle chicken pieces with salt and pepper; place on noodles. Combine soup, milk, ⅓ cup cheese, chives and sage; pour over chicken. Sprinkle with remaining cheese and paprika. Bake 45 minutes; add carrots. Bake additional 20 minutes, or until chicken is tender.

CRUSTY BAKED CHICKEN
Serves 4

2 cups potato chips, finely crushed
¼ teaspoon salt
¼ teaspoon pepper

¼ teaspoon curry powder
⅛ teaspoon ginger
1 (3-pound) frying chicken, cut up
2 eggs, beaten
¼ cup milk
½ cup butter or margarine, melted

Mix potato chips, salt, pepper, curry powder and ginger. Combine eggs and milk; pour butter into shallow baking dish. Dip chicken in chips, then in egg mixture, then in chips again. Put pieces side by side in dish; bake at 375 degrees for 45 minutes.

CHICKEN CHOLUPAS

4 chicken breasts, cooked, deboned and diced
3 cans cream of chicken soup
1 large can green chilies, diced
1 onion, finely diced
16 ounces sour cream
¾ pound Monterey Jack cheese, grated
¾ pound mild cheddar cheese, grated
12 small flour tortillas

Mix all ingredients together, except tortillas and only half the cheeses. Put 3 tablespoons mixture in each tortilla. Roll up and place in a greased baking dish. Pour rest of mixture over tortillas. Sprinkle remaining cheeses over all. Bake at 350 degrees for 45 minutes.

GINGER AND RUM ROASTED CORNISH GAME HENS

- 4 Cornish game hens
  Salt and freshly ground pepper
- 1 large garlic clove, crushed
- ¼ cup honey
- ¼ cup chicken stock
- ¼ cup soy sauce
- ¼ cup rum
- 1 tablespoon peanut *or* vegetable oil
- 1 teaspoon ground ginger

Preheat oven to 375 degrees. Season Cornish hens well with salt and pepper, inside and out. Combine remaining ingredients in bowl. Spoon 2 tablespoons of the mixture into each hen cavity. Tie the legs together and fold the wings back. Place the hens in a roasting pan. Brush each hen with the sauce. Roast for 55 minutes, or until tender. Baste the hens twice during the cooking time with the sauce.

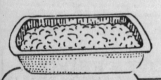

FAVORITE CHICKEN LOAF
Serves 6

- 1 cup soft bread crumbs
- 2 cups milk
- 2 eggs, lightly beaten
- ½ teaspoon salt
- ¼ teaspoon paprika
- 3 cups cooked chicken, diced ¼ inch thick
- ½ cup cooked peas
- ¼ cup chopped pimiento
- 1 (10½-ounce) can condensed cream of mushroom soup for sauce

In a bowl blend bread crumbs, milk, eggs, salt and paprika. Stir in chicken, peas and pimiento. Turn into a well-greased loaf pan (9 x 5 x 3-inch). Bake in a moderate 325-degree oven until firm, about 40 minutes. Serve with mushroom sauce made from soup.

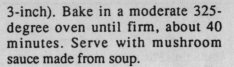

CHICKEN CHOW MEIN, AMERICAN-STYLE
Serves 4

- 1 tablespoon butter *or* margarine
- 4 tablespoons minced onion
- 1½ cups shredded, cooked chicken
- 1 cup celery, diced
- 1½ cups meat stock *or* water
- 2 tablespoons soy sauce
- 1½ tablespoons cornstarch
- 3 tablespoons cold water
  Chow mein noodles

Brown onion lightly in margarine. Add next 4 ingredients and simmer 15 minutes. Blend and stir into meat mixture; add cornstarch mixed in cold water. Cook until slightly thickened and clear. Serve hot on chow mein noodles.

CHICKEN-VEGETABLE-FRENCH-FRY CASSEROLE
Serves 8

This provides meat, potatoes and vegetables in 1 dish. Put together ahead of time, and it is ready to eat 35 minutes after popping in the oven.

- 2 fryer chickens, cut up
- ¼ cup (½ stick) butter
- ¼ cup flour
- 1 teaspoon salt
- 2 cups reserved chicken broth
- 1 (10½-ounce) can cream of celery soup
- 1 (10-ounce) package frozen peas and carrots
- ½ cup (1 stick) butter
- 1 (1-pound) box frozen french fries
  Parmesan cheese

Cook, cool and bone chicken. Save 2 cups of broth. In a buttered 9 x 13-inch pan, put good-sized pieces of chicken. Melt butter; add flour, salt, broth and soup. Cook until thick and smooth. Cook peas and carrots for 3 minutes. Drain. Mix with sauce and pour over chicken.

Melt stick of butter; stir frozen french fries in butter until coated. Place on top of other ingredients. Sprinkle generously with Parmesan cheese. Bake, uncovered, at 450 degrees for 20–25 minutes. If it has been put together earlier and refrigerated, bake for 35 minutes.

CROCK POT RAVIOLI CASSEROLE
Serves 8

- 1 (10-ounce) package frozen chopped spinach
- 1 (8-ounce) package twisty noodles
- 1 pound ground beef chuck
- 1/2 pound mild Italian sausage
- 1 onion, finely chopped
- 2 tablespoons oil
- 2 (8-ounce) cans tomato sauce
- 1 teaspoon salt
- 1 teaspoon oregano
- 1/2 cup shredded Parmesan or Romano cheese
- 1 cup (1/2 pint) sour cream
- 1 cup (4 ounces) shredded Monterey Jack cheese
- 3 green onions, chopped

Defrost spinach. Squeeze dry. Cook noodles in boiling, salted water until tender. Drain. Brown meats and onion in oil until crumbly. Add tomato sauce, salt and oregano. Cover. Simmer 30 minutes. Mix in spinach. Spoon half the noodles into a buttered crock pot. Top with half of meat mixture and half the Parmesan cheese. Cover with layers of remaining noodles, meat and Parmesan cheese. Spread with sour cream. Sprinkle with Jack cheese and onions. Cook on high (300 degrees) 1 hour.

BAKED CHICKEN

2 chicken breasts
1 tablespoon butter *or* margarine, melted
½ cup Parmesan cheese
2 tablespoons butter *or* margarine

Preheat oven to 400 degrees. Dip chicken in melted butter and coat with cheese. Melt remaining butter in a pie plate and place chicken in pie plate, skin-side up. Bake at 400 degrees for 50 minutes. Baste with juice during baking. Cover with foil if chicken browns too quickly.

QUICK CHICKEN BAKE
Serves 6

2 cups cooked chicken, cubed
1 can cream of chicken soup
1 cup sour cream
½ cup celery, diced
½ cup onion, chopped
½ cup water chestnuts, thinly sliced
1 cup cooked rice
Bread crumbs

Mix together and place in a buttered 2-quart casserole. Sprinkle bread crumbs on top. Microwave on HIGH for 6–8 minutes.

If you prefer cream of mushroom soup or cheddar cheese soup—go for it. Do not be afraid to experiment.

CRISPY SESAME CHICKEN
Serves 6–8

10 pieces chicken
½ cup butter
½ cup bread crumbs
1 cup grated Parmesan cheese
6 tablespoons sesame seeds

Preheat oven to 350 degrees. Rinse chicken and pat dry with paper towels. Combine bread crumbs, cheese and sesame seeds. Melt butter. Dip chicken into the butter and then the seasoned crumbs. Place chicken in a shallow pan (lining with foil helps with cleanup). Bake at 350 degrees for 1 hour.

PORK CHOP 'N' POTATO BAKE

1 can cream of celery soup
½ cup milk
½ cup sour cream
1 package hash brown potatoes
1 cup shredded cheddar cheese
1 can French onion rings
6 medium pork chops
Seasoned salt
¼ teaspoon salt
¼ teaspoon pepper

Brown chops and sprinkle with seasoned salt. Mix soup, milk, sour cream, potatoes, salt, pepper, ½ cup of the cheese and ½ can of the onion rings. Spoon into a greased casserole or 9 x 13-inch pan, and arrange chops over top. Cover and bake at 350 degrees for 40 minutes. Top with remaining cheese and onion rings. Bake, uncovered, 5 minutes more.

SOUPY PORK CHOPS

6 pork chops, ½ inch thick, fat removed
1 can tomato soup
1 package dry onion soup mix
1 medium onion, sliced
1 green pepper, sliced
1 cup mushrooms, sliced

Arrange chops in an oblong casserole. Mix remaining ingredients and pour over chops. Cover with waxed paper. Microwave at 70 percent for 30 minutes.

SALISBURY STEAK WITH ONION GRAVY

1 (10-ounce) can onion soup
1-1/2 pounds ground beef
1/2 cup fine dry breadcrumbs
1 egg, fork beaten
Dash salt
Dash pepper
1 tablespoon all-purpose flour
1/4 cup ketchup
1/4 cup water
1 teaspoon Worcestershire sauce
1/2 teaspoon mustard

In bowl combine 1/3 cup soup with ground beef, crumbs, egg, salt and pepper. Shape into 6 oval patties. In frypan brown patties. Drain off fat. Gradually blend flour into remaining soup, mixing until smooth. Add remaining ingredients, blending well. Add to frypan. Heat to boiling, stirring to loosen up brown bits. Cover, cook 5 minutes, stirring occasionally. Add patties to gravy in frypan. Cover and simmer an additional 15 minutes. These patties freeze very well; place patties and gravy in a "freezer to oven" container for convenience.

OVEN FRIED PORK CHOPS
Serves 4

3 tablespoons margarine *or* butter
1 egg, beaten
2 tablespoons milk
1 cup corn bread stuffing mix
4 pork loin chops (about 1½ pounds), cut ½ inch thick

Set oven to 425 degrees. Place margarine or butter in a 13 x 9 x 2-inch baking pan. Place pan in the oven about 3 minutes, or until margarine melts. Stir together egg and milk. Dip pork chops in egg mixture. Coat with stuffing mix. Place chops on top of melted margarine in pan. Bake 20 minutes. Turn. Bake 10–15 minutes more, or until pork is no longer pink.

REAL BAKED HAM

- 5 pounds ham
  Cider to cover
- ½ cup brown sugar
- 1 teaspoon mustard
- 20 whole cloves

Cover the ham with cold water and bring slowly to the boil. Throw out the water and replace with the cider to cover ham. Bring this to a boil; lower heat, keeping the liquid barely simmering for 20 minutes to the pound of ham; remove from heat and allow to stand in the liquid for 30 minutes. Take out ham; skin it and score fat with a sharp knife in a diamond pattern. Stud with whole cloves. Mix the sugar and mustard; rub well into ham. Bake in a preheated oven for an additional 10 minutes to the pound in a 400-degree oven. Carve; serve with sweet potatoes or a salad.

MUSTARD-GLAZED HAM LOAF
Serves 8–10

- 1½ pounds ground ham
- 1 pound boneless pork shoulder, trimmed and ground
- 3 eggs, slightly beaten
- ½ cup finely crushed saltine crackers (14 crackers) *or*
- ½ cup finely crushed bread crumbs (3 or 4 slices)
- ½ cup tomato juice
- 2 tablespoons chopped onion
- 1 tablespoon prepared horseradish
- ½ teaspoon salt
- ⅛ teaspoon pepper
- 1–2 recipes Mustard Sauce (recipe follows)

Mix ingredients. Shape into a 9 x 5-inch loaf in shallow baking dish. Bake in a 350-degree oven for 1¼ hours.

Meanwhile prepare Ham Loaf Mustard Sauce. Drain fat from pan. Pour Mustard Sauce over loaf. Bake 30 minutes more, basting with sauce occasionally.

Mustard Sauce:

- ½ cup brown sugar, firmly packed
- 2 tablespoons vinegar
- ½ teaspoon dry mustard

SASSY SAUSAGES
Serves 5–6

- 1 cup water
- ⅓ cup red cinnamon candies
  Red food coloring
- 3 red tart apples, cored and cut into ½-inch rings
- 1 pound pork sausage links
- 3 tablespoons water

In skillet, heat 1 cup water, the cinnamon candies and a few drops red food coloring until candies are melted. Place apple rings in syrup; cook slowly, turning occasionally, about 20 minutes, or until tender. Place links in another skillet; add 3 tablespoons water. Cover tightly; cook slowly for 8 minutes. Uncover, cook, turning sausages until well-browned. To serve, insert hot sausage link in center of each apple slice.

BURGUNDY STEAK
Serves 2

- 1 cup burgundy wine
- 1 tablespoon Worcestershire sauce
- ½ teaspoon dried leaf basil
- ½ teaspoon dried leaf thyme
- ¼ teaspoon dry mustard
  Dash garlic powder
- 2 (8-ounce) beef rib-eye steaks
- ¼ cup butter *or* margarine
- 4 frozen french-fried onion rings
- ½ cup fresh mushroom slices

In a small bowl, mix burgundy, Worcestershire sauce, basil, thyme, mustard and garlic powder. Place meat in a plastic bag; put in a shallow baking pan. Pour marinade into bag; seal bag. Marinate in refrigerator 8 hours or overnight, turning bag over occasionally. Melt butter or margarine in a large skillet. Add onion rings. Cook over medium-high heat until golden brown. Remove onion rings and keep warm; reserve butter or margarine in skillet; Drain steak; reserve ½ cup marinade. Cook steaks in butter or margarine in skillet until done as desired, turning several times. Place steaks on a platter; reserve drippings in skillet. Cook and stir mushrooms in drippings until barely tender. Stir in reserved marinade. Cook and stir until heated through. Pour over steaks. Top with cooked onion rings.

BARBECUED FLANK STEAK

- ¼ cup soy sauce
- 3 tablespoons honey
- 2 tablespoons vinegar
- 1 green onion, chopped, *or* 2 teaspoons onion powder
- ½ to 1½ teaspoons garlic powder
- 1½ teaspoons powdered ginger
- ¾ cup salad oil
  Flank steaks

Mix first 7 ingredients in large bowl; add steaks. Marinate at room temperature for 3–6 hours. Broil over hot coals until medium-rare or rare; slice diagonally, cutting in ½–¾-inch strips. Marinade will keep indefinitely in refrigerator if green onion is removed.

BREADED PORK CHOPS
Serves 6

- 6 pork chops
- ¾ cup fine bread crumbs
- 1 teaspoon salt
- ⅛ teaspoon pepper
- 1 egg, beaten
- ¼ cup milk
- ¼ cup boiling water

Add salt and pepper to bread crumbs. Beat egg and add milk. Dip chops in liquid and roll in crumbs. Put 3 tablespoons fat into skillet; brown chops. Place chops in a baking pan or dish and add boiling water. Cover and bake at 400 degrees for about 50 minutes. (I take the cover off for about the last 10 minutes.) These are delicious and so easy to prepare, too. The chops turn out very tender. This is one of my favorite pork chop recipes.

SAUSAGE 'N' CHEESE TURNOVERS
Makes 10 sandwiches

- 1 (10-ounce) can refrigerated big flaky biscuits
- ½ pound Italian bulk sausage *or* ground beef, browned and drained
- ¼ teaspoon Italian seasoning
- 1 (4-ounce) can mushroom pieces and stems, drained
- 4 ounces (1 cup) shredded mozzarella or provolone cheese
- 1 egg, slightly beaten
- 1–2 tablespoons grated Parmesan cheese

Heat oven to 350 degrees. Grease a cookie sheet. Separate dough into 10 biscuits; press or roll each to a 5-inch circle. In a medium bowl, combine browned sausage, seasoning, mushrooms and mozzarella cheese. Spoon about 3 tablespoons meat mixture onto center of each flattened biscuit. Fold dough in half over filling; press edges with fork to seal. Brush tops with beaten egg; sprinkle with Parmesan cheese. Place on prepared cookie sheet. Bake for 10–15 minutes, or until deep golden brown.

Tip: To reheat, wrap loosely in foil. Heat at 375 degrees for 10–15 minutes.

SALISBURY STEAK

- 2 pounds hamburger
- 1 can onion soup
- 1 cup bread crumbs
- 2 eggs, beaten
- 1 can tomato soup
- 1 can celery soup

Mix the hamburger, bread crumbs, onion soup and eggs as for meat loaf. Add salt to taste. Add more bread crumbs, if needed. Make into patties; dip in flour and brown on each side.

Arrange in a greased baking dish. Make a gravy of 1 can celery soup, 1 can tomato soup and 1 can water.

Pour over the patties and bake in a 350-degree oven for 1 hour.

BEEF RING WITH BARBECUE SAUCE

- 1½ pounds ground chuck
- ¾ cup quick-cooking oats
- 1 cup evaporated milk
- 3 tablespoons onion, finely chopped
- 2 tablespoons Worcestershire sauce
- 3 tablespoons vinegar
- 2 tablespoons sugar
- 1 cup ketchup
- ½ cup water
- 6 tablespoons onion, finely chopped

Mix together ground chuck, oats, evaporated milk and 3 tablespoons onion. Pack into an 8-inch ring mold and bake 10 minutes. Remove to a larger pan.

Combine remaining ingredients to form the sauce. Pour sauce over beef ring. Bake at 350 degrees for approximately 1½ hours. Baste frequently with sauce during baking time.

This has been a family favorite for years and is absolutely delicious!!

HAM CASSEROLE

- ½ pound egg noodles, cooked
- 2 cups ham, cubed
- 1 to 1½ cups cheddar cheese, shredded
- 1 can cream of mushroom soup
- ¾ cup milk
- 1 teaspoon dry mustard
- 1 box frozen peas

Pierce box of peas in several places. Microwave for 5 minutes; set aside. Combine ham, cheese, soup, milk and mustard in a 3-quart glass casserole. Add noodles and peas; stir to blend. Microwave on HIGH for 6–8 minutes, stirring one time.

SPARERIBS "ALOHA"

- 3 pounds spareribs
- ½ cup finely chopped onion
- ¼ cup green pepper, chopped
- 1 (16-ounce) can tomato sauce
- ½ teaspoon dry mustard
- 1 tablespoon Worcestershire sauce
- 1 (2½-cup) can crushed pineapple
- ¼ cup brown sugar

Cut every third rib about halfway through the strip. Sprinkle with salt and pepper. Place in shallow pan. Bake 1¼ hours at 350 degrees. Pour off fat. Mix remaining ingredients and let stand to blend flavor. Pour over ribs. Bake 45–50 minutes, basting frequently to glaze ribs.

SPANISH PORK CHOPS AND RICE
Serves 4

- 4 (1-inch-thick) pork chops (about 2 pounds in all)
- 1 tablespoon olive oil
- 2 onions, sliced
- 1 green bell pepper, cut into chunks
- 1 tomato, cut in wedges
- 2 cloves garlic, minced
- ½ teaspoon turmeric
- ¾ teaspoon pepper
- ½ teaspoon paprika
- 1 teaspoon ground cumin
   Salt to taste
- ⅔ cup rice
- 1⅓ cups chicken stock
- ⅓ cup black olives, pitted and cut up
- 2 tablespoons chopped parsley

Brown chops in oil over medium-high heat for about 8 minutes. Remove. Add onions and green pepper. Cover and cook 3 minutes. Add tomato, garlic, spices, salt and rice; stir 1 minute. Add stock; cover and simmer for 5 minutes. Add chops and any accumulated juices. Cover and cook until rice is done and chops are cooked through, about 20 minutes. Sprinkle with olives and parsley.

BROILED FISH FILLETS
Serves 4

- 4 fish fillets, ¼-inch thick (cod, haddock *or* fillet of sole)
   Marinade (used for meat)
   Parsley
- 4 lemon wedges

Marinate fish fillets for at least 30 minutes. Place fish in a broiler rack over a sheet of aluminum foil. Broil at medium heat on the 2nd oven shelf for 5 minutes. Turn fish with a broad spatula or pancake turner and broil for 4–5 minutes. Before serving, pour remaining marinade (heated, if desired), over fish. Garnish with parsley and lemon wedges.

Serve with a salad of spicy red beets.

TUNA AND CHEESE CASSEROLE

- ⅓ cup chopped onion
- 1 teaspoon butter *or* margarine
- 7 tablespoons (⅓ of a 10¾-ounce can) condensed cream of celery soup
- 2 teaspoons lemon juice
- ⅔ cup tuna, drained and flaked
- 1 cup cooked rice
   Salt to taste
   Black pepper to taste
- ¼ cup grated cheddar cheese

Preheat oven to 350 degrees. Cook onion in butter until tender, but not brown. Stir in remaining ingredients, except cheese. Turn into a buttered, shallow 6-inch casserole for 20 minutes, or until heated through. Top with cheese and bake 5 minutes longer.

BROILED SCALLOPS
Serves 3

- 1½ pounds scallops
- 6 tablespoons butter
- ½ teaspoon salt
- ⅛ teaspoon black pepper
- ⅛ teaspoon dry mustard

Wash; clean the scallops; pick them over for shells; season with the mixture of above seasonings. Place in drip-pan tray, with wire grill removed. Dot with butter. Broil at medium heat on 2nd shelf for 5 minutes. Turn the scallops with a broad spatula and broil for 2–3 minutes.

Melt additional butter to serve with the scallops.

BARBECUED LEMON CHICKEN

- 3 roasting *or* broiling chickens
- 1 cup salad oil
- ¾ cup fresh lemon juice
- 1 tablespoon salt
- 2 teaspoons paprika
- 2 teaspoons onion powder
- 1 teaspoon garlic powder
- 2 teaspoons crushed sweet basil
- 2 teaspoons crushed thyme

Have butcher split chickens and remove wings, backbone and tail. Clean well; place in shallow pan. Combine remaining ingredients; pour into jar. Cover; shake well to blend. Pour over chicken; cover tightly. Marinate overnight in refrigerator, turning chicken occasionally. Remove to room temperature 1 hour before grilling. Barbecue chicken

SWISS STEAK
Serves 4

- ¼ cup flour
- ¾ teaspoon salt
- ¼ teaspoon black pepper
- 1½ pounds round steak
- 3 tablespoons fat
- 1 medium onion, chopped
- 1½ cups stewed tomatoes
- ½ cup sliced carrots
- ½ cup sliced celery

Mix flour, salt and pepper. Dredge steak with flour; pound the flour into both sides of steak. In a Dutch oven, heat the fat; brown the steak well on both sides. Add vegetables; cover and simmer gently for 1½ hours.

PEPPER STEAK
Serves 6

- 1½ pounds round steak, ½ inch thick
- 1 cup sliced onion
- 1 cup beef broth
- 2 stalks celery, chopped
- 1 tablespoon salt
- ½ teaspoon garlic powder *or* 1 garlic clove, minced
- ½ teaspoon ginger
- 2 green peppers, cut in strips
- 1 cup sliced mushrooms
- 1 (1-pound) can tomatoes, chopped
- 3 tablespoons soy sauce
- 2 tablespoons cornstarch
- 1 cup water

Cut round steak into thin strips and brown in Dutch oven in small amount of oil and margarine. Add beef broth, onion, celery, salt, garlic and ginger; simmer, covered, for 35–40 minutes, or until tender. Add green peppers, mushrooms and tomatoes; cook an additional 10 minutes. Mix soy sauce and cornstarch in 1 cup water until smooth. Slowly stir into sauce and cook, stirring constantly, until thickened. Serve over rice. This can be made the day before serving and reheated in the microwave.

MEXICAN MEAT LOAF

- 1½ pounds ground beef
- 1 medium onion, chopped
- ½ cup chopped mushrooms
- ¼ cup chopped green pepper
- ½ cup taco sauce
- 2 tablespoons barbecue sauce
- 1 egg, beaten
- ½ cup tortilla chips, finely crushed
- ½ teaspoon salt
- Dash black pepper

Combine all ingredients; mix well. Pack into an oiled 8-inch loaf pan. Bake at 400 degrees for 1¼ hours, or until done.

You can use ground veal, pork or turkey if you like. Also may use ketchup instead of barbecue sauce. You can also melt some cheddar cheese on top during the last few minutes. Do your own thing!!

MEATBALL SUPREME
Serves 4

- 1 (10-ounce) can cream of vegetable soup
- ½ soup can of water
- 1 pound ground beef
- 1 egg
- ¼ teaspoon salt
- 2 tablespoons dry bread crumbs
- 2 tablespoons chopped onion
- 1 tablespoon chopped parsley
- Dash of pepper
- 1 tablespoon shortening

Blend soup and water. Measure out ¼ cup of this mixture; combine with beef, egg, salt, bread, onion, parsley and pepper. Shape 12 meatballs; brown meat in shortening. Add remaining soup. Cover and simmer for 20 minutes. Stir now and then. If sauce is thin, remove cover and cook a few additional minutes.

GREEN VEGETABLE MEAT LOAF
Serves 8

- 2 pounds lean ground meat
- 2 (10-ounce) boxes frozen chopped broccoli, thawed and drained
- 1 cup chopped onion
- ⅔ cup uncooked quick cooking oatmeal
- 2 large eggs
- ½ cup milk *or* water

- 1 (1.5-ounce) package meat loaf seasoning mix

Heat oven to 375 degrees. Lightly grease a 9 x 5 x 3-inch loaf pan. Put all ingredients into a large bowl. Mix with hands 3–4 minutes until well-blended. Press mixture into prepared pan. Bake 1 hour in the middle of oven. Remove from oven; cover loosely with foil and let stand 10–15 minutes. Drain off juice. This vegetable-laced meat loaf is delicious fresh from the oven, and even better the next day cold.

MEAT LOAF CHOW MEIN

- 1 pound ground beef
- 1 package Chow Mein Oriental Seasoning Mix
- ¾ teaspoon garlic powder
- ½ teaspoon salt
- ½ teaspoon pepper
- 2 eggs
- 1 can crispy Chinese noodles (optional)

Mix all ingredients together, except crispy Chinese noodles. Mold into 2 loaves. Bake at 350 degrees for 1 hour. Arrange Chinese noodles around loaves for garnish before serving.

SOUPER MEAT LOAF

- 2 pounds ground chuck
- 1 package dry onion soup mix
- 1 egg
- ½ cup ketchup
- ½ cup baked crumbs
- 4 slices American cheese

Mix all ingredients, except cheese; blend well. Divide mixture in half. Place half of meat in a ring mold. Place cheese strips over meat. Add remaining meat and seal well. Cover with waxed paper. Microwave on HIGH for 15 minutes. Rest 5 minutes or microwave at 50 percent for 25–30 minutes.

FRUITED PORK CHOPS

4 pork loin or rib chops, (about 1/2 inch thick)
1 can (8-1/4 ounce) pineapple chunks, drained
1 cup pitted prunes
1/2 cup dried apricots
1/2 cup bottled sweet and spicy French salad dressing

Cook pork over medium heat until brown. Drain. Place pineapple, prunes, and apricots on pork. Pour dressing over fruit and pork. Heat to boiling; reduce heat. Cover and simmer until pork is done-20-25 minutes.

PEPPER PORK CHOPS

6 thick cut pork chops

Pepper Sauce:
1 (8-ounce) can tomato sauce
1 (7-1/4-ounce) jar roasted red peppers, undrained
1 teaspoon oregano
2 garlic cloves, halved
1/2 teaspoon pepper
1/2 cup corn oil
1/3 cup chopped walnuts
1/4 cup grated Parmesan cheese
1/4 cup Marsala wine

Place chops in 13x9x2-inch baking pan. Cook in 350 degree oven until browned on both sides, turning once.
Meanwhile, place all sauce ingredients in blender; whirl until smooth and creamy. Pour sauce over chops and continue baking until chops are tender, about 1 hour.
To serve: Place on platter, garnish with alternating red and green pepper rings.

CREOLE PORK CHOPS
Serves 4-6

6 pork chops (1/2-inch thick)
3 tablespoons shortening
6 thin slices lemon
6 thin slices onion
6 teaspoons brown sugar
1/2 cup catsup
1/2 cup water

In a skillet, brown chops in shortening. On each chop place a lemon slice, and an onion slice. Mix together brown sugar, catsup, and water. Pour over chops. Cook covered until tender, about 1 hour.

LEMONY LAMB CHOPS
Serves 6

6 shoulder lamb chops (cut 3/4 inch thick)
1/3 cup water
1/4 cup lemon juice
1 tablespoon Worcestershire sauce
3/4 teaspoon salt
1/4 teaspoon dried oregano (crushed)
Dash freshly ground black pepper
1 tablespoon cornstarch
2 tablespoons water
1/4 teaspoon grated lemon peel

Trim excess fat from chops. In large skillet, cook trimmings until about 1 tablespoon of fat accumulates; discard trimmings. Slowly brown chops in fat on both sides (about 15 minutes). Combine the 1/3 cup water, lemon juice, Worcestershire sauce, salt, oregano, and pepper; pour over meat. Cover and cook over low heat for 30 minutes or until tender. Remove meat to warm platter.
Pour pan juices into measuring cup; skim off fat. Add water, if necessary, to equal 1 cup liquid; return liquid to skillet. Blend together cornstarch and remaining 2 tablespoons water. Add to skillet, along with lemon peel. Cook and stir until thickened and bubbly. Pass lemon sauce with meat.

HERB-GRILLED LAMB CHOPS
Serves 4

4 large loin or 8 rib lamb chops
1 teaspoon thyme
1 teaspoon oregano
1 teaspoon rosemary
3 small bay leaves, crushed
Grated rind and juice of 1 lemon
Pinch of paprika
6 tablespoons oil
Salt and pepper
Butter

Trim chops of excess fat. Mix herbs, lemon rind, and paprika. Rub mixture well into both sides of chops. Arrange chops in large shallow dish; pour lemon juice and oil over them. Season lightly with salt and pepper; place in refrigerator for 3 hours, turning occasionally. When ready to cook, drain chops and place on hot griddle. Sprinkle any leftover dried herbs onto coals. Cook chops 16-20 minutes, turning once or twice.

SPARERIBS MILWAUKEE STYLE

4 pounds country style spareribs (trimmed, cut in serving pieces)
1 (12-ounce) can beer
1/2 cup dark corn syrup
1/2 cup finely chopped onion
1/3 cup prepared mustard
1/4 cup corn oil
1 to 2 tablespoons chili powder
2 cloves garlic, minced or pressed

Place ribs in large shallow baking dish. In medium bowl stir together beer, corn syrup, onion, mustard, corn oil, chili powder, and garlic. Pour over ribs. Cover; refrigerate overnight. Remove ribs from marinade. Grill 6 inches from source of heat for about 40 to 45 minutes or until tender, turning and basting frequently, about 40 to 45 minutes or until tender.

POT ROAST WITH SOUR-CREAM GRAVY

Serves 6-8

2 tablespoons salad oil
4-5-pound bottom round beef roast
1 medium onion, sliced
1 cup dry red wine
1 cup water
2 tablespoons flour
1/4 cup cold water
1 teaspoon salt
1/4 teaspoon black pepper
1/2 cup sour cream

Heat oil in Dutch oven; brown meat on all sides. Add onion, wine, and water. Cover and simmer gently for 3-4 hours or until tender. Remove meat and keep warm. Drain off all but 1-1/2 cups liquid. Stir flour into cold water until blended; slowly stir into liquid in pan. Add salt and pepper. Cook, stirring over low heat, until thickened. Slowly blend in sour cream. Serve gravy with sliced pot roast.

ROAST TURKEY WITH BROWN RICE AND SAUSAGE STUFFING

Serves 10-12

1 (10- to 12- pound) turkey
Salt
Pepper
Melted butter or margarine
12 ounces mild bulk sausage
1 large onion, chopped
2 cloves fresh garlic, minced
1 medium green pepper, chopped
3 cups water
1 teaspoon sage
2 cups quick-cooking brown rice

Rinse turkey; pat dry. Rub salt and pepper into neck and body cavities. Secure drumsticks lightly with a string. Insert meat thermometer into center of thigh next to body, but not touching bone.

Roast uncovered on roasting rack in 325-degree oven 20 to 22 minutes per pound, basting occasionally with melted butter. Turkey is done when meat thermometer registers 170 to 175 degrees and thick part of drumstick feels soft when pressed with thumb and forefinger, or drumstick moves easily.

Meanwhile, lightly brown sausage in large saucepan, stirring to crumble. Drain off excess fat. Add onion, garlic and green pepper; sauté lightly. Add water, 1 teaspoon salt, 1/8 teaspoon pepper, sage, and rice.

When turkey is done, remove from oven and let stand 20 to 30 minutes before carving. Bring rice to a boil. Pour into greased 9 x 13- inch glass casserole. Cover with aluminum foil; bake 25 to 30 minutes at 325 degrees or until water is absorbed.

ROAST LEG OF LAMB WITH APPLE-MINT SAUCE

Serves 6

Leg of lamb
1 teaspoon salt
1-1/2 teaspoons ground ginger
1/8 teaspoon pepper
1/4 cup butter
Flour
1/2 cup beef broth or bouillon
2 tablespoons minced mint or 1/2 cup apple cider or apple juice
1 onion, minced
1 teaspoon sugar

Place lamb on rack in shallow baking pan. In small bowl, mix together salt, 1/2 teaspoon ginger, pepper, and butter. Rub butter mixture generously over lamb. Sprinkle with flour. Bake in preheated 450 degree oven for 15 minutes. Meanwhile cook remaining 1 teaspoon ginger, broth, mint, cider, onion, and sugar over low

heat for a few minutes. Reduce oven temperature to 325 degrees. Cook lamb, basting frequently with sauce 20 minutes per pound, or until meat thermometer registers 145 degrees for medium-rare, 160 degrees for medium or 170 degrees for well-done.

POT ROAST DINNER

3-5 pounds pot roast
1 package dry onion soup
1 can cream of mushroom soup

Put meat in pan and add the soups. Cover and bake at 350 degrees for 3 hours. Add peeled carrots and potatoes; cover and continue to bake 1 hour or until vegetables are cooked through.

If I'm expecting a house full of guests, I put all the ingredients in the slow cooker the night before or early morning.

DUTCH MEAT LOAF

Serves 6

1 pound ground beef
1 pound bulk pork sausage
1-1/2 cups bread crumbs
1 (8-ounce) can tomato sauce (1 cup)
2 tablespoons brown sugar
3/4 cup water
1 egg
1 teaspoon salt
1/2 cup chopped onion
1 tablespoon vinegar
2 tablespoons prepared mustard

In mixing bowl combine ground beef, sausage, bread crumbs, onion, 1/2 cup tomato sauce, egg, and salt. Shape into loaf in baking pan. Bake 30 minutes at 350 degrees. Drain off excess fat. Combine rest (1/2 cup) of tomato sauce, brown sugar, vinegar, prepared mustard, and water. Bake 45 minutes longer. Baste loaf several times during the baking process.

CHICKEN-IN-A-SHELL
Serves 6

6 baking potatoes
2 tablespoons butter or margarine
1 (10-3/4 ounce) can cream of
  chicken soup
1 cup Parmesan cheese, grated
3 tablespoons fresh parsley,
  chopped
1-1/2 cups cooked chicken, cubed

Bake potatoes until done; cut potatoes in half lengthwise; scoop out insides and reserve, leaving a thin shell. Mash potatoes with butter; add 1/2 cup cheese and remaining ingredients. Spoon into potato shells; sprinkle with remaining cheese. Arrange potatoes in shallow 3-quart baking dish. Bake 375 degrees for 15 minutes.

CHICKEN A LA KING

4 chicken breasts
Salt and pepper
3 heaping tablespoons flour
3 heaping tablespoons butter
2 cups milk
1 small jar diced pimientos
1 small jar sliced mushrooms
3 tablespoons minced parsley
3 tablespoons sherry

Season chicken well; boil until tender; cool and cut into bite-size pieces. Melt butter; add flour and stir until mixed. Add milk and cook until sauce is thick and creamy. Add cut-up chicken, pimientos, mushrooms, parsley, and sherry. Season to taste and serve hot in patty shells or on toast.

FISH HASH

2 tablespoons butter
2 cups flaked cooked fish
2-1/2 cups diced boiled potatoes
1/3 cup cream
2 tablespoons minced onion
1 teaspoon lemon juice
1/2 teaspoon salt
1/8 teaspoon pepper

Melt butter in skillet. Combine remaining ingredients and place in skillet; fry slowly until well heated and slightly browned, about 10 minutes. Serve with parsley.

FISH AU GRATIN
Serves 3-4

1 pound frozen fillet of sole, flounder,
  or haddock
1/3 cup mayonnaise
1/4 cup grated Parmesan cheese
2 tablespoons fine dry bread crumbs

Brush each fillet with mayonnaise. Mix cheese and crumbs. Roll fish in crumb mixture. Place in baking dish. Sprinkle with remaining crumb mixture. Bake in preheated 375 degree oven until fish is lightly browned and flakes easily when tested with fork, about 20 minutes for frozen fish, 15 minutes for thawed or fresh fillets.

HADDOCK-SHRIMP BAKE
Serves 6

1 can shrimp, drained
2 pounds frozen haddock, thawed
1 can shrimp soup
1/4 cup melted margarine
1 teaspoon grated onion
1/2 teaspoon Worcestershire sauce
1/4 teaspoon garlic salt
1-1/4 cups crushed Ritz crackers

Place shrimp and haddock in greased 13 x 9 x 2 inch baking dish. Spread soup over top. Bake in preheated 375 degree oven for 20 minutes. Combine remaining ingredients; sprinkle over fish mixture. Bake for 5 more minutes.

FILLET OF PERCH DIJONNAISE
Serves 2-3

1 (12 oz) package frozen perch fillets
2 tablespoons onion, finely chopped
1 tablespoon butter
1/4 pound sliced mushrooms
2 tablespoons cooking sherry
1 tablespoon Dijon mustard
1 tablespoon freshly chopped parsley
Salt and pepper to taste
1/4 cup dry cracker crumbs
1/3 cup grated Swiss cheese

Preheat oven to 400 degrees. Sauté onion in butter until soft. Add mushrooms and stir over high heat 2 minutes. Stir in sherry, mustard, parsley, and seasonings. Sprinkle half of crumbs in greased 7-1/2 x 11-3/4 inch baking dish. Arrange fish over crumbs in a single layer. Spread mushroom mixture over fish. Sprinkle on remaining crumbs; cover with cheese. Bake 15 minutes. Garnish with sautéed mushrooms.

FLOUNDER BORDELAISE

1 pound fillet of flounder, frozen
2 tablespoons butter
1 clove garlic
1/2 small onion, finely diced
1 cup canned tomatoes, drained and
  chopped
1/2 cup red cooking wine
1 tablespoon minced parsley
Pinch ground thyme
1/2 teaspoon salt
1/4 teaspoon black pepper
1/2 cup fresh bread crumbs

Cut slightly thawed fish into 1-inch slices. Heat butter in large skillet. Sauté onion and garlic for 1 minute. Remove garlic and discard. Add remaining ingredients, except bread crumbs. Simmer, uncovered, until fish flakes, about 5 minutes. Stir in crumbs. Serve with a side dish of rice or thin spaghetti seasoned with butter, Parmesan cheese, and some of the fish sauce.

LEMON CHICKEN
Serves 4

2 boneless chicken breasts
1 onion, chopped
1/4 cup lemon juice
1 tablespoon margarine
2 egg yolks
1 tablespoon flour
1 cup chicken broth

Cut chicken breasts in half. In skillet, slowly sauté onion in margarine until tender. Add chicken; brown. Add 1 cup chicken broth; cover and simmer 30 minutes. Put egg yolks into bowl along with lemon juice and flour. Mix well. Pour over chicken and stir until thickened (about 10 minutes). Use sauce from chicken to serve over broccoli, if desired.

BAKED CHICKEN WITH ORANGE SOY SAUCE
Serves 4

1 (2-1/2 pound) chicken, cut up (skin removed)
2 tablespoons soy sauce
1/4 teaspoon salt
1/2 teaspoon celery seed
1/2 teaspoon garlic powder
1/4 teaspoon ground ginger
2/3 cup orange juice

Preheat oven to 400 degrees. Place chicken in 13x9-inch baking pan in a single layer. Top with soy sauce, salt, celery seed, garlic powder, and ginger. Pour orange juice over chicken. Bake 40-45 minutes, until juices run clear when chicken is pierced with a fork. (220 calories per serving)

CHICKEN CACCIATORE

1/4 cup flour
2-1/2 to 3 pounds chicken, cut up and skinned
2 tablespoons oil

1 (32-ounce) jar Prego
1 medium onion, sliced
1 medium green pepper, sliced
1 teaspoon Italian seasoning
1 teaspoon garlic powder
 Salt and pepper
1/4 cup red wine
1 (16-ounce) can tomatoes, undrained and cut up
Hot cooked pasta

Place flour in dish; roll chicken pieces in flour, coating well. In large skillet, brown chicken on all sides in hot oil. Drain excess oil from skillet. Add remaining ingredients, except pasta. Cover; simmer 30-40 minutes or until chicken is fork tender, stirring occasionally. Serve over hot pasta.

HONOLULU CHICKEN

1 broiler/fryer, cut up
1/4 cup flour
1/4 teaspoon salt
Dash of pepper
Oil
1 (10 ounce) jar peach preserves
1/2 cup barbecue sauce
1/2 cup chopped onion
2 tablespoons soy sauce
1 (6 ounce) can water chestnuts, drained and chopped
1 green pepper, cut in strips
Hot cooked rice

Coat chicken in seasoned flour; brown in small amount of oil Drain. Mix preserves, barbecue sauce, onion, and soy sauce. Pour chicken; cover. Simmer 40 minutes or until chicken is tender. Add water chestnuts and green pepper the last 10 minutes of cooking time. Serve with rice.

FAST AND EASY CHICKEN KIEV
Serves 4

1 package boneless, thin chicken breast fillets
4 tablespoons margarine
1 teaspoon chopped chives
1/2 teaspoon tarragon
1/4 cup flour
1 egg
1/2 cup dry bread crumbs
Hot cooked rice

Preheat oven to 400 degrees. Spread chicken breasts flat on work area and sprinkle with salt and pepper. Place 1 tablespoon margarine on center of each breast; top with 1/4 teaspoon chives and 1/8 teaspoon of tarragon. Fold chicken to enclose margarine completely. Beat egg and 1 tablespoon water in small bowl. Coat chicken rolls with flour; dip in egg, then coat with bread crumbs. Place rolls, seam side up, in 13x9-inch baking pan. Bake 20 minutes. Serve with rice.

MARINATED CHICKEN BREASTS

1 cup sour cream
1 teaspoon Worcestershire sauce
1 teaspoon paprika
1 teaspoon salt
1/4 teaspoon pepper
1 tablespoon lemon juice
1 teaspoon celery salt
1 small garlic clove, crushed
6 split chicken breasts (3 chickens)
Bread crumbs
Butter or margarine

Mix sour cream and next 7 ingredients. Marinate chicken breasts 4 hours or, preferably, overnight. Before baking, roll each piece in fine bread crumbs. Place in baking dish. Dot with plenty of butter or margarine. Bake at 350 degrees for 1 to 1-1/2 hours. May cover when completely baked and turn oven to warm. Will hold 2 hours with no harm to flavor.

MARINATED HAM WITH SAUCE VERONIQUE

Serves 8-12

1/4 cup firmly-packed brown sugar
2 tablespoons honey
2 teaspoons Dijon-style mustard
1 (3- to 4-pound) boneless ham
2 cups dry white wine

Combine brown sugar with honey, mustard, and pat over top of ham. With metal skewer or long-tined fork, poke ham in several places. Pour wine over ham. Cover with plastic wrap and refrigerate for 3 to 4 hours, turning ham over several times to marinate.

Roast ham, uncovered, in preheated 325 degree oven for 1-1/2 hours, basting frequently with marinade. Serve with Green Grape Sauce.

Green Grape Sauce
2 cups seedless green grapes
2 tablespoons minced parsley
1 cup chicken stock
1/2 cup dry white wine
3 tablespoons cornstarch
1-1/2 tablespoons lemon juice
1 teaspoon Dijon-style mustard
1/8 teaspoon dried ginger
1/2 cup whipping cream

Cut grapes in half into small bowl. Add parsley and set aside. Combine chicken stock, wine, cornstarch, lemon juice, mustard and ginger in stainless steel or enamel saucepan over medium heat. Bring mixture to a boil, stirring constantly until slightly thickened. Stir in cream. Heat through. Remove sauce from heat. Stir in reserved grape mixture. Makes 3-1/2 cups of sauce.

HAM CROQUETTES

2 cups ground cooked ham
1 tablespoon oil
3 tablespoons margarine
1/4 cup flour
3/4 cup milk
1 teaspoon grated onion

1/2 cup fine dry bread crumbs
1 beaten egg
2 tablespoons water
Oil to deep fry

Melt margarine and add oil; stir in flour. Add milk, all at one time. Cook and stir until bubbly and thick, then cook 2 minutes longer. Stir in meat and onion. Cover and chill thoroughly. Divide into 12 balls and roll each ball in crumbs. Flatten balls somewhat, then dip into a mixture of egg and water; roll in crumbs again. Fry in deep fat for 2 minutes, turning once. Drain well and serve immediately.

Great way to use leftover ham!

EASTER-ELEGANT FILLED PORK TENDERLOIN

Serves 5-6

1-1/2 to 2 pounds pork tenderloin
2 tablespoons butter
1 cup onions, thinly sliced
1/4 cup snipped dried apricots
1/4 pound fresh mushrooms, sliced
1/2 cup fresh parsley, chopped
1/2 cup golden apricot nectar
1 cup hot wild rice, cooked according to directions

With sharp knife, cut tenderloin lengthwise, do not cut all the way through. Set aside. In a skillet, sauté onions, apricots, and mushrooms in butter; cook, stirring 3-5 minutes. Add parsley and golden apricot nectar; cook gently 2 minutes longer. Add to hot wild rice; mix thoroughly. Spread center of tenderloin with wild rice mixture. Tie meat securely with string. Brush surface with oil or butter. Set on rack in baking pan. Bake at 350 degrees for 1 hour. Remove string; slice and serve.

NO-HAM BALLS

2 pounds ground beef
1/4 teaspoon onion powder

1/8 teaspoon garlic powder
1/8 teaspoon liquid smoke
1 egg
1/2 cup water
1/4 teaspoon dry mustard
1 tablespoon Morton's quick tender salt
1/2 cup milk
1 cup fine graham cracker crumbs

Mix all ingredients together and shape into small balls. Place balls into a 9x13 inch ungreased baking pan. Bake uncovered in a 350 degree preheated oven for 25-30 minutes; then pour sauce over top of meat balls and return to oven for 15 minutes.

Sauce:
1 teaspoon dry mustard
1 (10-3/4-ounce) can tomato soup
3/4 cup packed brown sugar
1/4 cup vinegar

Mix all ingredients together. These meat balls are great to put in a slow cooker.

GOLDEN GLAZED HAM LOAF

Serves 8

1 pound lean ground ham
1 pound ground pork
1 cup soft bread crumbs (2 slices)
1/3 cup chopped onion
1/4 cup milk
1 egg
1/8 teaspoon pepper
1 cup orange marmalade
2 tablespoons lemon juice
1 tablespoon prepared mustard

Preheat oven to 350 degrees. In a large bowl, combine all ingredients, except marmalade, lemon juice, and mustard; mix well. In a shallow baking dish, shape into loaf. Bake 1-1/2 hours. Meanwhile stir together marmalade, lemon juice, and mustard. Use 1/3 to 1/2 cup sauce to glaze loaf during last 30 minutes of baking. Heat remaining glaze and serve with loaf.

VEAL PARMESAN
Serves 4

1 pound veal round steak
1/2 cup dry bread crumbs
1/4 cup grated Parmesan cheese
1/2 teaspoon salt
1/4 teaspoon pepper
1/4 teaspoon paprika
1 egg
3 tablespoons water
1 (8-ounce) can tomato sauce
1/3 cup salad oil
1/2 teaspoon oregano

Cut meat into four serving-size pieces; pound until 1/4 inch thick. Stir together bread crumbs, cheese, salt, pepper, and paprika. Beat eggs slightly. Dip meat into egg; dip into crumb mixture, coating both sides. Heat oil in large skillet; brown meat on both sides. Reduce heat; add water. Simmer in covered skillet for 30-40 minutes. Remove from skillet; keep warm. Pour tomato sauce in skillet; stir in oregano. Heat to boiling; pour over meat.

STUFFED BREAST OF VEAL
Serves 4

1 (4-5 pounds) breast of veal
1 medium-size loaf stale hard Italian bread
1 (3-ounce) box white raisins
2 tablespoons pignoli nuts
2 tablespoons chopped fresh parsley
1 large whole egg
1 cup shredded mozzarella cheese
1 large clove garlic, crushed
1/4 teaspoon salt
1 (3-ounce) container mushrooms, stems and pieces

Make a pocket in veal. Slightly soak bread in water and squeeze dry through a strainer. Mix remaining ingredients with 3/4 of bread (reserving rest if needed, according to size of pocket). Stuff 3/4 full, allowing for expansion. Sew pocket closed. Season outside of veal with paprika for color.

Place veal in baking pan with cover (or glass baking dish covered with aluminum foil). Add 1 cup water or 1 cup dry wine, plus 1/2 cup water.

Place in 350-degree oven and baste occasionally. Cooking time is approximately 3 hours. Remove cover for last half hour only, to brown.

VEAL PARMIGIANA

3/4 teaspoon salt
1/8 teaspoon pepper
1 cup crushed corn flakes
1/2 cup Parmesan cheese
2 eggs, lightly beaten
1/3 cup oil
6 veal cutlets
1 (15-ounce) can Hunt's tomato sauce special
1 teaspoon oregano
1/4 teaspoon garlic salt
6 slices Mozzarella cheese

Combine salt, pepper, corn flake crumbs, and Parmesan cheese. Dip each cutlet into eggs, then crumbs; repeat. In large skillet, heat oil; brown cutlets on each side. Add a few tablespoons of water; cover and cook over low heat for 30 minutes. In saucepan, combine tomato sauce, oregano, and garlic salt. Heat to warm. Place veal in dish; cover with slices of cheese and sauce. Bake in 375 degree oven for about 10 minutes.

PORK IN CIDER SAUCE
Serves 4

1 pound boneless pork, cut into bite-size strips
1 tablespoon shortening
2 cups apple juice or cider
1/4 cup grated onion
8 teaspoons cornstarch
2 tablespoons brown sugar
1 teaspoon salt
1/2 teaspoon ground cinnamon
4 tablespoons cider vinegar
2 medium apples, cored and coarsely chopped
2 cups or more hot cooked rice

In a large saucepan or Dutch oven brown pork strips in shortening. Drain off fat; be sure browned bits are left in the pan for flavor. Add 1 cup only of the cider and the onion. Bring to boil. Reduce heat; cover and simmer about 40 minutes or until meat is tender.

In a bowl, combine cornstarch, brown sugar, salt, and cinnamon. Blend in remaining apple cider and vinegar. Add to pork mixture along with apple. Cook and stir until mixture is thickened and bubbly. Cook and stir 2 minutes more. Add salt and pepper to taste.

Serve over hot rice.

PEACHY HOLIDAY HAM

IMPORTANT: First take off as much gelatin from ham as possible. Use a 3-pound ham, but a 5-pound canned ham works just as well. Place ham in glass casserole dish; set aside.

I saucepan, mix and heat until boiling:

1/2 cup water
1 tablespoon fresh lemon juice
2 tablespoons white granulated sugar
1/2 tablespoon powder from a packet of French's Mi Casa Chili Seasoning Mix, spicy style
3 pinches arrowroot or 6-9 pinches cornstarch
2 tablespoons Worcestershire sauce
1 (16-ounce) can sliced peaches with juice

Pour the above mixture over ham. Place a small piece of aluminum foil over ham so the top does not get tough. The sides are left open. Turn occasionally, once or twice during cooking time. Bake at 350 degrees for 3-5 hours, depending on size of ham. Cook a 3-pound ham for 3-4 hours.

BURIED GOLD MEAT LOAF

-1/2 pounds ground beef
 eggs, beaten lightly
 slices wheat or white bread
  soaked in milk and squeezed dry
 cup instant mashed potatoes
 tablespoons Parmesan cheese
 tablespoons chopped parsley
 alt and pepper to taste
 /8 teaspoon nutmeg
  cup flour
  tablespoons vegetable oil
  cans beef bouillon
  hard-cooked eggs, shelled

In a bowl combine first 9 ingredients. Flatten mixture on waxed paper; place hard-cooked eggs down the center. Roll up, shaping into a loaf. Roll in flour. In a small roasting pan, brown on all sides. Add the beef bouillon; cook slowly for 1 hour. (Add more bouillon if the loaf becomes dry). Remove loaf from pan; let stand 5-10 minutes. Slice carefully to retain the shape of the egg; arrange on platter. Serve reduced cooking juices separately.

HIGH PROTEIN MEATLESS LOAF
Serves 8

1-1/2 cups crunchy peanut butter
1-1/2 cups cooked beans of your choice, lightly mashed
1/2 cup onion, finely chopped
1/4 cup wheat germ or bran
1/2 teaspoon basil
Salt and pepper to taste
1-1/4 cups soft wheat bread crumbs
1-1/2 cups American cheese, grated
1-1/2 cups milk
3 tablespoons fresh parsley, chopped
4 eggs, well beaten
2 cups tomato sauce, heated

Combine all ingredients except tomato sauce; mix well. Turn into a greased 9x5x3-inch loaf pan. Bake 350 degrees for 45 minutes. Unmold on serving platter; serve with heated tomato sauce.

REUBEN MEAT LOAF

2 pounds ground beef
2 cups bread crumbs
1 egg
1 tablespoon catsup
1 teaspoon salt
1 (8-ounce) can sauerkraut, rinsed and drained
1 cup shredded Swiss cheese
1/4 pound pastrami, chopped
1/4 cup sour cream
1 tablespoon mustard

Combine beef, crumbs, egg, catsup, and salt in bowl; mix well. Combine sauerkraut, cheese, pastrami, sour cream, and mustard. Place one third of meat mixture in loaf pan. Spread with sauerkraut mixture. Repeat meat mixture and sauerkraut mixture, topping with meat mixture. Bake at 350 degrees for 60 minutes.

CHICKEN LOAF

3 cups cooked chicken, cut in pieces
1/2 cup chicken broth, without fat
3 slices bread, crumbled
1/2 cup rice, cooked
1-1/2 teaspoons salt
1/4 teaspoon pepper
1/2 cup milk
1 tablespoon onion, minced
1 tablespoon green pepper, chopped
1 egg

Heat chicken broth and add chicken, crumbs, rice, salt, pepper, milk, onion, green pepper, and beaten egg. Press firmly into greased loaf pan and bake in 325-degree oven for 1 hour. If gravy is desired, use 3 tablespoons flour with 2 cups of chicken broth.

CORNED BEEF LOAF
Serves 6

2 cans corned beef
3 eggs
3/4 cup fresh bread crumbs
3/4 cup milk
1/4 teaspoon poultry seasoning or mustard

Grind the contents of two cans corned beef; add to this the beaten eggs, and bread crumbs (which have been soaked a few minutes in the milk); add the poultry seasoning or mustard. Stir the mixture thoroughly, adding more milk, if necessary, to give the right consistency. Put into a deep dish and bake 1 hour in a 325-degree oven.

GREAT SALMON LOAF

1 (1-pound) can red salmon, drained
1/2 cup mayonnaise
1 can celery soup
1 egg
1 cup cracker crumbs
1/2 cup chopped onion
1 tablespoon lemon juice
1 teaspoon salt
Cucumber Sauce (recipe follows)

Mix all ingredients together. Put into buttered baking dish. Bake at 350 degrees for approximately 50 minutes. Serve with Cucumber Sauce.

Cucumber Sauce:
1/2 cup mayonnaise
1 cup sour cream
2 teaspoons lemon juice
1/4 cup chopped cucumber

Combine ingredients and blend well.

FISH CREOLE

1 pound sole or orange roughy fillets
1 (8-ounce) can tomato sauce
1 (2.5-ounce) jar sliced mushrooms
½ green pepper, diced
¼ teaspoon garlic powder
¼ teaspoon oregano
3 green onions, sliced
1 stalk celery, diagonally sliced
3 tablespoons water
1 teaspoon instant chicken bouillon

Rinse fish and pat dry. Arrange in 3-quart oblong baking dish with thicker portions toward outside of dish. Combine remaining ingredients in a 4-cup glass measure; pour evenly over fish. Cover with plastic wrap; microwave on HIGH for 8–10 minutes, or until fish flakes easily. Let stand 5 minutes.

SALMON STEAKS

2 (8-ounce) salmon steaks
1 tablespoon butter
½ tablespoon lime juice
1 green onion, chopped
⅛ teaspoon ground pepper
⅛ teaspoon dill weed

Place salmon steaks on microwave-safe plate; place a paper towel over top of steaks and microwave on HIGH for 3–3½ minutes. Set aside. Combine butter, lime juice, onion, dill weed and pepper in small dish; microwave on HIGH for 30–45 seconds until melted. Pour over salmon. Garnish with lime slices.

SHRIMP STIR-FRY

1 head bok choy, sliced (about 8 cups)
1 large red pepper, chopped
1 tablespoon cooking oil
2 cloves garlic, minced
8 drops hot pepper sauce
1 teaspoon sesame seed
12 ounces uncooked fresh shrimp, well-drained
1 tablespoon water
2 teaspoons cornstarch

Combine bok choy and red pepper in a 2-quart bowl; microwave on HIGH, uncovered, for 5–6 minutes; stir once or twice; set aside. Combine oil, garlic, hot pepper sauce and sesame seed in casserole; microwave on HIGH, uncovered, for 2–2½ minutes, stir in shrimp; microwave on HIGH, uncovered, for 2–2½ minutes until shrimp are pink; stir once. Combine water and cornstarch in a 1-cup glass measure; mix well. Drain juices from vegetables and from shrimp into measure; blend well. Microwave on HIGH, uncovered, for 1–1½ minutes, or until mixture boils and thickens. Add to shrimp along with vegetables; toss lightly to coat. Microwave on HIGH, uncovered, for 1–2 minutes, or until heated through.

SAUSAGE WEDGES

½ pound bulk pork sausage
1 cup (4 ounces) shredded cheddar cheese or American
2 tablespoons diced onion
¾ cup milk
4 eggs, beaten
1 teaspoon dried parsley
2 tablespoons butter

Crumble sausage in a 9-inch pie plate. Cover with paper towel and microwave for 3–4 minutes on HIGH. Drain off fat; sprinkle cheese over sausage; stir in onion. In a medium bowl combine milk and eggs; add parsley and butter. Pour over sausage; cover with plastic wrap and microwave 4 minutes on HIGH. Stir; cover and microwave for 6–8 minutes on MEDIUM (50 percent). Let stand, covered, 5 minutes.

BACON AND SWISS CHEESE QUICHE

1 (9-inch) single crust pie shell
½ pound bacon (9–11 strips)
2 tablespoons flour
¼ teaspoon salt
½ teaspoon ground nutmeg
⅛ teaspoon cayenne pepper
¼ cup chopped onion
2 cups half-and-half
4 eggs
⅓ cup grated Swiss cheese
Paprika
Parsley flakes

Microwave pie shell in a glass pie plate on HIGH for 5–7 minutes; rotate ½ turn after 2½ minutes. Cool. Arrange bacon in single layer on microwave bacon rack; top with paper towels. Microwave on HIGH for 9 minutes, or until crisp. Cut into bite-sized pieces and sprinkle over bottom of crust.

In a 1½-quart casserole combine flour, salt, nutmeg, cayenne and onion; whisk in half-and-half to blend well. Microwave on HIGH for 4–6 minutes, whisking every minute until hot and thick. Meanwhile in small bowl beat eggs to blend; add about ¼ of half-and-half mixture to eggs and whisk well. Then add mixture back to warm half-and-half; microwave on MEDIUM HIGH (70 percent) for 3–5 minutes. Pour into pie shell. Distribute cheese evenly over top, then sprinkle with paprika and parsley; microwave at MEDIUM (50 percent) for 6–9 minutes. Let stand 15 minutes.

Creative Cooking

INDEX

INDEX